The Sex Pistols
Invade America

The Sex Pistols Invade America

The Fateful U.S. Tour, January 1978

Mick O'Shea

McFarland & Company, Inc., Publishers
Jefferson, North Carolina

LIBRARY OF CONGRESS CATALOGUING-IN-PUBLICATION DATA

Names: O'Shea, Mick, author.
Title: The Sex Pistols invade America : the fateful U.S. tour, January 1978 / Mick O'Shea.
Description: Jefferson, North Carolina : McFarland & Company, 2018. | Includes bibliographical references and index.
Identifiers: LCCN 2018019049 | ISBN 9781476669397 (softcover : acid free paper) ∞
Subjects: LCSH: Sex Pistols (Musical group)—Performances—United States. | Concert tours—United States. | Punk rock music—History and criticism.
Classification: LCC ML421.S47 O75 2018 | DDC 782.42166092/2—dc23
LC record available at https://lccn.loc.gov/2018019049

BRITISH LIBRARY CATALOGUING DATA ARE AVAILABLE

ISBN (print) 978-1-4766-6939-7
ISBN (ebook) 978-1-4766-3184-4

© 2018 Mick O'Shea. All rights reserved

No part of this book may be reproduced or transmitted in any form or by any means, electronic or mechanical, including photocopying or recording, or by any information storage and retrieval system, without permission in writing from the publisher.

Front cover: The Sex Pistols at the Longhorn Ballroom in Dallas, Texas, on January 10, 1978 (© Robert Bayley)

Printed in the United States of America

McFarland & Company, Inc., Publishers
Box 611, Jefferson, North Carolina 28640
www.mcfarlandpub.com

To the memory of Margaret Moser (1954–2017) and Lauren Griffin (1981–2017), who both sadly lost their respective fights against illness while the book was going to press. Margaret, a renowned journalist and music enthusiast, not only provided her recollections of the Randy's Rodeo show, but also offered an insight into the Sex Pistols as a musical and cultural force. Lauren, wife of Freddi Griffin, wasn't even born at the time of the tour, but it was her enthusiasm that proved the deciding factor in persuading Freddi to share his tale for the first time. Rest easy, ladies.

Acknowledgments

This book wouldn't have been possible without Rory Johnston, John Holmstrom, Roberta Bayley, John "Boogie" Tiberi, Barry Cain, Ebet Roberts, and Richard McCaffrey. Sincere thanks also to Bob Merlis, Chris Salewicz, Peter Perrett, and Sylvie Simmons.

I'm also wholly indebted to a number of other people who were in attendance at each of the seven tour venues, be they members of the support acts, workers at the venues, freelance photographers, law enforcement officers, or audience members.

The Great SouthEast Music Hall, Atlanta, Georgia: Sharon Powell, Lynn Stroud, Darryl Rhoades, Freddi Griffin, Lauren Griffin, Rex Patton, Jonny Hibbert, Doreen Cochran, Tony Storch, David T. Lindsay, John F. Wiley, Jarboe Living, Steve May, Alun Vontillius.

Taliesyn Ballroom, Memphis, Tennessee: Bruce Van Wyngarden (chief editor at the *Memphis Flyer*), E. Winslow "Buddy" Chapman, Tom Graves, Ward Archer, Stacy Hall, Jeff Golightly.

Randy's Rodeo, San Antonio, Texas: Sig McKenna Izbrand, Margaret Moser, Bill Bentley, Ken Hoge, Jesse Sublett III, Joe Pugliese, Kathy Valentine, Donjon Evans, Nancy Gray.

Kingfish Club, Baton Rouge, Louisiana: Smiley Anders, Melissa Eastin, Tim Parrish, Eddie Flowers, Greg Ellis, "Electric Earl" Reinhalter, Cyril A. Ruth, John Guarnieri, Getty Freeman, Carlton Freeman, Kevin Bourgeois, Brad Orgeron, Gaylon Keeling, Sean McLaughlin.

Longhorn Ballroom, Dallas, Texas: Doug Groom, Saran Knight, Gabi Berlin, A. Lamar St. John, Trudie "T Rudie" Arguelles, Helena "Hellin Killer" Roessler, James "Bucks" Burnett, George Gimarc, Lannie Flowers, T. Tex Edwards, Jim Parrett, Mike Haskins, Barry "Kooda" Huebner, Clarke Blacker, Bob Childress, Don Broughton.

Cain's Ballroom, Tulsa, Oklahoma: Larry Schaeffer, Dana Martin, David Blue, Annette Weatherman, Tate Wittenberg, Ellis Widner, Tom Dutton, Richard Galbraith, Greg Sewell, Vernon L. Gowdy III.

Winterland Ballroom, San Francisco, California: Hugh Brown, Penelope Houston, Greg Ingraham, Jane Weems, Devorah Ostrov (a.k.a Betty Fremont), Theresa K., Pleasant Gehman, Kristian Hoffman, Susan A. Campbell, Dan Young, Jerry Pompili.

Thanks also to Phil Singleton at the God Save the Sex Pistols website.

Also a huge thank you to the following Facebook pages: I Have Been to the Great Southeast Music Hall, San Antonio; Texas Punk Rock Archive; Raisin' Cain: The History of Cain's Ballroom

Special mention to: Tasha "Bush" Cowen, Shannon "Mini B" Stanley, Matt Whapshott, Lisa "T-bag" Bird, Paul Young (not the singer), Roop & Debs, Joel & Aggie from The Old

House at Dorking, Ziggy P & Mel, Gemma and Donna (a.k.a The Girls), Boo & Alex, Zoe Meadows, Dan, Jeannie & "Pinks," Tony Makin & Pads, Kat & Jordan, James "Spunky" Willment, "Scouse Mark" Rudge, Michelle West, Chris "Hammy" Hamilton, Johnny Diamond, Charlotte Belmont, Jack & Kat, Steve & Julie Pyke, Luke Dillon and Mike Harrison.

Table of Contents

Acknowledgments   vii
U.S. Tour Dates   xi
Preface   1
Introduction   3

One. Sex Pistols Will Play   7
Two. Atlanta   16
Three. Memphis   34
Four. San Antonio   54
Five. Baton Rouge   75
Six. Dallas   94
Seven. Tulsa   118
Eight. San Francisco   140
Nine. Endgame   165
Ten. Aftermath   178

Chapter Notes   187
Bibliography   191
Index   193

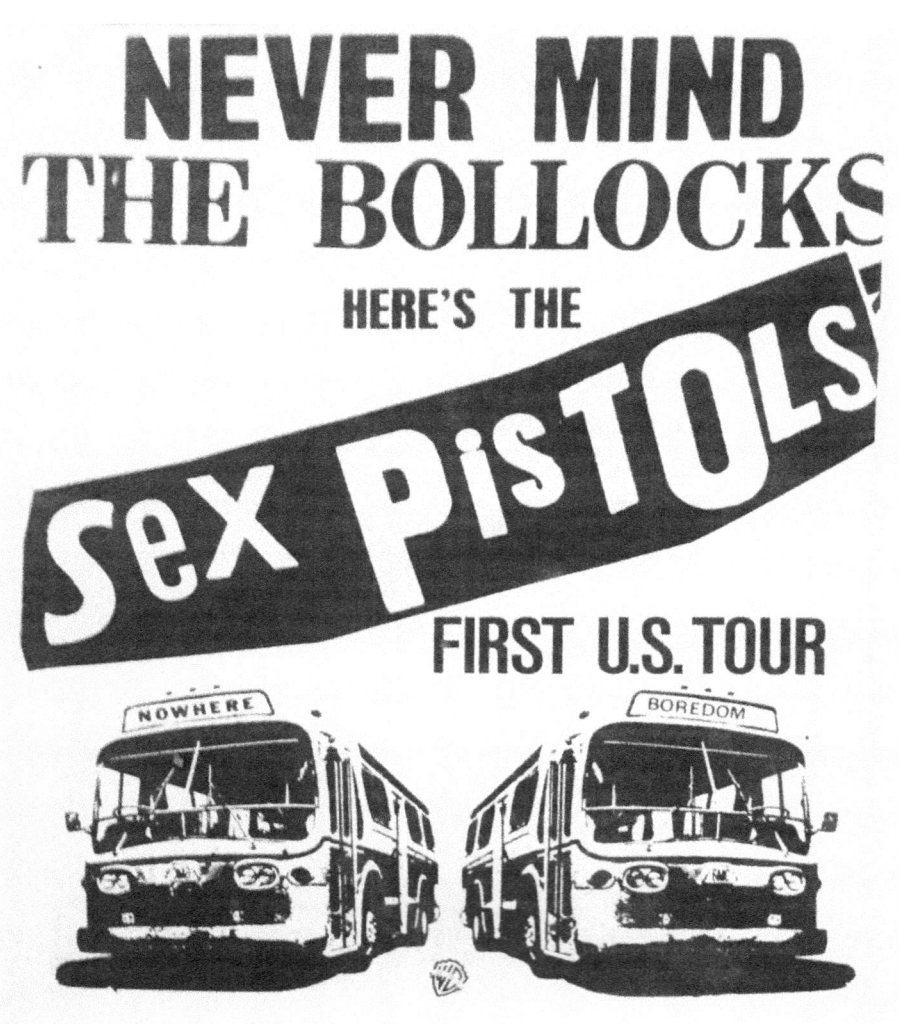

Cover of the U.S. tour promo package (courtesy Rupert Tracy).

U.S Tour Dates

1977

Thursday, December 29: Leona Theatre, Homestead, PA. Cancelled.
Saturday, December 31: Ivanhoe Theatre, Chicago, IL. Cancelled.

1978

Sunday, January 1: Agora Ballroom, Cleveland, OH. Cancelled.
Tuesday, January 3: Alexandria Roller Rink, Alexandria, VA. Cancelled.
Thursday, January 5: Great SouthEast Music Hall, Atlanta, GA.
Friday, January 6: Taliesyn Ballroom, Memphis, TN.
Sunday, January 8: Randy's Rodeo, San Antonio, TX.
Monday, January 9: Kingfish Club, Baton Rouge, LA.
Tuesday, January 10: Longhorn Ballroom, Dallas, TX.
Wednesday, January 11: Cain's Ballroom, Tulsa, OK.
Saturday, January 14: Winterland Ballroom, San Francisco, CA.

Preface

I was 15 when the Sex Pistols flew out from Heathrow in early January 1978 to undertake their inaugural U.S. tour. I'd somehow managed to miss the brouhaha surrounding their now-legendary appearance on *Today* at the beginning of December 1976, but there had been no escaping the media backlash following the release of "God Save the Queen" the following May. According to the UK tabloids, the Pistols were four degenerates who couldn't play their instruments, yet even the most cursory listen to *Never Mind the Bollocks, Here's the Sex Pistols* puts an end to that spurious myth.

By the time of the U.S tour the Sex Pistols had released four singles, signed with three major UK record labels, employed two bass players, and scored a UK No. 1 album. Within a six month period—December 1976 to June 1977—they had also enjoyed the sobriquet of being the scourge of the British Establishment. Despite being front-page news in the UK, however, the Pistols' anarchic antics had largely gone unnoticed in America. *Rolling Stone*'s Charles M. Young had visited London to interview the band during the summer of '77, but it wasn't until Warner Bros. successfully beat off competition from several other U.S. labels to secure the rights to distribute *Never Mind the Bollocks* in North America and Canada in October 1977 that the American media finally sat up and took notice.

Being the scourge of the British Establishment gave the Pistols plenty of kudos among the disillusioned and disenfranchised, but the flipside to this was their largely being prevented from performing live in the UK. Indeed, in the wake of the release of "God Save the Queen" the Pistols played just 13 UK dates throughout the whole of 1977. There was talk of a full UK tour set for March/April 1978 in the music press, and my friends and I were thrilled at the prospect of getting to see the Pistols in the flesh. (All this would be rendered moot, of course, owing to the Pistols' acrimonious implosion in San Francisco at the tour's finale, but we were still at school and in all likelihood have been refused admission.)

Though I avidly followed the U.S. tour in the UK music press, I was blithely unaware of the Pistols' manager Malcolm McLaren's shenanigans in his insisting on a tour of America's Deep South. A compromise was eventually reached whereby the tour included three northern dates as well as a final show in San Francisco.

Hindsight has proved in McLaren's favor, however. By stubbornly insisting the Pistols play in off-the-rock-'n'-roll-radar outposts such as Memphis, San Antonio and Baton Rouge, McLaren sowed the seeds for a culture clash akin to the one that had engulfed the UK; a clash that would continue to resonate across America throughout the 1980s and beyond.

While accounts of the Pistols' ill-fated U.S. tour have appeared in print elsewhere, *The Sex Pistols Invade America* covers the tour from varying perspectives, with many people sharing their experiences for the first time. The book also strives to separate fact from the many fallacies that surround those twelve days of mayhem when the Sex Pistols wended their way across an unsuspecting USA.

Introduction

> *"Apart from Sid, the Pistols weren't self-destructive, nor were they on the road to hell—quite the opposite. We were out to wreck the system, but certainly not wreck ourselves."*
>
> —John Lydon[1]

The year 1977 had proved somewhat turbulent for the Sex Pistols. There were, of course, several mitigating reasons for what had been twelve months of seemingly never-ending turmoil. In January, they'd been unceremoniously dumped by their record label, EMI, following an unseemly scene at Heathrow airport while awaiting a flight to Amsterdam for a short promotional tour. That the press reportage would prove to be as speculative as it was specious was of no consequence to EMI's hierarchy. In truth, the band's fate had already been sealed owing to their now-legendary appearance on *Today* on Wednesday, December 1, 1976.

Today was a regional news magazine show that was broadcast live within the London area at 6 p.m. from Monday to Friday. The Pistols had been invited onto the show at the eleventh hour to talk about their impending UK tour to promote their debut single, "Anarchy in the UK" (EMI 2566); a 30-second clip of the promo video would also be aired. The show's host, the curmudgeonly Bill Grundy, had other ideas, however. Instead of asking about the tour, Grundy boorishly tried to belittle the Pistols, before willfully baiting guitarist Steve Jones to "say something outrageous." Jones, who'd downed a couple of complimentary bottles of wine in the Thames TV hospitality suite before going before the cameras, duly obliged.

In 2008, the *New Musical Express* (*NME*) revealed the Pistols' expletive-laden teatime tête-à-tête with Grundy to be the most requested clip in Thames' 40-year history. However, in the immediate wake of the interview, the Pistols were pilloried from pillar to post; the resulting media backlash resulting in all but three of the 19 dates being cancelled by either indignant venue owners or outraged local councils.

Ironically, the invitation for the Pistols to appear on *Today* had only come about owing to the then all-powerful Musicians' Union refusing to grant clearance for the promo video to Queen's latest single, "Somebody to Love," so that it could be aired at the close of that evening's show. As EMI held a 50 percent share in Thames, someone at the label sought to salvage the situation by suggesting the Pistols. Had it not been for the pedantic posturing of the Musicians' Union, the Pistols' career would have most certainly taken an entirely different path. There would have been no "Filth and Fury" banner headlines,[2] and the Anarchy Tour would have been undertaken without any noteworthy incidents. EMI would have released a follow-up Sex Pistols single (most likely "Pretty Vacant") towards the end of January 1977, with the intention of releasing an album in the April as scheduled.

The year 1977 would see Queen Elizabeth II celebrate her Silver Jubilee, and McLaren, among others within the Pistols camp, were making noises about "God Save the Queen" being the follow-up single. The band had recorded a demo version of "No Future," as the song was originally titled, but with EMI's chairman, Sir John Read, occasionally taking afternoon tea at Buckingham Palace there was little likelihood of a release ever coming to pass.

The Pistols newfound notoriety following the parting of the ways with EMI meant there'd been plenty of interest from various record companies. The frontrunners in the race for the Pistols' signatures were CBS and Richard Branson's Virgin Records, so it came as something of a surprise when the news broke that the band had signed with the American label A&M Records.

A&M had established a reputation for being the home of soft rock and easy listening with artists such as Burt Bacharach, the Captain & Tennille, and the Carpenters on its roster. The label's London-based managing director, Derek Green, had, somewhat naively it has to be said, signed the Pistols "sight unseen" on the back of a demo tape McLaren had presented him several weeks earlier. Indeed, Green's naivety was such that he remained unaware of Vicious having replaced founding bassist Glen Matlock until the press conference unveiling the Pistols as A&M's latest acquisition.

Green was already ruing the hastiness of his actions when the Pistols got themselves embroiled in further mischief at A&M's UK offices following the mock contract signing outside Buckingham Palace. McLaren was duly summoned to Green's office and left again within the hour clutching a severance check for £75,000. A&M had already pressed 25,000 copies of "God Save the Queen" (AMS 7284), but upon the termination of the contract the singles were routinely destroyed. (A few copies would survive the cull and ultimately find their way onto the black market.)

Speaking in 2007, McLaren would liken record companies to being "just another whore down the street."[3] However, while the A&M sacking had garnered further column inches in the media, the Pistols had found themselves regarded as pariahs within the music industry. So much so, that the only "whore" willing to offer her wares was Virgin. McLaren was loath to sign with Branson's "hippy label," but with the clock counting down on the Silver Jubilee celebrations, "God Save the Queen" was in serious danger of being left to wither on the bough. Branson would subsequently be knighted for "services to entrepreneurship," yet raised no objection to the Pistols sticking a safety pin through the queen's nose for the sleeve to "God Save the Queen" (VS 181).

Unsurprisingly, the BBC issued an immediate blanket-ban on the Pistols' new single, while the Independent Broadcasting Authority quickly followed suit in banning airplay on all commercial radio and television stations. Despite such draconian measures, however, "God Save the Queen" sold upwards of 150,000 copies a day and was sitting at #2 on the UK Singles chart during Silver Jubilee week. (Conspiracy theories have since abounded about the shadowy forces of Whitehall purposely rigging the chart in order to spare the Establishment's blushes.)

Never Mind the Bollocks' supposedly "offensive" artwork had resulted in further embargos and a farcical court case following its release in October 1977. The album's lead single,

"Holidays in the Sun" (VS 191), would also be denied radio airplay for referencing the Nazi concentration camp Bergen-Belsen within the lyric. (The picture sleeve would also have to be withdrawn shortly after the single's release owing to the Belgian Travel Service issuing an Infringement of Copyright summons.)

♪ ♪ ♪

The British Establishment might well have had it in for the Sex Pistols, but the fatal shot that holed the band below the waterline was self-inflicted with Matlock's ousting soon after their return from Holland at the start of the year. Willfully replacing the band's sole recognized tunesmith with someone who glorified in being a non-musician was utter folly. Sid Vicious (born Simon John Ritchie) undoubtedly had image and attitude to spare, but in terms of musical creativity the cupboard was bare and the Pistols' powder would never be dry again. Steve Jones has since come to accept that Matlock's departure was perhaps fated. "Maybe the chemistry would've sustained us to do another album if Matlock hand hung around, but it wasn't our destiny. The Sex Pistols were born to crash and burn, and that's exactly what we did."[4]

Matlock and Rotten's mutual dislike would have brought a parting of the ways at some juncture. Yet had the Pistols not appeared on *Today*, they would have continued as an EMI act, and Matlock would most likely have remained in the band beyond February 1977. And of course, had Matlock remained a Sex Pistol then Vicious' own sad trajectory would have been somewhat different….

Branson's perseverance in landing the Pistols paid off when *Never Mind the Bollocks* gave Virgin their second UK No. 1 album. However, any hopes Branson had been harboring on cashing in on the highly lucrative North American territory were soon dashed when McLaren blithely chose to ignore the U.S. clause in the Pistols' Virgin contract by signing with Warner Bros. for a reported £250,000 (£50,000 was to secure the U.S. rights, while the remaining £200,000 was to be ploughed into the ongoing Sex Pistols movie project).

The U.S. clause within the Virgin contract stated that the Pistols would sign with Virgin, so long as Virgin matched whatever offers came in from American labels. Branson was said to be beside himself at McLaren's duplicity. Insult was soon added to injury when Warners rush-released *Never Mind the Bollocks* in time for the all-important Christmas market, putting an end to the demand for the import copies that Virgin had been shipping into the U.S. via Canada. (Warners also released "Pretty Vacant" [WBS 8516] as the lead single from the album.)

The year did, however, end on something of a constructive note for the Sex Pistols. As they were scheduled to bring their Never Mind the Bans Tour to a close at Ivanhoe's in Huddersfield, West Yorkshire, on Christmas Day, a benefit matinee performance was staged for the children of local striking firemen. (Invites were also extended to the children from one-parent families in the town, but it's the children of the striking firemen that everyone remembers.)

The Pistols were determined to bring a little festive cheer and arrived at Ivanhoe's armed with a plethora of *Never Mind the Bollocks* promotional merchandise including copies of the album, T-shirts, posters, badges, and "Anarchy in the UK" handkerchiefs, and a dozen or so customized skateboards with yellow boards with pink wheels to match the album's artwork. A banquet was also been laid on, the centerpiece being a huge cake into which Rotten happily launched himself headfirst to instigate a food fight.

Little would have anyone guessed that afternoon as cake and mince pies flew through the air that this would prove the Pistols' last UK date—at least with Vicious in the lineup. Reflecting on that day, Jones said that while interband relations were getting pretty dark by that time, he wasn't harboring any thoughts that the end was nigh. That despite the growing tensions between Rotten and McLaren, between himself and Cook and Rotten and Vicious, and even betwixt Rotten and Vicious, it still hadn't felt like "the writing was on the wall yet."[5]

♪ ♪ ♪

More than 80 people were interviewed for this book. Each interview by the author is cited on first reference; after that, all otherwise unattributed quotations originate from those interviews.

ONE

Sex Pistols Will Play

Sex Pistols Lose Battle to Beat U.S. Ban
    Britain's top Punk rock band, the Sex Pistols, were last night banned from entering America.
    The ruling came from the U.S. Embassy in London as the band prepared to fly to New York for a 19-day sell-out tour which was due to start with a concert tonight.
    They were banned because lead singer Johnny Rotten and three other members of the band have criminal records.
    —George Lynn, *The Sun*, December 30, 1977

No one at Warner Bros. was expecting *Never Mind the Bollocks* to emulate its UK success on the *Billboard* chart, but the positive feedback—particularly from the label's own WEA (Warner–Elektra–Atlantic) stores—was indicative that America was finally ready to embrace the Sex Pistols. Bob Regehr, head of Warners' Artist Relations Department, would be overseeing the tour. Once he'd received confirmation from McLaren that a window would be kept free for the first two weeks in January 1978, he set the tour ball in motion by contacting Premier Talent Agency in New York.

Premier Talent had been founded in the early Sixties by Frank "The Tank" Barsalona. Barcelona believed the key to any artist's success came on the stage rather than in the recording studio, and set about single-handedly revolutionizing the concert business by offering an alternative to the shoddy package tours and 15-minute sets that were typical of the day.

Regehr's next step came in flying McLaren's U.S. representative, Rory Johnston, to New York to meet with Premier Talent's Executive Vice-President Barbara Skydel. "I was dealing with all the American label activities from a management perspective," Johnston explained. "Premier Talent was the hottest rock agency in America at that time, and Warners were keen for me—or Malcolm—to meet with Barbara and Frank. But I also met with Jeff Franklin at ATI [American Talent International], and a couple of other booking agents. Malcolm either didn't want to or couldn't make the trip, but was satisfied that I could decide which agency we'd go with.

"I'll always remember going out to dinner with Barbara and Sid Bernstein. Sid was a very interesting guy. He was responsible for putting the Beatles on at Shea Stadium the first time. He and Barbara took me to a very posh New York steakhouse, and they actually let me in there in my leather jacket and ripped jeans. I think Sid and Barbara had to clear it with the restaurant first … this was 1977, after all. It was definitely a set-up to get us to sign with Premier, and it worked. But I knew Premier would be the best bet when Barbara didn't immediately throw me out of her office when I told her we only wanted to do a tour of Texas. Although the Pistols signed with Warners in October '77, negotiations had started earlier in the year. I definitely made two trips to New York to speak with Premier. The steakhouse trip was early September, and the second would have most likely been in October following the signing."[1]

Johnston was enrolled as a student at the Hammersmith College of Art when he'd first encountered McLaren and the fledgling Sex Pistols. "To pay the rent I worked nights as a barman both at Dingwalls in Camden Town, and the Portobello Hotel, which was situated close to Basing Street Studios. Attending Hammersmith at the same period was Mick Jones, who would of course later form the Clash. I became friendly with Mick based on common interests in music. I was living in Ladbroke Grove, and as he only lived a couple of stops further along the Hammersmith tube [subway] line we'd run into each other all the time. Mick was very influential in getting me interested in the emerging pre-punk scene. Incidentally, Joe Strummer worked a few hours a week at the Portobello as a dishwasher."

Owing to UK licensing laws at the time, pubs would close at 11 p.m. Hotel bars could remain open at the discretion of the management, but for guests only. The Portobello's night receptionist, Alan Jones, worked at SEX (McLaren and Vivienne Westwood's shop on the King's Road), however, McLaren would occasionally bring the four Sex Pistols along for some after-hours drinking. "The Portobello was a magnet for musicians, artists, fashion designers, TV and film industry types, et cetera," Johnston continues. "It had a very casual

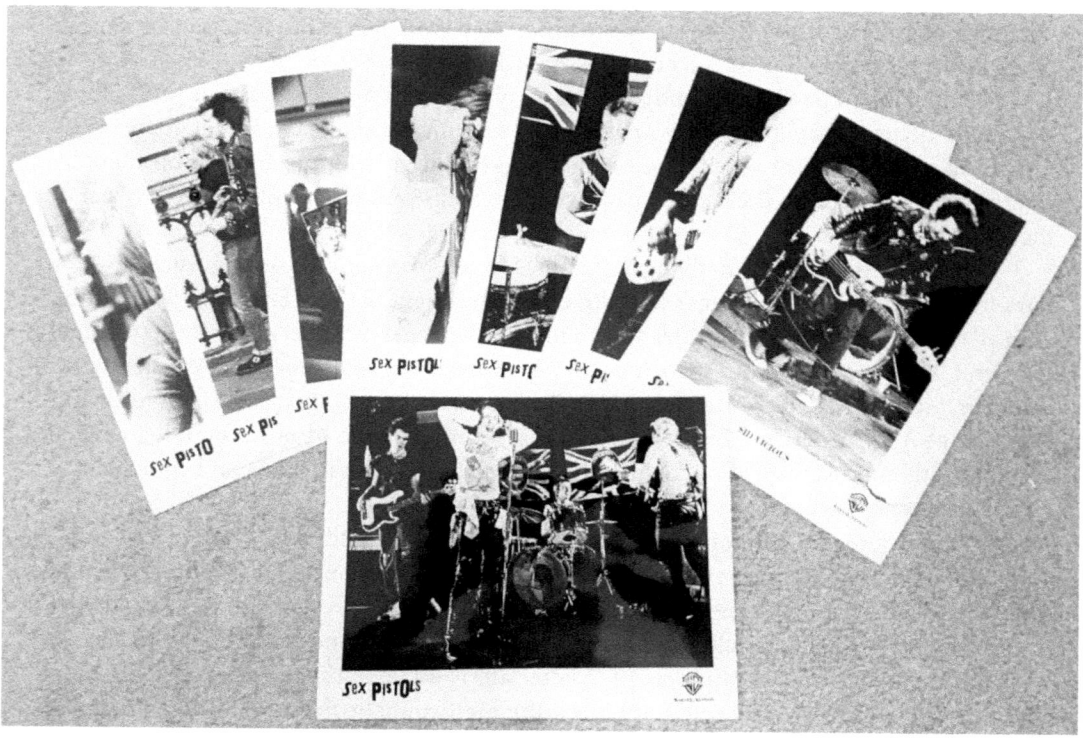

Stills from the U.S. tour promo package (courtesy Rupert Tracy).

'the lunatics are running the asylum' atmosphere where sometimes you couldn't tell who was working there and who was a guest.

"It was Alan who introduced me to Malcolm, and also took me to one of the Pistols' early shows. I can't remember which one it was now, possibly the first 100 Club date [March 31 1976]. I honestly didn't expect them to be all that good, but I was hooked after two songs. I was completely floored at their energy and the tension in the music. The atmosphere was both electric *and* dangerous. I remember thinking, 'Finally, here's a band to blow away the cobwebs and expose the raw nerve that had been missing from rock 'n' roll for years!'"

After graduating from Hammersmith during the summer of 1976, Johnston relocated to New York and got a job working for the Wartoke Concern, a management and publicity company that looked after Patti Smith and ex-Velvet Underground founder John Cale, among others. "I knew Jane Friedman, who managed John and Patti, from my working at the Portobello. In fact, I stayed with Jane during my time in New York before heading over to LA a few months later. Punk was beginning to explode back home by the time I arrived in LA, but this of course was light years before email, or faxes, so communications were terrible. International calls were very expensive, and as the U.S. music press viewed punk as being a bunch of snotty-nosed kids that couldn't play their instruments, news from London was hard to come by."

Johnston was, however, aware of the Pistols' signing with EMI, and their subsequent firing. "On a whim, I called Malcolm and offered my services as an 'experienced' music person based on my experiences with Wartoke. Amazingly, he agreed. He said he needed help planning a trip to LA with his lawyer Steven Fisher and asked me to set up some meetings with labels and publishers? I remember thinking, 'Shit! What the fuck do I do now?'

"While I was working from my office in LA—actually a pay phone on Hollywood Boulevard—the Pistols were hurtling towards another label deal in the uproar following the ejection from EMI. Malcolm and Vivienne were living in a small flat in Wandsworth, as I remember. Most of the time when I called he'd be in bed. I'd keep the calls as short as possible to save money. I was generally making it up as I went along, based on what I could glean from the calls and whatever press I could find. Anyway, a few weeks later I picked up Malcolm and Stephen at LAX in my very banged up '63 Ford Thunderbird. I'd started to reach out to some of the bigger labels including MCA, Epic, Casablanca, and Warner Bros. Capitol was off the list because of their relationship to EMI.

"The first visit was hysterical. Malcolm arrived in full bondage gear, with his trousers tied together at the back of the knees. Stephen was dressed in full English lawyer uniform: black jacket, grey pinstripe trousers, stiff shirt, and a black tie with a Windsor knot. They looked absolutely bizarre! It was meant to be a 'welcome to LA' meeting at A&M. I think [co-founder] Jerry Moss wanted to vet Malcolm himself after Derek Green had decided to sign them in London, but was beginning to get cold feet because of the band's public bad behavior. When we arrived at the A&M offices people just stopped and stared open-mouthed at Malcolm and Stephen, but the end result of the meeting was that the signing would go ahead. I was due to start working out of the A&M offices, soon after. My job was to be overseer of the operation to make sure A&M kept the Pistols' message pure, which was basically, 'Go fuck yourself!'"

While McLaren was in LA he brokered a deal with Freddie Hornik, the Czech-born fashion entrepreneur who had breathed new life into the ailing Granny Takes a Trip after taking ownership of the legendary King's Road boutique in London in 1969. Hornik had since opened GTaT outlets in New York and LA, the latter store having recently relocated from Doheny Drive in West Hollywood to Sunset Strip. The second issue of the recently launched *Slash* magazine (July 1977) featured an "Anarchy in the Sunset Strip" Seditionaries spread, with Johnston serving as an ad hoc model.

As Johnston had played a part in getting the Pistols signed with A&M, he had expected to be kept in the loop as to what was happening. When a week passed without any word from London he decided he could wait no longer. "I was due to start working out of A&M's offices the following day so I called Malcolm to ask if everything was all right. As usual it was one of those calls where he was half asleep. He said, 'Oh, hi, Rory, didn't you hear? We got kicked off the label again.' Of course, I hadn't heard a fucking thing because there was no way to communicate easily. I was stunned as I had start label hunting all over again."

Johnston had also proved instrumental in the Pistols signing with Warners. "I had met with several labels aside from Warners, all of whom were very keen to sign the Pistols. Casablanca Records were very hot at the time with Kiss and Donna Summer, and their head, Neil Bogart, tried very hard to persuade me. So did MCA. The reason I ultimately chose Warners over the others was partly because I knew Linda Stein, who managed the Ramones who were signed to Seymour Stein's Sire Records. Sire were already in the Warners system, which to my mind meant they had some familiarity with the whole punk ethos.

"Another thing that tipped it for me was the quality of the Warners team in LA—in

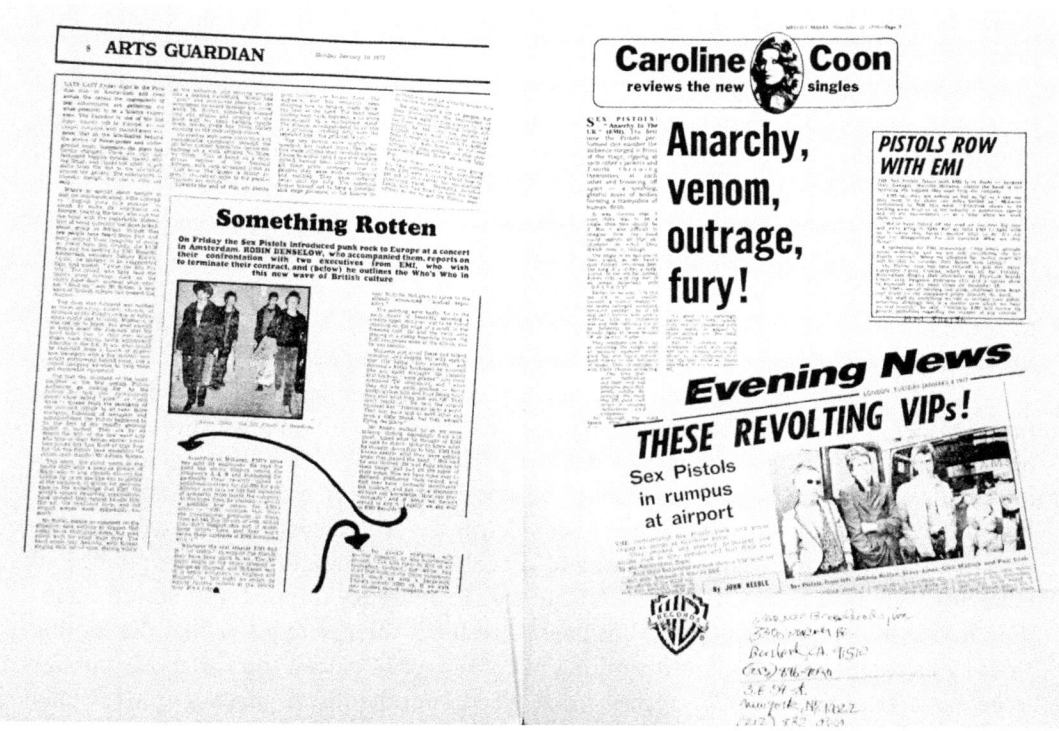

Copies of press coverage contained in the U.S. tour promo package (courtesy Rupert Tracy).

particular Bob Regehr, Carl Scott, and of course [executive] Mo Ostin, who I felt got the Pistols and Malcolm on a level that nobody else I'd met in the U.S. labels did. At the time, Warners were massively successful with Fleetwood Mac and Rod Stewart, and I felt confident we would get any support we needed for marketing and touring. Warners had also just brought over Derek Taylor from the Beatles' Apple Corps as creative director, and I felt that both as a Brit and someone who'd dealt with craziness surrounding the Beatles for many years, he would be a useful ally if we ran into issues with the label over imaging and packaging."

♪ ♪ ♪

The Sex Pistols had undertaken conventional overseas tours in Scandinavia and Holland during 1977, but McLaren was anxious about Warners treating the band as just another commodity. The thought of the Pistols becoming just another staid touring act was anathema to his way of thinking. As such, he made it plain that his charges wouldn't simply follow the careworn formula of playing America's seaboards and the major cities dotted in between—especially Los Angeles and New York.

A Sex Pistols show in New York would have undoubtedly attracted substantial attention within the U.S. media, if only because it would allow a guilt-edged opportunity to run comparisons between the UK punk scene and what was happening down on the Lower East Side. If he'd have been asked why he was eschewing New York in the lead-up to the U.S. tour, McLaren would have no doubt seized upon the adage about there being little point in "preaching to the converted." In reality, however, he was wary of coming face-to-face with those within New York's rock cognoscenti who—having churlishly denigrated his earnest attempt to breathe life into the flat-lining New York Dolls during the spring of '75— were now accusing him of having stolen ideas from what he'd witnessed at CBGBs to create his own punk fiefdom back in London.

Speaking with Legs McNeil and Gillian McCain in 1996, McLaren readily admitted to his having returned to London with "the image of this distressed, strange thing called 'Richard Hell' [born Richard Lester Meyers], and this phrase, 'The blank generation.' Richard Hell was a definite, 100 per cent inspiration. In fact, I remember telling the Sex Pistols, 'Write a song like "Blank Generation,"' but write your own bloody version. Their version was 'Pretty Vacant.'"[2]

John Lydon, unsurprisingly, remains adamant that his use of safety pins—at least at the time of his being invited to front the nascent Sex Pistols in August 1975—had simply been to keep his threadbare wardrobe from falling apart rather than as fashion accouterments. Had McLaren had his way, there would have been no need for an approach to Lydon, of course, as he'd wanted Richard Hell to accompany him back to London to work with Jones, Cook, and Matlock. Hell had initially proved receptive to the idea and might well have followed McLaren to London had he not been in the grip of early heroin addiction.

McLaren had made a similar petition to Syl Sylvain. Like Hell, the corkscrew-haired ex-New York Doll had also pondered the possibility of uprooting to London to rejuvenate his career—even going so far as to present McLaren with his '74 Gibson Les Paul Custom to vouchsafe his intentions. Sylvain would ultimately decide to stick with the devil he knew, however, and accompanied Dolls' front man David Johansen to Japan to add gravitas to a makeshift Dolls line-up for a highly lucrative 10-date July tour.

In the interim, McLaren had penned Sylvain a seven-page missive outlining his vision for the Sex Pistols (which currently resides in the Rock and Roll Hall of Fame in Cleveland). Upon receiving back word from Sylvain, instead of shipping the Les Paul back to its rightful owner, McLaren had gifted the guitar to Jones on the understanding that he switch from lead vocals to guitar.

Bob Regehr was desperate for the Pistols to play New York and mooted the idea of the band playing Madison Square Garden at $1 a head. McLaren, however, wasn't for budging, although he would begrudgingly consent to the Pistols performing on NBC's late-night show *Saturday Night Live*. McLaren's initial proposal for the Pistols to undertake a tour of Texas hadn't gotten beyond Johnston's initial meeting with Barbara Skydel. "Texas was a dangerous and scary place back then," Johnston explained. "The idea behind playing shows only in Texas was to get an honest reaction like the Pistols were getting in Britain and Europe. And you could say Malcolm achieved a victory of sorts as two of the dates were in Texas."

Labeled "Unsuitable": The artwork for the U.S. version of *Never Mind the Bollocks* was pink/green rather than the standard yellow/pink (courtesy Rupert Tracy).

McLaren had also insisted that Warners issue the Pistols and their tour entourage with airline tickets valid for whatever destination the holders might require. On this, Warners had offered no resistance.

The tour was to commence with a show at the 1,800-seater Leona Theatre in Homestead, Pennsylvania, on December 28, 1977, with two other northern Rust Belt dates booked at Chicago's Ivanhoe Theatre (December 31) and Cleveland's Agora Ballroom (January 1, 1978). The Cleveland outfit Pere Ubu was booked as support for the northern dates.

Following a show in Virginia at the Alexandria Roller Rink on January 3, the tour would then head for Georgia's capital, Atlanta, before swinging through the Deep South that had so captivated McLaren during his on-the-road adventures with the Dolls. The final tour date at the 5,400-capacity Winterland Ballroom in San Francisco (January 14) only came about owing to Rory Johnston's digging his heels in. "Winterland was down to me telling Malcolm that we had to do something to pacify Warners. He'd gotten his way with not playing LA, but I told him that we had to play California, and that we ran the risk of Warners pulling tour support if we didn't. I'm not sure Warners would have pulled the support, but the threat worked."

McLaren had one last caveat up his sleeve. As the Pistols would be playing predominately to working-class audiences, he insisted that the ticket prices for all the dates should be pegged at $2. Not surprisingly, this didn't go down well with the promoters, and a compromise was reached whereby ticket prices—with the exception of Winterland, where tickets would retail at $5—were raised to $3.50, with Warners agreeing to cover any shortfalls.

♪ ♪ ♪

Given the furor surrounding the Sex Pistols' every move, *Never Mind the Bollocks* had hardly needed promoting in the UK. As such, the Never Mind the Bans Tour was
simply to allow fans an opportunity to see the Pistols performing onstage. With the Bans tour climaxing at Ivanhoe's on Christmas Day, the leg-weary Pistols would have been left with a two-day break before heading to America. What no one had anticipated, however, was McLaren's choosing to leave it until the eleventh hour before applying for the visas that would allow the Pistols into America. He might not have been expected to know all the ins and outs of the U.S. State Department's policy regarding the all-important visas, but he surely knew enough to know that the Pistols' collective criminal past would prove problematic.

Jones had the most convictions, but these were petty offences ranging from breaking and entering, drunk and disorderly, and use of a motor vehicle without insurance. Cook had two convictions for theft against his name, while Vicious could boast two charges of assault and his being caught in possession of an illegal weapon (flick-knife). By far and away the most serious conviction as far as the U.S. Embassy officials were concerned, however, was Rotten's drugs conviction from the previous March.[3]

Rory Johnston was half-expecting the visa applications to be denied. "The unwritten rule regarding drugs offences is that your first visa application will always be turned down. Malcolm knew that as well as I did, the Stones being a classic example! The second application would have been approved, but his leaving it late in applying for the visas royally fucked things up! Those northern shows that were cancelled would have been great for the Pistols."

Considering the sizeable outlay Warners had invested in the Pistols, rather than hang around to test the veracity of Johnston's "unwritten rule" the label sent its top legal eagle, Ted Jaffe, into battle.

Jaffe, who'd first made a name for himself serving as John F. Kennedy's commissioner of foreign claims, had joined Warner Bros. from Atlantic Records following Warners' purchase of Atlantic in 1968. He'd been Atlantic's vice-president at the time and had overseen the sale.[4]

Jaffe had secured the Rolling Stones' entry into America in November 1969 when the band's visas were denied owing to various drug offences and was therefore confident of achieving similar success with the Pistols. Speaking with *The Washington Post*, he pointed out that the Pistols' collective offences were more "misdemeanors" than "heinous crimes" and that none of the Pistols had spent a single day behind bars or paid out any "serious, substantial fines."

Jaffe's argument would carry the day as on December 30, the U.S. State Department issued the Sex Pistols with two-week visas. There was, however, one non-negotiable proviso. Warners would have to post a $1 million surety to guarantee the band's behavior during the tour. That Warners put up the seven-figure bond is evidence of how much the label believed in the marketability of the Pistols.

Regehr might have been anxious to break the Pistols in America, but he was equally keen to protect the label's $1 million surety. Though he'd been happy to deal with Rory Johnston during the negotiations for the album rights, he decided to bring in someone he could rely on to oversee the tour.

With his shoulder-length hair and dead slug moustache, Noel Monk wouldn't have looked out of place in the Eagles or the Doobie Brothers. He'd cut his rock teeth working as the stage manager at the Fillmore East in New York had spent the last ten years overseeing tours by the likes of Johnny Cash, the Moody Blues, and the Rolling Stones.

"It wasn't so much that "Boogie [Tiberi] and I were out of our depth," Johnston counters. "But I was new to the touring game, and the stuff that Boogie had done with the Pistols in the UK and Europe was nothing compared to what was expected on a U.S. tour. Warners simply had too much at stake. They needed to take control. I'd already recognized that we needed an experienced tour manager for the tour." (John "Boogie" Tiberi had taken over the day-to-day running of the Pistols in February 1977 around the time of the Matlock/ Vicious interchange.)

"I did manage to bring my friend Dwayne 'DW' Warner on board. I used to work occasionally at a bar called the Sundance Saloon Calabasas out in Topanga Canyon, which was a mecca for local and national bands at the time, and was as funky as you could get. Wayne worked there as a bouncer, and he and I struck up a friendship. Dwayne ultimately fell under Monk's influence and command, but he proved to be very good at dealing with Sid when things got rough. Being a bouncer, he knew how to diffuse potentially dangerous situations as smoothly as possible." (In Noel Monk's book *12 Days on the Road: The Sex Pistols and America*, Warner is referred to as "E.X.")

The general misconception surrounding the tour is that the U.S. Embassy's initial stance in refusing to issue the visas had also resulted in the cancellation of the Pistols' appearance on *Saturday Night Live*. The *SNL* slot, however, was scheduled for Saturday, December 17, 1977—twelve days before the opening U.S. show. This would have meant postponing the opening dates of the Never Mind the Bans Tour at Brunel University, Uxbridge, and Mr. George's, Coventry. The *SNL* slot would have fallen through because of the visas issue, but if McLaren had made his application at the time, the Pistols would have received clearance to enter America in time for the tour.

Johnston was certainly left bewildered by McLaren's lackadaisical attitude regarding the visas. "Warners had pulled off a major coup getting the Pistols onto *Saturday Night Live*. The show had a huge audience, and hardly anyone in America would have heard of the band at that point. Once it had been put in place, I spoke with the director, Lorne Michaels, in the run-up to the show. *SNL* might go out live, but it takes all the previous week to sort out the show's running order, booking the celebrities, putting the sketches in place, etc. I didn't find out the Pistols wouldn't be flying out until the last minute. I mean, I flew to New York to meet the band at JFK and take them to the NBC studios! I know the Pistols had some UK shows booked in December, but I never did find out why Malcolm didn't apply for the U.S. visas in time. He must have known the Pistols would need visas—not to mention a carnet to get the band's equipment in and out of the country! I mean, if he had, it would have brought the problems getting the visas to the fore much sooner, and would have saved the northern dates."

In hindsight, the *Saturday Night Live* fiasco encapsulates McLaren's mindset regarding his managerial duties at the time. The Pistols' loss, however, would prove Elvis Costello's gain.

Costello had started out as a singer-songwriter on London's pub rock circuit before gaining recognition on the punk/new wave scene. He happened to be midway through his own debut U.S. tour with his backing band, the Attractions, when *SNL*'s producers made the call. (This, apparently was only after the Ramones had rebuffed *SNL*'s advances.)

Costello was signed to Colombia Records in America and had reluctantly agreed to the label's request that he perform "Less Than Zero" from his debut solo album, *My Aim Is True* (which had just been released in the U.S.). Costello, however, couldn't see what relevance a song castigating Oswald Mosley, the former British Union of Fascists, would have to an American audience. In a show of rebellion that McLaren would surely have approved, Costello brought the song to a halt midway through and, having apologized to the bemused studio audience, he led the Attractions into "Radio Radio."

Costello had penned "Radio Radio" (which would be released as a single in the UK in October 1978) as a protest against what he perceived to be the commercialization of radio broadcasts. Coincidentally, the lyric included a reference to the BBC's banning of the Pistols' "God Save the Queen."

In a mock salute to McLaren, the Attractions' drummer Pete Thomas took to the studio stage sporting a T-shirt bearing the words "Thanks Malc." While it undoubtedly made for interesting television, Costello's on-air antics resulted in a suspension from his appearing on *Saturday Night Live* by the show's producers. It would be twelve years before Costello again graced the *SNL* stage.

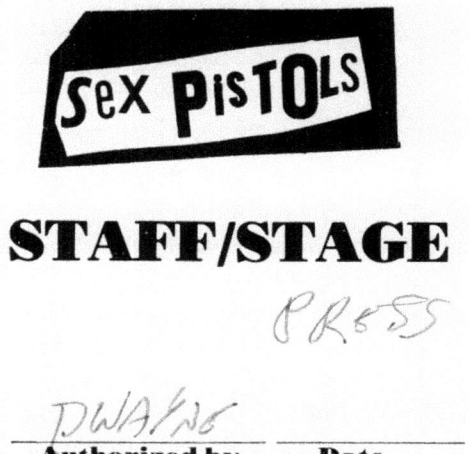

U.S. tour press pass signed by Dwayne Warner (© Richard Galbraith).

Two

Atlanta

> We were paid a pittance of ten dollars a day on the road. The food was not exactly high quality, and it was all pretty shabby. Going to America was all about imagining this wonderful spectacle, and in a way that's exactly what we got, though not according to the rules of the day.
>
> —John Lydon[1]

The Sex Pistols flew into New York during the early evening of Tuesday, January 3, 1978. McLaren wasn't due to fly out until the day of the opening show in Atlanta, so the task of chaperoning the Pistols fell to Boogie Tiberi. The 26-year-old Tiberi, an Anglo-Italian, had been working as a photographer in an advertising studio in London's Soho when he'd happened upon Joe Strummer's band, the 101ers, playing one of their residency shows at the Elgin pub in Ladbroke Grove. Having been captivated by charismatic Strummer, he'd started taking photos of the 101ers before agreeing to become the band's manager. Indeed, it was he who was responsible for booking the then-unsigned and relatively unknown Sex Pistols as support for the 101ers at the Nashville Rooms in West Kensington in early April 1976. This was the show, of course, that would change the course of rock history as on seeing the Pistols, the savvy Strummer had scented the coming wind of change and decamped from the 101'ers to join forces with Mick Jones and Paul Simonon to form the Clash.

Like Strummer, Tiberi had also been captivated by the raucous young upstart Sex Pistols and had followed Strummer into the Clash fold. He'd initially been impressed with Clash manager Bernard Rhodes' vision, before tiring of the latter's "left-of-center" rhetoric. "Bernard was a very interesting character, with some very interesting ideas, but I quickly sensed that it wasn't going to work. I'd been the one running the show with the 101ers, and Bernard wanted 'complete control' of what Joe, Mick, and Paul were doing. I took a month out before deciding I'd better do something, so I went to see Malcolm at his shop. I was vaguely aware that Nils [Stevenson, the Pistols first road/tour manager] was no longer involved with the Pistols. Malcolm told me to come back the next day as he 'might have something' for me. I went back the next day, and that's when he offered me the job as road manager. It was around the time of Glen leaving. Malcolm said that he'd need to get a reference from Bernard. And I'm still not sure that he was joking."[2]

As with their departure to Amsterdam nigh on a calendar year earlier, the Pistols had supposedly caused a rumpus at Heathrow airport, swearing and spitting at each other as they'd made their way through the departure lounge. One fellow passenger likened the band's behavior to that of a "pack of wild animals."[3]

Tiberi, however, says this was simply more tabloid propaganda. "It simply didn't happen. Sure, the band were all excited to be going out to America. But they were worn out both physically and mentally from the December Holland and UK tours. On the UK tour, instead of staying out on the road, we returned to London after every show, which was pretty grueling. What people tend to overlook about the Pistols is that they were very workmanlike and professional. When we got to Heathrow, they knew the routine as they'd done it all before with the bags, passports, et cetera. It was when we went through to the departure lounge that we found the press waiting for us. There was about a half dozen of them, and it was they who started goading the band, swearing at them in the hope of getting a reaction. The band were used to it, but for me it was still quite disturbing. I was thinking, 'Why behave like that?' I was also puzzled how they knew which flight we'd be taking. Of course, what I should have realized at the time was that Malcolm had tipped them off. I was privy to most of the stuff Malcolm got up to with the press, but he kept that one to himself."

A throng of reporters had gathered at the Pan Am terminal to await the Pistols' arrival. As far as Noel Monk was concerned, however, pandering to the press wasn't part of his remit. Pausing long enough to allow the *New York Post* to grab a shot of the Pistols for its morning edition, he and his security team bundled the band aboard a bus to ferry them to the Delta Airlines terminal and a connecting flight bound for Georgia's state capital.

Tiberi was aware of the reception committee that awaited them in New York as McLaren had briefed him on the surety Warners had had to put up to get the Pistols into America. "Somebody at Warners had briefed Malcolm about the need to protect their surety, and to make him understand the reasoning behind Monk's hiring his own security. When we got off the plane at JFK, Monk was waiting for us on the other side of the barrier. He motioned us through, saying everything had been taken care of. I don't even remember us having to show our passports. The problem was that the tour bus we'd hired to take us to Philly for the original opening tour date was staying in New York. We were flying onto Atlanta, but for some reason Warners had decided to rent a bus to ferry us to the next terminal—probably to keep the Pistols away from the press. They'd cordoned a section off for us, but the bus was too big to fit under the portico, so we had to get off again and wait for a smaller bus. A CBS film crew was there to film the Pistols' arrival. It made the evening news, and what you see is the band climbing into what was effectively a minibus. You can see the footage in the *Swindle* where Steve is gurning through the window. It made the evening news. Malcolm must have somehow caught CBS' clip, because when we arrived at the hotel in Atlanta there was a telex waiting for me that said, 'Too much press!'

"Noel Monk was strictly a company man and was going to do whatever it took to keep Warners' surety safe. He wasn't remotely interested in the Pistols, and decried the music. Thankfully, Rory's friend [Dwayne Warner] understood intuitively what the Pistols were about and acted as a sort of buffer. The question that still baffles me to this day is, 'What was Noel Monk's brief on that tour?' I mean, literally within hours of meeting him I could see he was totally wrong for the job. Who was it that hired him? When Malcolm arrived two days later, I remember asking him that same question and Malcolm didn't have any answer."

Rory Johnston met up with the band at Atlanta's Hartsfield airport. "I'd already sent Dwayne on ahead to meet up with Noel Monk. I'd been delayed in LA going over last-minute details of the tour at Warners' offices in Burbank. I'm not sure why Malcolm had to stay behind in London. It might have had something to do with the *Swindle* project, because I know he was meeting with potential directors to replace Russ Meyer around that time. But it could also have been something to do with the shop. Malcolm's mindset was that the shop [since renamed Seditionaries] was just as important as the Pistols or the film; they were all intertwined strands, if you like.

"I don't remember there being any press waiting for the band in Atlanta. There were a few fans though. They were mainly female as I recall, and all interested in Sid funnily enough. I thought it strange at the time, as I'd always thought of John being the focal point. The band paused long enough to sign a few autographs and then we were on our way."

Monk had booked the Sex Pistols into a Squire Motor Inn on the corner of Piedmont Road NE and Squire Place in Buckhead. (A block of luxury apartments now stands on the site.) Monk had chosen Buckhead—an affluent uptown district in the northern section of Atlanta—as it was a short drive to the Great SouthEast Music Hall, where the Pistols were set to get the tour underway two days hence.

The flight from New York to Atlanta had added another four hours to the Pistols' transatlantic odyssey. Despite their having been on the move for some fourteen hours, not everyone was ready to hit the hay. Upon arriving at the Squire Motor Inn, and discovering there was a strip joint named the Tattletale Lounge within walking distance of the hotel, Rotten and Vicious shrugged off their jet lag and set off in the strip joint's general direction. However, the duo returned a few minutes later bemoaning their having been stopped by a passing patrol car and warned off from venturing out looking the way they did.

Rory Johnston's mind was on other matters, but says he vaguely remembers Rotten

The Sex Pistols come face-to-face with the American public for the first time at their opening U.S. tour date at the Great SouthEast Music Hall, Atlanta. Left to right, Vicious, Jones and Rotten (© Alun Vontillius).

and Vicious' sloping off. "It had been a long day, and to be honest all I could think off was getting up to my room. The hotel was out in the 'burbs a bit. I think the idea was to keep us isolated as much as possible from the fans that were viewed as a 'potential liability.' In hindsight, it's not surprising John and Sid were stopped. But at the time, I didn't realize how much risk was involved in stuff like that outside of major cities such as New York and LA. What is surprising is Monk allowing John and Sid to wander off on their own—if only because they wouldn't have had any real idea as to where they were going.

"Of course, had I known how bad Sid was into the smack by then I would have stepped in. But the tour hadn't started yet, and no one outside of the band and Malcolm knew the full extent of Sid's problem. Warners had really only spoken to Malcolm through me up to that point, so they were equally in the dark as to how strung out Sid was. Malcolm should have laid everything out about Sid from the offset, but all he was thinking about was trying to create the same buzz about the Pistols in the U.S. as he had in the UK."

Vicious had been hooked on heroin almost as long as he'd been a Sex Pistol thanks to his beloved girlfriend Nancy Spungen having introduced him to the drug as a means of cementing their love. His dependency on both Nancy and heroin became so all consuming that McLaren hatched up a plot to kidnap the bottle-blonde Philadelphian and bundle her onto the next available flight to New York while her unsuspecting lover was at the dentist. The plot had foundered, however, owing to Spungen's frantic screams drawing unwanted attention from passers-by. McLaren had begrudgingly allowed Nancy to remain with Vicious in their Maida Vale drug enclave, but he'd been adamant that she remained behind in London while the Pistols went to America.

"Nancy wasn't allowed to travel anywhere with the band," says Tiberi. "And it wasn't a case of it being a question that Sid couldn't ask. He didn't want Nancy there, either. She was at the Christmas Day Huddersfield show. She connived her way up there by ordering a cab on the Pistols' account. You can imagine how that went down with Malcolm.

"Nancy didn't want Sid to go America. Sid was her meal ticket ... if you know what I mean. She didn't have anyone else in London, and with Sid in America she wouldn't have any money. I never went near that place [Pindock Mews] if I could help it. I hated it there.... Everyone did. She got her revenge, though, because when Sid was out on the road he didn't have easy access to smack. But those few days between Christmas and flying out to America she got him more and more stoned. At that time Sid only had a 'minor habit' ... what we called 'clucking.' But that week made such a difference, as she [Nancy] immersed him in the stuff. He developed an internal agenda where he was now only interested in 'getting and using.'

"Another thing most people fail to understand—and I'm not imagining this—is that Sid was on probation the whole time he was in the Pistols. When I came on board—which was the day after Sid joined the band—the Pistols were already a tight, professional band, and Sid was either going to fit in or he wouldn't—especially with Paul, as he was the driving force onstage, setting the tempo for the songs. And Steve and John had built up a symbiotic relationship from the 100 Club Punk Festival onwards [September 1976]. I was really impressed with their work ethic. I must have seen them sixty times in all and—not counting the U.S. shows—they put in maybe two lackluster performances.

"Sid's probation wasn't, you know, 'set in stone.' There wasn't a pantomime trapdoor beneath his feet, but he knew the ground rules and followed them ... at least until we got to America. But of course, and again I'm not imagining this, there was a real chance that Sid would have been let go had the U.S. tour been delayed … a 'for his own good' kinda thing. When Glen left the Pistols were a three-piece with a bass player. John, Steve, and Paul were the core. They were the ones that recorded the album."

♪ ♪ ♪

The Great SouthEast Music Hall—or the Great SouthEast Music Hall Emporium & Performing Arts Exchange, Inc., as the 500-capacity venue was formally known—was housed above a bowling alley within the long-since demolished Broadway Plaza shopping mall on Piedmont Road. Robert Christgau, the New York music critic, who was covering the Pistols' opening show for the *Village Voice*, certainly thought the GSEMH a strange choice. "If the Sex Pistols believe that by skipping punksymp sanctuaries like New York, Boston, Los Angeles, and Detroit on their first American tour they'll get to confront the true Amerika head-on, then I hope they take their debut to heart, because they opened in a shopping center."[4]

The GSEMH's then general manager, Sharon Powell, who was 20 at the time of the Pistols' visit, takes umbrage at Christgau's withering putdown. "Atlanta was regarded as a 'musical mecca' at that time, and the Great SouthEast Music Hall was one of *the* premier clubs in the U.S. Whenever a record company sent one of its new acts out on a promotional tour, Atlanta was a popular stop."

Powell is also quick to stress that Atlanta was far from the southern ideal that McLaren had imagined. "Atlanta has always been sort of a separate entity from the rest of the South. Malcolm thought that by having the Sex Pistols doing shows in the South they were really gonna hit us with shock and awe. What he didn't understand was that punk had been a serious part of our music for years. The Great SouthEast Music Hall was patterned after the Bottom of the Barrel in Union City [New Jersey], and so we were initially influenced by the New York punk scene: the Dolls, Iggy, the Ramones, etc. We also loved the Clash, but we were listening to the Pistols very early on.

"The Ramones were regarded as 'old hat' to some by the time the Pistols were here. The Pistols were new and more edgy. I was carrying my firstborn son at the time of the show, and *Never Mind the Bollocks* was about all he heard in the womb. Atlanta also had its fair share of punk-orientated bands such as the Restraints and Angelust. The Fans had released their own EP the previous year, and Phillip 'Fly' Stone from the Nasty Bucks often dressed in trash bags onstage."[5]

Restraints' bassist Dave Barge would be in attendance at the show and remembers his encountering Vicious backstage. "I was wearing an original NSDAP [Nationalsozialistische Deutsche Arbeiterpartei] badge and a hand-made swastika earring. Sid immediately asked, 'Kin I 'ave that?' 'What?' 'That Nawtzee badge.' I gave the badge to him, and was rather pissed when I learned that he gave it to a drag queen just a few hours later!"[6]

Powell's duties at the GSEMH were usually office-related, but on band nights she would work "front of house." On the night of the Pistols' show, however, she would find herself on crowd control. "Imagine a five-foot, two-inch, 110-pound child hippie girl out there calming the punks. Truth is, for some reason my demeanor made it an easy task for me as I was willing to go where my most brawny bouncers would not. I think that in the South, no matter what your social status, if a small woman walks up to you and gives you 'the look of warning,' you stop."

The first thing that caught the eye upon entering the GSEMH lobby was the boarding on the walls, as each performer—from singer-songwriter Jonathan Edwards who played the opening night while the seating was still being installed, to Darryl Rhoades and the Hahavishnu Orchestra, who'd brought down the curtain on the hall's 1977 live calendar—would be handed a magic marker and encouraged to leave a personal message for posterity. Powell says the Pistols would have signed one of the boards as every band was asked to do so, and none that she can remember ever refused. The boards were lost, however, when the GSEMH was forced to relocate to Cherokee Plaza on Peachtree Road during the summer of 1978 (the GSEMH would close for good in August 1979).

The Emporium served up a variety of sandwiches, sides, and platters named in honor of artists who had either played the GSEMH or hailed from the South. People could feast on a "Tom Waits Watcher," a "Melissa Manchester," or the "Earl Scruggs Stack." Despite the media intensity surrounding the Sex Pistols' visit, however, Powell says there were no plans to add a "Bollocks Burger" to the menu.

"Somebody say something?" Rotten challenges a heckler while tour manager Noel Monk (in glasses) and Glen Allison (longer hair, with back toward Rotten) look on from in front of the stage (© Alun Vontillius).

A selection of draft beers were served up in buckets bearing the GSEMH logo of a woman with her Medusa-like tresses a writhing mass of stenciled musicians.

♪ ♪ ♪

Certain sections within the UK music media viewed the news the Sex Pistols would be heading to America as their prostituting themselves to the Warner Bros.' dollar. However, the Pistols weren't the first UK punk-related act to play in the United States as the Damned had played shows in New York and LA the previous April. Could this have perhaps proved a factor in McLaren's refusal to play either city? The Damned's visit had gone unnoticed outside of the UK music media, but the thought of following a trail blazed by his adversaries would still have offended McLaren's sensibilities.

McLaren's antipathy towards the Damned and their management, Jake Riviera and Dave Robinson—who'd also founded Stiff Records to which the Damned were signed—primarily stemmed from their having pipped the Pistols to the post in releasing the first recognized UK punk single ("New Rose," BUY 6). McLaren would exact revenge of sorts in throwing the Damned off of the Anarchy tour after one performance.

While the Pistols were out on the road Tiberi was often called upon to run the soundboard, while his Glitterbest colleague Stephen "Roadent" Connelly operated the lighting. Warners were intent on establishing the Pistols in the U.S. and would therefore have provided a professional sound engineer to accompany the tour. This, of course, was contrary to McLaren's way of thinking as he preferred to keep the chaos at optimum levels whenever possible. Connelly had been left behind in London, but Tiberi would again be running the soundboard regardless of whether the venues had their own in-house engineers. "I wasn't professional by any means, but enjoyed doing it. Malcolm wanted me to operate the sound on the U.S. tour simply because the in-house operators wouldn't necessarily know the songs."

The GSEMH did employ its own in-house engineer in Steve May. By his own admission, May, who would run the legendary 688 Club in Atlanta during the 1980s, wasn't familiar with the Pistols' music as he'd yet to hear them either on vinyl or the radio, but had little trouble recognizing them when they arrived for the soundcheck the day before the show.

"Steve Jones and Paul Cook came up first. They wanted to take a look at the gear which we'd rented for them. When John came up to the stage from the dressing room they were mainly concerned with checking the gear and levels as opposed to rehearsing any actual songs. Sid showed up later still, and seemed to have trouble with his amp. It was an Ampeg SVT, but I believe the trouble was more of an operator malfunction than the amp itself. Sid wasn't interested in anything other than where he could make a drug connection. He asked me and the other guys that I'd brought in to assist me if we could get him any drugs, but I wasn't about to touch that."[7]

May's right-hand man, Alun Vontillius, doesn't recall the Pistols going to any great efforts at the soundcheck either. "I do remember the rider asking for all mixer channels to be available, and cleared—'zeroed out'—and the stage to be cleared also. As I was kneeling in front of the side full monitor on stage right, Johnny pointed his vocal mic directly into his monitor causing such a loud, shrill feedback. It knocked me backwards.

"The show itself was pretty much like that—*loud!* Malcolm had me bring all the faders up into distortion on most channels, so really there was no real mix to speak of. The rider also called for all lighting gels to be removed. The phrase was 'Artist will provide gel.' Of course, the Pistols didn't, and it was 'all white light all up full.'

"My other abiding memory from that night is of being offered $300 to let the NBC News crew in the downstairs back door when I went outside for some fresh air before the show. I foolishly said, 'No.'"[8]

The Pistols had outgrown the need for support acts in the UK, but Warners were keen for U.S. audiences to get value for their money. The honor of kick-starting the tour in Atlanta fell to local Sixties covers act the Dynamic Atlanta Cruis-O-Matic (usually truncated to Cruis-O-Matic). Rex Patton, the band's bassist, still isn't sure why Cruis-O-Matic was offered the slot. "We were friends with the GSEMH's general manager, Glenn Allison. He liked our band, but I wasn't ever sure why we were chosen. I hung out at the music hall a lot, and Glenn introduced me to the girl who worked PR there—I subsequently married her. The Pistols gig happened during her first week on the job, and I remember Glenn asking me if we wanted the date to my face. So it might have been as simple as the fact that he needed an opening act, and I was just right there at the time."[9]

It was at the soundcheck that Patton and the rest of the guys from Cruis-O-Matic were introduced to the Pistols. "They were all right guys until someone from the press walked in," Patton continues. "Then they would kick a mic stand or something to keep their image up. Sid couldn't play at all, but Steve and Paul were good and Rotten did cut a seedily charismatic figure. They didn't bother to watch us soundcheck, though. Instead, as I later heard, they went off on a tour of the strip bars and transvestite clubs."

Doreen Cochran, who tended bar in the Emporium, was so excited about seeing the Pistols that she arrived at the GSEMH around 9 a.m. on the day of the soundcheck. "I was 22 at the time and into punk rock, because at the time I was dating a guy named Dan Baird who played guitar in the Nasty Bucks. It was Dan that turned me on to the Ramones and the Sex Pistols."[10]

Cochran had to content herself with many hours of thumb-twiddling before the Pistols arrived, but as luck would have it she bumped into Rotten while he was scouring the place in search of alcohol. Cochran duly guided him to the Emporium. "I hung out with Johnny right up until show-time. It was *absolutely* non-sexual, however. I need to stress this! Just because you work at a music hall most people think you must be fucking the band. I found Johnny fascinating, but like I say, I was with Dan at the time.

"We were having some drinks, and, strangely enough, Johnny told me that he thought the band would break up when they got out to San Francisco. He said how he didn't think it could last much longer. I still don't know why he said that, 'cos it was nothing I said. We were still talking when Sid comes in. He's leaning on the bar and he's just kinda looking at me, and he starts drooling on the bar. Johnny kinda reprimanded Sid. He told him there was no point doing what he was doing because nobody was watching."

With Cochran tagging along, the Pistols' first port of call upon "completing" their soundcheck was the Backstage, a bar on Cheshire Bridge Road. They hadn't been there long, however, when Rotten grabbed Cochran by the arm and pulled her towards the door. He didn't care where she took him; his sole concern simply being to escape the pressures of being a Sex Pistol if only for a few hours.

Directly across the street was a transvestite club called the Locker Room, where, according to Lydon's autobiographical recollections, there were cubicles to the rear where punters could enjoy a free blow jobs from obliging "John Wayne look-a-likes in dresses" while watching triple-X films being run on a loop. "It's not what you'd think the South was all about. It's funny how the city fathers could allow that stuff to go on, and then condemn the Sex Pistols on stage."[11]

"Johnny said, 'Look at those geezers! They look just like birds, don't they?'" Cochran adds. "One of the female impersonators fell for Johnny in a big way. I think her name was 'Rusty,' and her forte was these glow-in-the-dark tennis balls that she'd swing around. They had the 'quarter movies,' where you shove in a quarter and you'd get porn. There were these little holes in the walls between the rooms, and he [Rotten] bent down and looked in one of the holes. I said, 'Don't do that!' and he said, 'Why?' I said, 'You might get a dick in your eye!' He just laughed."

♪ ♪ ♪

Alex Cooley, the local promoter responsible for booking acts at the Great SouthEast Music Hall, would subsequently cite the Pistols' appearance as being a "pivotal moment," even though he was honest enough to add that he didn't realize it at the time. "I got a call saying this band the Sex Pistols was the hottest thing in England and they wanted to tour the States. So I booked them and the world's press descended upon us. There were stringers from every major U.S. news organization there including ABC, NBC, CBS, Hearst, and Gannett. I sat backstage with the guys and they really didn't know what was going on. No one did! So we had to deal with all of that.... And the guys just didn't know what to think. Those scrawny kids from the wrong side of the tracks in London were as pleasant as could be, [but] they tore it up on the stage and people ate it up with a spoon. It opened my eyes. Music was becoming much more raw ... much more real."[12]

Steve May remembers the Pistols staying put in the dressing room prior to show time. "I was a bit confused being a fan and actually perplexed that a band playing their first U.S. tour, and this first gig seemed so unattached. Little did I know the turmoil going on between Malcolm and John, or the band versus Sid. The dressing room was a bit crowded with reporters. There was also a bunch of young kids—aged between 13 and 16—that were writing pieces about the Sex Pistols for local fanzines. These kids were absolutely awestruck with Rotten, and he paid way more attention to them than any of the more established press."

According to Rex Patton's recollections, Cruis-O-Matic opened with a medley of Johnny Rivers' "Secret Agent Man" and the Who's "The Kids Are Alright" (both released in 1966). The crowd was largely receptive throughout their 50-minute set, but Robert Christgau was rather less complimentary when writing up his *Village Voice* critique. Callously rechristening them the "Shitheads," he mused their only being allowed on the same stage as the Pistols owed to their being the very antithesis of the headliners.[13]

Jonny Hibbert, Cruis-O-Matic's saxophonist/vocalist, surprisingly doesn't bear any grudges against Christgau. "No, I never held that against him. You see, if we had have been Sex Pistols wannabes then it probably wouldn't have been much of a show. And if the hall had booked a Sex Pistols wannabe band it wouldn't have been the same show. We'd played all the larger clubs in Atlanta and were fairly well-liked, so our being chosen to open for the Pistols.... Well, let's just say it made sense to us. Of course, our punk friends were less sure. The way I see it, the Sex Pistols were lampooning the British Establishment, and we were lampooning them as it were."[14]

The "lampooning" came towards the end of the set with the arrival onstage of the Hahavishnu Orchestra's Darryl Rhoades sporting a "Kill Me" T-shirt and a large papier-mâché safety-pin fastened about his head. "We were known for satire and skewered all things on the social spectrum while concentrating heavily on the music scene," Rhoades explained. "We'd recently played the Bitter End in Greenwich City NYC, when we were joined on stage by Iggy Pop for a piece titled 'Boot in Your Face.' The song sounded very Ramones-like, and after the song was done, we would say, 'Right, now I wanna do another song for my fadda.' Then we would play the song again making fun of how so many of the punk songs sounded similar. So, when I read the review by Christgau in the *Village Voice* where he talked about us doing two songs back to back that sound exactly alike, I knew he didn't get the joke. He didn't get the joke of Cruis-O-Matic opening for the Sex Pistols either. They were intentionally put on the bill to incite the audience even more. They were all dressed as prep guys playing songs that you'd hear at a frat party, and I was brought on to do a song to make fun of what that night was about. When I came onstage I did all the things that the Pistols were told not to do. I spat on the crowd and was pelted by tomatoes, which begs the question: who brings fresh fruit to a rock concert? I like to think that I took the 'bullet' for the Pistols since the audience probably had a limited amount of ammo.

"It certainly was an event. The line started early outside the hall while we were inside doing soundchecks and bracing for what we knew would be a media storm. Videos cameras and photographers were lighting up the room; it was electric, but I remember feeling the same about this show as I had listening to disco. It was pumped up by media and its popularity was a result of the hype. The only thing that impressed me about the Pistols that night was Steve Jones' musicianship. On stage, it was more about posing than music, and Sid was doing his best to hang onto the planet but didn't have much of a grip. Johnny had all the charisma and energy on stage and commanded attention."[15]

Hibbert also admits to being impressed with Steve Jones's guitar style. "He and Paul Cook were excellent that night. I didn't care much for Johnny Rotten, though. He was nice enough, just not particularly friendly. Sid was somnambulant. I'm surprised he was able to play."

♪ ♪ ♪

Singer/songwriter Jarboe (Jarboe la Salle Devereaux), who would go on to join the experimental rock outfit Swans in the mid–Eighties, says she and her friends got to the Great SouthEast Music Hall early on the day of the show. "My two friends and I arrived there during the morning. We already had tickets, and we were the only ones outside the hall for quite some time before people slowly began showing up and forming a line behind us. The press also began to show up, and they stood to the right side of the line—there were a lot of them. We were interviewed by Robert Christgau inside. He was making his way through the audience asking questions. He asked us if we were there for the music or the fashion. We responded, 'The music, of course!' While we were waiting, the Sex

Chris Wood, left, and David Barge, center, of Atlanta punk pioneers The Restraints check out the competition from across the pond, with an unidentified onlooker. Barge would gift Vicious his treasured NSDAP badge after the show ... and be left upset when the bassist later gave the badge to a local drag queen (© Alun Vontillius).

Pistols walked by to the left of us. There was no fanfare, and they sort of bopped by waving their hands as they proceeded into the venue. When the doors were finally opened, the press rushed in before us and the other audience members. So it was chaotic and rushed getting in and fighting for a place in front of the low stage."[16]

One of those standing directly behind Jarboe and her friends was 26-year-old David T. Lindsay. Lindsay, an independent record label exec from neighboring Decatur, had been introduced to the Sex Pistols through *Rolling Stone*'s Charles M. Young when the latter visited Atlanta the previous September to interview Darryl Rhoades.

Young had recently returned from interviewing the Pistols. He'd also accompanied the band to Wolverhampton on the SPOTS tour (Sex Pistols on Tour Secretly). His report—"Rock Is Sick and Living In London"—would appear in the October 20, 1977, issue of *Rolling Stone*, which had also featured Rotten on the front cover. "He [Young] had brought along an advance copy of 'Pretty Vacant' with him to the interview," Lindsay explained. "I was at Darryl's New Year's Eve show [at the GSEMH] when they announced advanced tickets for the Sex Pistols. I immediately went to the box office and paid for a pair."[17]

Lindsay had bought his ticket in advance because he was desperate to see whether the Pistols would live up to what he'd read about them in Young's article. Imagine his consternation when his friend, Farrell Roberts, who worked the lighting at the GSEMH, called to give him the heads-up that the management had announced the advance tickets were being put back on sale.

Sharon Powell is so proud of her association with the GSEMH that she started the "I have been to the Great SouthEast Music Hall Facebook page." She was adamant that Lindsay's memory was playing tricks on him. "The tickets for every show had to be handstamped. They were numbered, and had to be checked out of the safe, numbered, recorded, etc. For the Pistols' show, we also took the extra step of the hole-punch with a safety pin."

Lindsay, however, was equally obdurate. "They most certainly did start selling tickets early on in the day of the show. And Farrell called to warn me! The problem apparently stemmed from fire marshals threatening to shut down the club if they went over capacity as no one had any idea what to expect from the Pistols' notoriety. I feigned illness to get off work and went straight over to the venue—changing out of my suit during the drive over there. If my tickets had been secure, I doubt I'd have left work early."

Lindsay would be vindicated when—at the time of writing—a photograph appeared on the GSEMH Facebook page of a hand-written notice stating that ticket reservations were only being honored till 7 p.m. The notice also advised that the hall would not be held responsible for any injuries incurred and that patrons entered at their own risk.

Lynn Stroud, who is married to renowned guitar-for-hire Peter Stroud (best known for working with Sheryl Crow, Don Henley, and Stevie Nicks), was 25 in January 1978. She was more of a mainstream music type of fan but had felt near-compelled to catch the Sex Pistols—if only to see what all the fuss was about. "The press was all abuzz about the band, so my girlfriend Paula and I decided that we should go down to the venue very early and maybe catch a glimpse of these 'media devils' in person."[18]

On gaining entrance, Stroud and her friend headed for the bar. They hadn't been seated long when they heard some commotion out in the lobby and assumed that it was the Sex Pistols arriving. Stroud says that a short time later one of the Warners' team came into the bar and, having identified himself as such, invited the women to accompany the

Pistols to a nearby restaurant. "Victoria Station is a steak and prime rib joint located just down the street from the Great SouthEast Music Hall. We gathered in the lobby by instruction when suddenly we were surrounded by more record company or tour people … and finally the Sex Pistols themselves. They pushed open the lobby doors for us to exit out to the van and we were blinded by the lights from the cameras of several local television cameras glaring into our faces. 'Sorry mom,' was all I could think to say.

"Johnny Rotten took the limelight, jutting his face toward the cameras and spitting like a camel. We hurriedly rushed up the steps into the van behind him. The rest of the band was already ahead of us. Johnny looked up and saw us cautiously trying to decide where to sit and offered up his seat to either of us. As we cruised down Piedmont Road towards the restaurant, the spitting, whirling dervish had reverted into a kindly, polite Englishman, making funny conversation. He thought it hilarious to be thousands of miles from London and yet be on his way to Victoria Station. He was showing complete respect, as though that moment with the press had been more of an epileptic seizure than the real deal of how he behaves."

Stroud says that while Rotten continued to behave like the perfect gentleman inside the restaurant, Vicious was soon playing to the gallery. "Dinner was like a scene from *Animal House*, but Sid was clearly not acting! He was not quite with reality. He began to build statues out of his mashed potatoes much like Richard Dreyfus in *Close Encounters*. But then he took it a step further and began to throw the mash around. No one was affected outside of our entourage since we were in a side dining space to ourselves, but his child-like behavior obviously set him apart from his band mates in terms of 'authenticity' of the toxic image that preceded their arrival. I had to scrub potatoes off my jeans before returning to the hall for the show."

♪ ♪ ♪

It was going on for 10 p.m. when the opening act of what was to become a seven-part tragedy got underway. "My name's John and this is the Sex Pistols," Rotten announced as the Pistols launched into the opening number, "God Save the Queen." With his ginger coif jutting out at disparate angles, Rotten was nattily resplendent in a (soon-to-be-discarded) suit jacket, waistcoat, white shirt and striped tie, and with a pair of swimming goggles nestled incongruously about his neck. As "God Save the Queen" drew to its discordant close, Rotten admonished the crowd for not dancing and enjoying themselves. "Forget about starin' at us, just fuckin' dance and have some fun. We're all ugly and we know it."

Vicious was showing off the newly acquired ringed bondage belt that he'd purchased at Hollywood Hots, a sex store selling leather and bondage implements that the Pistols had reportedly visited the previous afternoon. Having removed his battered motorcycle jacket, he strutted about the stage throwing shapes a la Dee Dee Ramone; his gaunt deathly pallor and scared concave chest giving rise to Rotten's comment: "See the fine upstanding young men Britain is chucking out these days."

A temporary concession stand had been set up close to the stage—manned by Alex Cooley. Aside from the obligatory album, people could purchase promo merchandise similar to what had been doled out to the kids at Ivanhoe's on Christmas Day. (A few of those gathered at the front of the stage are sporting *Never Mind the Bollocks* T-shirts and badges.)

The second number was "I Wanna Be Me." Rotten had penned the song's lyric as a scathing diatribe against certain "typewriter god" reporters within the UK music press who had unfairly criticized the Pistols over their supposed non-musicianship. As with "God Save the Queen," however, the song was marred by Jones' ongoing problems with his Les Paul. So much so that Rotten drolly put the woeful sound emanating from Jones' Fender amp down to "God's punishment."

The Pistols were primarily in America to promote *Never Mind the Bollocks*, so the crowd would have perhaps anticipated the majority of the set to comprise of songs from their debut long-player. With the exception of "Liar," every other song from the album featured in the set list. What might be seen as overkill, however, was simply a means to an end, as the Pistols had but 16 original songs within their canon.

In his *Village Voice* review Christgau wrote how an excited Bob Regehr had rushed across midway through the show to declare Rotten "a fucking superstar."[19] In between "Holidays in the Sun" and "EMI," the superstar playfully enquired of the crowd if the Pistols were the "worst thing you've ever seen?" Resident Atlanta music fan John F. Wiley had begrudgingly accompanied his friends to the show fully expecting to hate every minute. "Being a Stones fan, I had no appreciation for punk, which seemed dumbed-down. Yet surprisingly, I found myself liking the Pistols' sound—especially the 'in-your-face' cynicism of 'God Save the Queen.' Someone in the audience had brought in a pig's ear, and during the show it was being tossed around and onto the stage."[20]

Sharon Powell saw very little of the Pistols' performance as she was staffing the front desk, but "thoroughly enjoyed" what she did see. "I remember thinking the Sex Pistols weren't so scary. In fact, they weren't so much different from some of my friends! I don't know if they were giving us a 'toned down' performance that night, or if we were still jaded from the jet-lag. I think that the Pistols were sort of like a 'Holy Grail' for the folks that were heavy into the scene, and that when they were not as outrageous onstage as perhaps was hoped by some, it was taken as being not as good of a show as was expected."

Drummer Cook sporting a Warner Bros. *Never Mind the Bollocks* promo T-shirt behind Rotten (© Alun Vontillius).

The view from the rear of the hall. One audience member would liken the Pistols' arrival in the United States as the "largest media rodeo since the last chopper lifted off the roof of the Saigon Embassy" (© Alun Vontillius).

Lynn Stroud admits to the show being "a blur of songs" she wasn't familiar with. "I was just a typical rock fan. I wasn't into punk, so this was all new to me. But I was certainly taking in every bit of this new movement of music and these stranger-than-strange punk icons from England who had our country in a tizzy. Paula was all about it. She definitely had had a better time than I did during the set, being a fan of their sound and angst. We'd sat with the band in the dressing room before the show and during the five-minute warning, Sid, with his own fingernails, clawed himself down his chest until he drew some blood before heading on stage."

Doreen Cochran watched the Pistols' performance perched on the side of the stage as Rotten had charged her with keeping an eye on his supply of Heineken and cigarettes. "It was just fun to be at the happening. I was handing out his butts to the girls in the audience. I couldn't hear a thing from where I was sitting—the best seat is always by the soundman. The show was alright, but not my favorite. I have the CD of the show somewhere, and I think you can hear me at the end saying 'Johnny spat on me.'"

After the show, Cochran went backstage and chatted with Rotten about the crowd's reaction. "He was a little upset that people seemed kind of subdued. He said that back in England people in the crowd would practically throw each other at the stage. I told him that it was different in America, and that most of the kids who were at the show didn't know what 'anarchy' was."

Cochran had relocated to Atlanta from her native Decatur in 1975 and was content with her life working at the Great SouthEast Music Hall. She was dating a happening musician on the local music scene (Baird would go on to form the Georgia Satellites a couple of years later), and now here she was shooting the breeze with her new best buddy Johnny Rotten of the nasty, notorious Sex Pistols. Indeed, Cochrane might well have gone on to be the talk of her alma mater, Columbia High, had the quiet kid that had sat behind her in home room not gunned down John Lennon a couple of years later.

♪ ♪ ♪

The irony surely wouldn't have been lost on the Pistols on discovering their first stateside interview was to be aired on NBC's *Today*, which at the time was America's highest-rated early morning "infotainment" show. With Monk and his team anxious to keep the band's location away from the media, Warners' director of publicity, Bob Merlis, had booked a suite at the Westin Peachtree Plaza Hotel in downtown Atlanta where the band would face questions from NBC News anchorman Jack Perkins.

Merlis was enjoying his second stint with Warners, having rejoined the label in 1974. He'd been in his current role for the last 18 months or so. As such, he'd been designated to meet the Pistols' upon their arrival in the U.S. He'd been at LAX awaiting a flight to Pittsburgh when a call to the office alerted him to the Pistols' visa applications having been denied.

Though Merlis had been privy to the inter-office gossip surrounding Warners' signing of the Sex Pistols, he was meeting the band in person for the first time. "Oh there was a great deal skepticism in the office," he says today. "The Sex Pistols were regarded by some of my colleagues as being 'barbarians' that should be kept at arm's length, but we were already moving with the times and the 'punk rock revolution.' Our 'punk baptism,' as it were, came in working with Sire and the Ramones, so it was a case of 'bring on the Sex Pistols.' My boss, Bob Regehr, was a bit of a risk-taker. His approach was, 'Let's see what happens....'

"I was unfamiliar with the Sex Pistols' music as I hadn't heard the album at that time. But of course, I knew all about the band from the adverse publicity they were generating in England. Like Bob, I fully believed we could turn the Sex Pistols into a successful act in the U.S. I don't think they would've gotten as big as say, Led Zeppelin or the Who, because they were so anti-establishment. But they would have recorded more albums—pretty much like the Clash did. Johnny Rotten was extremely charismatic, Cook and Jones were already very accomplished musicians, and Sid would have gotten more accomplished on the bass ... maybe.

"I don't know whether A&M Records were able to distribute the Sex Pistols' music in America, as I'm not familiar with what was stated in their contract. I'm assuming they would have done so, as they were an American label. I can't be sure on this, but I'm guessing it would probably have been different with EMI because their U.S. arm—Capital Records— were very conservative They passed on the Beatles because they deemed them too avantgarde, remember, so I should imagine a band like the Sex Pistols would have been even more off-putting for Capitol's hierarchy."[21]

Merlis says he was unaware of the $1 million surety that Warners had agreed to post on the Pistols as per the U.S. State Department's stipulation when granting the visas, but Rory Johnston says he isn't surprised at this. "I don't know how clued in Bob would have been regarding the financial side of things. Most of the money stuff would have been handled at a Mo Ostin/Bob Regehr level."

NBC's report, which was aired the morning after the Pistols' show, began with footage of NYPD Port Authority officers awaiting the band's arrival at JFK while a female voiceover said how the authorities had been warned the Sex Pistols might attack their fellow passengers before the footage switched to Perkins standing in front of the stage at the Great South-East Music Hall after the Pistols had departed the stage.

Perkins, an ex-war correspondent, went into a dry monologue about the publicity that had preceded the Pistols; how they "spat on audiences, vomited on stage, and sang of anarchy." The screen then switched—albeit briefly—to footage of Perkins in conversation with Vicious and Cook at the hotel with Perkins' voiceover bemoaning Rotten and Jones' no show and the band's supposed $10 demand to give a "bleep, bleep interview." From photographs taken that afternoon, Rotten and Jones do at least put in an appearance at some juncture, but the omission of any actual interview material suggests Perkins' wallet stayed in his pocket.

"Jack Perkins was the wrong guy for the interview, totally *the* wrong guy for the job!" Merlis reflected. "I booked a nice room at a downtown hotel. The band showed up, only he didn't really want to talk to them. They picked up on that, and started doing things like demanding payment to do the interview. They would have done it for free if he hadn't been such a jerk!"

With the non-interview over, and the Pistols having departed for a nearby "sex devices store" (Hollywood Hots), the camera focuses on Perkins sitting alone in the hotel room—again delivered in a deadpan monotone—trying to conjure up the supposed scene of carnage the band had left in their wake which amounted to some spittle stains and cigarette butts on the carpet, the dregs of an afternoon's beer and booze on a nearby table. "Perkins tried to make the room look 'rock group trashed,' which it wasn't by any means," Merlis scoffed. "If I smoked, which I don't by the way, it would have looked like a room that I might have occupied for a couple of hours. But he tried to paint it as anarchy and carnage! After the band departed the hotel, he set about playing up the band's supposed bad reputation. I think he was really disappointed they didn't throw a TV out of the window or something."

Jeff Calder, an aspiring guitarist recently relocated to Atlanta from his native Florida, likened the Pistols' arrival in the U.S. as being the "largest media rodeo since the last chopper lifted off the roof of the Saigon Embassy." He encountered Perkins loitering in the GSEMH lobby with his camera crew, "eyeballing a handful of Georgia's Dracula punks with disdain." From their conversation, Calder quickly sized up the reporter's distaste for his assignment. "Perkins did not like the Sex Pistols. 'I just don't get it,' he told me. Earlier in the day, he'd attempted to interview the Pistols at their hotel room. The Pistols agreed to speak with Perkins, if he would pay them five dollars [sic]. 'Did you give it to them?' I asked. 'Hell, no!' he snorted, indignant a journalist of [his] stature could somehow be on the take."[22]

Tony Storch was working at WRAS-FM in Atlanta, the college radio station of Georgia State University. "Back then we were playing music nobody would touch. I guess nowadays it goes under the guise of 'classic rock' … or not-so-classic rock. In any case, I got a free ticket for the Sex Pistols, which was fairly normal back then. I was 22 at the time of the show, and was also working part-time at another commercial radio station. I recall informing an older gentleman that I was going to see the Sex Pistols and getting into an awkward conversation with him. He was a very conservative southern gentleman and had a real problem with what the Pistols represented, which was basically 'sex, drugs, and rock 'n' roll.'

Promoter Alex Cooley (standing, right) looking perplexed as the Pistols vacate the stage. He'd booked the Pistols on being told they were the "hottest thing in England," yet would subsequently recall how "those scrawny kids from the wrong side of the tracks in London were as pleasant as could be" (© Alun Vontillius).

"I didn't know what to expect that night, but I recall being rather surprised by the number of people wearing black with pins and assorted metal in their faces. I had never seen anything like that before … or at least if I had, not to that degree. I was dressed rather more conservative: blue sweater and a red shirt with a four-inch collar! When the Pistols took the stage there was this incredible, palpable surge of energy and volume. When the band blasted into their first song the crowd—almost on cue—started violently gyrating and dancing wildly. It was unlike anything I'd ever seen, yet seemed natural given the intensity of their music and show.

"I've since read about people thinking the Pistols couldn't play, but I'd have to disagree as they held it together pretty tight. I know we in the audience had a sense we were present at some historical marker—it being the first North American concert and all. Afterwards, I saw an NBC crew questioning people as they walked out. I was somewhat media savvy, and knew they'd like a short soundbite so I gave them one.

'How was it?'

'It was vicious … and rotten.'"[23]

♪ ♪ ♪

The general consensus in regard to the Pistols' U.S. debut in Atlanta is that the audience was predominantly made up of people from the media. Some estimates have a 75 percent press/audience ratio. Sharon Powell says that while this is an exaggeration, the media did heavily outnumber the paying customers. "During the time period that the Pistols played the hall, we were in a state of flux, and there was a running joke that there were many more media than there were actual customers."

The vast majority of those reporters would write unfavorable reports, but the Pistols did at least have the satisfaction of knowing they'd had to pay for the privilege of putting their poison pens to paper. The Pistols' "no freebie" policy had extended to the coterie of photographers anxious to capture the Pistols within their lens.

One of the freelance photographers shuffling for elbow room in front of the stage was Bob Gruen. Gruen was familiar with the Pistols as he'd befriended McLaren during the spring of '75 while the latter was in New York, and had paid a visit to SEX during a visit to London the following year. "I'd made some money with the Bay City Rollers. My son, who was one or two years old at the time, was living in Paris so I went to visit him. And then I went to England. The only phone number I had was Malcolm McLaren's. I'd met him when he was working with the Dolls. He took me to a club called Louise where I met the Sex Pistols, the Clash, Siouxsie and the Banshees, Billy Idol … and a lot of other musicians who at that point were just kids wishing they were in bands.

"The pictures were printed in *Rock Scene*. It was new, way before something like *Rolling Stone* would recognize it. I think the first time *Rolling Stone* mentioned the Sex Pistols was when they were already a major group and were on the cover. After having traveled with Ike and Tina Turner, the New York Dolls, and Alice Cooper, to me they [Sex Pistols] weren't that unusual. They were just a bunch of wild, crazy guys, and I'd seen that already. Which is maybe partly why I was there? I was able to do it as a job and not be overwhelmed by it."[24]

Gruen's visit had conveniently coincided with the Pistols signing to EMI, allowing him to accompany the band to EMI's offices in Manchester Square to capture their contract signing for posterity. On a subsequent trip to London he accompanied the Pistols into the recording studios (Lansdowne Road) while they were recording "Anarchy in the UK."

Gruen's intention had been to fly down for the day, stay overnight at the Squire Motor Inn (where the Pistols were also booked), and then return to New York the following morning and hole up in his darkroom to develop the photos he'd taken of the Pistols.

In his 1990 book, *Chaos: Sex Pistols* (Omnibus Press), Gruen says his intention had been to snap some shots of the Pistols getting on the tour bus before heading for the airport, that he'd overslept, and that he'd then happened upon Vicious and the "tour manager," and had accompanied them to the airport. While speaking with Legs McNeil and Gillian McCain six years later, however, he says he'd been saying his saying his goodbyes when McLaren—realizing there was a spare seat on the tour bus taking them the 400-mile overnight drive to Memphis—invited him along for the ride.[25]

Gruen's mind must have been playing tricks on him, however, as the Pistols and their entourage—with the exception of Tiberi and Vicious—flew to Memphis. Their arrival at Memphis International the following morning was captured for posterity by Ebet Roberts.

THREE

Memphis

Barry Cain reports on the start of the Sex Pistols' American tour:
Johnny leaves his heart in Finsbury Park
Atlanta, Georgia—"Hullo, my name's John and this is the Sex Pistols" and into "God Save the Queen."
And so the band belly-flopped into one of the worst gigs they have ever played.
—*Record Mirror*, January 14 1978[1]

Whenever the Sex Pistols needed to hit the ground running they more often than not they tripped over their own shoelaces. And so it had proved in Atlanta. They couldn't even cite ring-rustiness for their putting in what was clearly a below-par performance, as they'd played 17 shows in December—their busiest month to date in terms of live shows. *Billboard* magazine chose to call it as they saw it, declaring: "*Sex Pistols Shoot Blank on First Atlanta U.S. Gig*." Despite his own less-than-complimentary assessment of the Pistols' opening U.S. show, *Record Mirror*'s Barry Cain believes there were mitigating circumstances for their poor showing. "Atlanta was a totally different vibe to a UK punk gig. In the UK, the aggression was honest and aimed at the sky, whereas in the U.S. the aggression was perfidious and aimed at the Pistols. A pure lack of understanding! Punk in a place like Atlanta, back then at least, could only ever be a fashion statement. I mean, what the fuck did 'God Save the Queen' mean to your average American?"[2]

Cain's introduction to the Pistols had come with interviewing Rotten at the end of November 1976, just prior to the band's appearance on *Today*. He'd also been the sole music journalist allowed to bear witness to Sid Vicious' unveiling as a Sex Pistol at the Notre Dame Hall in London the previous March.

Cain had only been working at *Record Mirror* for several weeks by the time he interviewed Rotten. He was of course already aware of the Pistols, but like many of his peers had assumed they would prove to be more hype than substance. It took but a solitary hearing of the promo copy of the "Anarchy in the UK" single that EMI had delivered to the paper's north London offices to bring about a rethink, however.

"When I heard 'Anarchy' my heart just went 'boom!' Then, when I discovered that John was an Islington boy like me, I thought it would be interesting to interview him. So when the opportunity did arise, I grabbed it. The interview was early in the evening at EMI's offices in Manchester Square. I think he was a tad relieved when he found out that I'd also grown up in a shit bit of Islington, and had ducked and dived as much as he had. It was a great interview, and John was, and still is, a wonderful interviewee."

When subsequently writing up the interview, Cain would declare the Pistols to be as "subtle as a sawn-off shotgun."[3] Yet little could he have known as he wrote up the interview that an unsuspecting world was about to get both barrels.

Cain had also leapt at the chance to fly out to the U.S. to report on the Pistols' tour, but owing to *Record Mirror*'s budget restrictions he'd only been able to cover the opening two shows. "Back then, record companies were more than generous when it came to press hospitality. The four weekly music papers [*NME*, *Sounds*, *Melody Maker*, and *Record Mirror*] were selling going on a million copies between them every week, and wielded immense power. So the fact that Virgin refused to pay the expenses of any journalist—including the national guys—was unprecedented. There had been death threats towards the band apparently, and the chance of a dead Sex Pistol was enough to send editors scurrying for their checkbooks. Virgin knew the force was strong with this one—unbridled free publicity and not a single hotel bill to pick up.

"Alf Martin, who was the editor at *Record Mirror*, asked me to go over and cover the two opening shows in Atlanta and Memphis. It was one of the last jobs I ever did as a staff writer. If I could get an interview, fine, but it wasn't important. The paper sorted the flights and hotels and even gave me some spending money. I was good to go, and hot to trot—a fucking adventure!"

With Virgin having left the UK-based reporters to their own devices, Cain hadn't anticipated any favors from anyone attached to Warners' press office. "I seem to recall no British journalists were allowed access to the Pistols. The only interviews were with American media. But this suited me down to the ground, 'cos 'I'm a lazy sod,' ha-ha."

Safe in the knowledge that gaining an interview with the Pistols wasn't a prerequisite, Cain nonetheless thought it only polite to pop backstage and say hello to the band. Finding his way through to the dressing room barred by a Stetson-wearing, 6-foot-5, 280-pound bearded behemoth (Glenn Allison), he walked up and asked Allison to inform the Pistols that "Barry Cain from *Record Mirror* says 'hello.'" Allison duly obliged, and returned a couple of heartbeats later to inform Cain—with deadpan delivery: "The Sex Pistols say 'hello' back."

It was a scene that wouldn't have looked out of place in *Spinal Tap*, but Cain says he was relieved. "It would've meant shorthand notes and transcriptions and … well, work! Besides, I didn't want to hang out with the Pistols—they probably couldn't do much but stay in their hotel rooms anyway because I guess it was a mite dangerous for them to venture out onto those Deep South mean streets. And to be honest, I'd never

Johnny Rotten. Walter Dawson, the *Memphis Commercial Appeal*'s resident pop columnist, thought the Pistols were "the first shot of real rock 'n' roll to come along in a long time" (© Tom Graves).

been down South before and so wanted to sample some of that renowned southern hospitality."

Cain would, however, inadvertently end up conversing with a Sex Pistol while awaiting his flight to Memphis. "I think I'd heard Sid had gone missing in Atlanta, but it was still a surprise when he turned up out of the blue with Glenn Allison. Sid came and sat next to me in the airport waiting lounge, his arm swathed in bandages after he'd slashed it with a broken bottle or something. Good looking guy up close. McLaren had ideas of Sid headlining in Vegas after the split. Might even have done it too."

♪ ♪ ♪

Before leaving Atlanta, Noel Monk had approached Glenn Allison with an offer to serve as additional security for the remainder of the tour. Monk knew Allison from their having worked on rock tours together in the past. Allison's unexpected departure from the GSEMH meant extra duties for Sharon Powell, but she wasn't going to stand in his way. "Some of the staff probably thought it was a bit cheeky, but most of us thought it was just fine. We were all music business folk, and we expected each other to get road gigs from time to time."

Vicious's going AWOL had presented Monk with an unnecessary headache. He was determined to keep to his schedule, however. Johnston says he and McLaren, and possibly Tiberi, stayed behind in Atlanta in the hope of locating Vicious. Realizing the three wouldn't have the first clue as to where to look for the errant bassist, Monk delegated Allison to assist them in their hunt for Vicious.[4]

Lynn Stroud and her friend Paula had already gotten way more than they'd ever imagined when purchasing their tickets, but their involvement with the Pistols was far from over, as Stroud explained. "After the show, we offered to take the band out on the Atlanta social scene. Sid was ordered back to his room by the record company watchdogs, and Johnny either went back to his room or elsewhere as he didn't join us. I took Steve and Paul to the Place on Paces, which was close by, and at that time was a good late night pub for drinks, music, and backroom billiards. I shot a game of pool with Steve and actually beat him, which doesn't say much for his skills since I had played maybe twice in my life before that. Steve and Paul were very normal from what I could gather comparing it to my exposure to other musicians of the rock world. Nothing out of the ordinary other than being typical 'artist heads'.... Very nice artist heads, in fact."

Stroud's friend Paula had opted to stay behind at the hotel with Vicious. "She loved the volatility of Sid's personality. She was always up for adventure, while I was the more cautious, logical, in-control one. Paula's adventures with Sid continued in a chaotic direction, which she summarized for me at the end of the night. She told me how Sid had gotten more and more riled up at his enforced confinement. They started making a lot of noise, apparently jumping up and down on the beds, acting like school kids, causing a ruckus; Sid was also throwing things against the wall. Paula thought it was a blast seeing this side of him, and it was—or so she thought—all in good fun. His true intent, of course, was to get Paula to take him somewhere where he could score some drugs.

"At some point, the record company watchdogs came in to settle Sid down. When Sid threatened to leave with Paula, they ripped the phone out of the wall. They told him he wasn't going anywhere, and told Paula to leave. She said they locked him in his room from the outside somehow, but apparently it didn't work. When Place on Paces closed I drove

Steve and Paul back to the hotel. As soon as they exited my car and headed up the steps to their rooms, a shadowy figure jumped out of the nearby bushes and into the passenger side of my car. My heart stopped for a second, but then I looked again.... It was Sid! He'd recognized me while watching his band mates exit my car, so I guess he figured I must be 'one of them.' He ducked down low in the seat and said, 'Lynn, get me out of here quick!'"

Having been forced to go cold turkey since leaving London, Vicious was suffering a withdrawal that no amount of alcohol was going to shake. Unbeknown to Stroud, Vicious had established contact with a local drug supplier back at the GSEMH and had pocketed Rory Johnston's wristwatch as a means of paying for his fix.

"It was an antique Omega that my dad gave to me, and I was actually blaming myself for being an idiot in losing the watch," says Johnston. "I was sharing a room with Sid, and I remembered seeing him eying the watch earlier. It was shortly after Sid had left that I noticed my watch was no longer on the bedside table where I'd left it. I thought, 'The bastard's taken it as collateral!' I was angry at the time, but you couldn't stay angry with Sid because he never meant any harm."

Lynn Stroud only knew Vicious' drugs liaison by "distant association," and therefore had no idea where the guy lived. Vicious, however, already had all the relevant info. "Sid had the guy's address and phone number. He said that he could get me there if I would just drive him. 'Sure,' I said calmly, knowing with certainty that I wasn't taking him anywhere. 'Just wait here a minute, let me run up to the room where your mates are going. I want to thank the guys from Warner Brothers for dinner and say good night. I'll be right back.' I knocked on their room door and said, 'Uh, fellas, your prisoner is in my car down by the lobby.' They shot out of that room and down the stairs like the FBI on a raid. Unfortunately by the time they reached my car, Sid had already lost his patience, or suspected my intent, and was long gone. Apparently, word had it later, that he got out on Piedmont Road and hitch-hiked to the 'drug-connection-person's' apartment where it is said that he got the drugs he wanted and stayed the whole night."

Vicious' "drugs liaison" was Freddi Griffin, a talented drummer, who was well-known for being one of the more flamboyant characters on Atlanta's alternative music scene. Having been a professional musician for several years, Griffin's first impression of the Sex Pistols was not a good one. "It seemed like a terrible start to a tour; the band was obviously already having problems, and Sid looked like he was 'jonesing.' The whole backstage deal was kind of a drag. I didn't feel like hanging around for very long, so I decided to go over to The Hothbrow, a nearby bar, and have a cocktail before going somewhere else. I'm sure I was probably also 'on a mission.' I.e. to score some coke or whatnot."

Griffin knew Stroud at the time of the Pistols' Atlanta show, but the two hadn't spoken for years. "I had no idea Lynn had been hanging out with Sid that night. At least it finally solves the mystery of how he arrived at my apartment. I'd always assumed it was some wanna-be groupie who'd overheard me talking to Sid. Anyways, Sid showed up at the apartment I was sharing with a friend. We'd been home for a while, and Sid managed to escape his handlers and make his way to our apartment, which, lucky for him, wasn't that far away from the band's hotel. He was dope-sick and wanted some heroin but we didn't have anything like that. This was when we were having 'tea parties' [PCP, a.k.a. phencyclidine or "angel dust"] so we offered him some of that and he shot up.

"I know doing PCP when you're dope-sick sounds horrible, but Sid seemed to dig it.

He kept saying, 'I want another whoosh, Joey!' He was a huge Ramones fan apparently, and decided that I resembled Joey Ramone. He said something like, 'I don't want to call you 'Freddi'; you're Joey.' I think it was his way of getting closer to me, he felt that we were getting to be mates or something. At first we were having a good time listening to Ramones records and talking. I think I had managed to find him a Tuinal or something so he wouldn't be so miserable. Besides, Sid was so messed up that being dope-sick was just part of life; he was so spaced out that his brain couldn't keep up with his addiction. He talked to me a bit about what he was going through with his band mates. How he used to be close friends with Johnny, and sort of friends with Steve."

Sometime during the night Vicious offered to trade leather jackets with Griffin. "There was no way that was going to happen! I had a new Harley motorcycle jacket, and Sid's jacket was absolutely disgusting. It reeked of body odor, vomit, and various other stenches. In fact, he was the worst-smelling person I'd ever met, and he held that place of dubious honor until 1992 when I was in the studio recording with GG Allin. That's pretty fucking awful!

"Sid also threatened to jump off the balcony for some reason. I told tell him, 'Go ahead, if you must!' He'd been saying shit like that every five minutes. I didn't really expect him to do anything at that point. Besides, our apartment was on the second floor. And although it was a little high because it was on the back of the building, unless he dove out on his head, jumping off the balcony would've probably just pissed him off! Unfortunately, while scattering my records all over, spilling drinks, and roaming about, an ornamental dagger that had been designed to look like Excalibur apparently caught Sid's eye. At some point the dope sickness either got to be too much for Sid, or the PCP turned on him. He grabbed the dagger and locked himself in the bathroom. Before anyone even knew what he was doing, he managed to deeply gash his left arm. Of course, we didn't know it at the time, but this was just the first instance during the tour where Sid managed to do himself fairly serious harm. Aside from feeling horrible, I guess he was also still trying to live up to his image of being 'Sid Vicious.'"[5]

According to Griffin, sometime the following morning, McLaren and Glenn Allison arrived at his door. "I'm still not sure how they tracked him down. Poor Sid didn't want to leave, but of course he didn't have any say in the matter. Malcolm wasn't going to take no for an answer; he was rattling Sid's breakfast meds in front of him. More Valium, I suppose.

"Apparently Malcolm had made the rounds of the local musicians and groupies until he found someone who knew who Sid had been with. So Sid rejoined the tour unwillingly, but he actually wanted to stay with me—at least as long as he could keep playing my records and doing drugs! I felt bad for him when he was led off. There seems to be some confusion in the books I've seen about how and where Sid was located. Some say that Glenn Allison tracked him down at Piedmont Hospital, although that version seems somewhat unlikely as Sid wasn't the type to seek medical attention."

Rory Johnston is adamant that Griffin is mistaken about it being McLaren that arrived at his door. "There's no way it could have been Malcolm as I was with him the whole time. People are surprised that Malcolm entrusted Glenn Allison—a guy we'd only just met—with delivering Sid to Memphis, but you have to remember Warners were calling the shots. Whatever Monk said went, and Malcolm had to fall into line. I was convinced the band

Three. Memphis

Rotten, foreground, and Vicious were undoubtedly the focal point, but it was Jones and drummer Cook's playing that left the greatest impression on U.S. audiences (© Ebet Roberts).

drove to Memphis, but maybe everyone flew from Atlanta and we all missed the plane. It would mean we'd recovered Sid by then. It's funny because I remember getting on board a bus in Atlanta after they'd arrived, but possibly that was a local rental? We were late getting to the show in Memphis, so maybe we all missed the first plane and were running late?

"Malcolm and I definitely went to the airport alone. I know this because we ended up missing our flight to Memphis. Atlanta is a fucking huge airport, and I can still picture us dashing through the departure lounge. We missed the damn thing by a hair's breadth. The plane hadn't taken off yet, but the gate was closed and they wouldn't let us through."

Ebet Roberts' photos are undeniable proof that the Pistols flew from Atlanta to Memphis, and Johnston vaguely remembers their taking receipt of the state-of-the-art tour bus in Memphis. "That's the only way any of it makes sense. If we didn't pick up the tour bus until Memphis, how else would the band have got to Memphis? I've probably confused myself because of our traveling by bus during our stay in Atlanta."

Johnston never did see his prized Omega watch again, but Griffin says Sid didn't offer him a watch or anything else that night. "I never personally saw Sid with any watch. And I wouldn't have been interested in it even if I had offered it. I wasn't a drug dealer of any kind at the time. I had connections for coke, PCP, and all sorts of pills—hell, it was the Seventies—but unfortunately for Sid, I didn't know anyone at the time that had heroin. Sid didn't pay or trade for anything that night; that's why he wanted to stay."

♪ ♪ ♪

Memphis is hailed the world over as the birthplace of rock 'n' roll owing to Sam Phillips' Sun Studio at 706 Union Avenue being the place where Elvis had first stepped up to the mic. Presley was now dead of course; his having suffered a fatal heart attack the previous August aged just 42. The lip-quivering, perfectly coiffed Elvis of '56 might have been little more than a sepia-toned memory by the time of his demise, but the King was nonetheless still worshipped on high by millions around the world, many of whom had made the pilgrimage to Graceland. Noel Monk claims that while awaiting Vicious' arrival in Memphis, Rotten, Jones and Cook had visited Graceland to pay their respects at Presley's gravesite.[6] Lydon, however, refutes this in *No Irish, No Blacks, No Dogs*, saying that while Jones and Cook might have done so, he'd gone so far as to avert his gaze when the tour bus had passed by Graceland's gates en route to the show.

The 725-capacity Taliesyn Ballroom (which would be torn down the following year to make way for a Taco Bell), was situated a little ways farther along Union Avenue from Sun Studio. "The Taliesyn—pronounced 'Tal-is-syn'—was a big ballroom attached to the 20th Century Club, the latter of which was almost demolished but is now, today, being restored as a high-end restaurant," says Tom Graves, who was 23 and recently married at the time of the Pistols' visit to Memphis. "The Taliesyn and 20th Century building were fine old edifices, but terribly dilapidated. It was crumbling inside, needed painting, and was perfect for the Sex Pistols. I was afraid that the amplification that night would cause the ceiling to cave in. I had never been to a concert there before. I don't know who found it, but, ordinarily, I don't think they used the place for concerts. So it was a strange venue to have it at in the first place."[7]

Stacy Hall, a 19-year-old art student in January '78, says the Taliesyn was an appropriate place for the Sex Pistols to play as it was "glamorous but shoddy." "The Taliesyn, or Xanadu as it was originally called, was a lovely old mansion originally built for debutante coming-out parties and wedding receptions. However, countless hundreds of high school graduating class and college fraternity parties had left the Taliesyn a wreck, always smelling a little like vomit. It was beat up, but it certainly was historic. And it was a blow to the city when the Taliesyn was razed in order to open a Taco Bell, of all things."[8]

Graves says that punk rock had pretty much passed most of his fellow Memphians by. "Memphis at that time did not know much of anything about the so-called 'punk movement.' The Ramones were unheard of here. When the Sex Pistols blitzed into Memphis, probably not one in ten people in the audience had ever heard one note of their music."

Graves first became aware of the Pistols on seeing Charles M. Young's reportage on the band in *Rolling Stone*. "Their name alone seemed calculated to outrage the status quo including the staid rock press. They brought danger back to rock 'n' roll, and I knew they were going to be a force to be reckoned with. I immediately wanted to check them out. Their album wasn't available in any of the record stores in the entire Memphis area, but I did manage to find an import copy of 'Pretty Vacant' in Peaches Records on Park Avenue. I had no idea what to expect when I gave the record its first spin, but from its repeated guitar signature followed by a thunder of drums—then the nastiest-sounding power chords this side of the Who's *Live at Leeds*—I was completely hooked. My wife, somewhat predictably, hated it, as did every friend I pigeon-holed into listening to the song."

As with Tom Graves and many others, 23-year-old aspiring folk guitarist Jeff Golightly had first read about the Pistols in *Rolling Stone* and had been thrilled on discovering Memphis was included on the band's U.S. tour itinerary. "I just kept seeing articles in the papers about this horrible band from England that was pissing everybody off. The local media here in Memphis were acting as if the world was about to end, and all the good church people would go to hell if they allowed the concert to take place. That intrigued me to no end. I just knew it was something I needed to see and be a part of. For years we had been saddled with the Fleetwood Macs, the Eagles, and other snooze rock. I personally was ready for a change back to rock 'n' roll."[9]

The *Memphis Commercial Appeal*'s resident pop columnist, Walter Dawson, was another thrilled to hear the Pistols were coming to Memphis. "I thought it was great. I thought it was the first shot of real rock 'n' roll to come along in a long time. On the other hand, the fact that it was a joke was nice too. And the people who didn't get the joke included the Memphis Police Department and city leaders, who actually sent police officers to Atlanta. They had all these ideas that the Sex Pistols were going to come in and jerk off on stage and all this stuff."[10]

"I'd personally had never heard of the Sex Pistols but there was some discussion [in the department] about their act," E. Winslow "Buddy" Chapman, who was the city's chief of police at the time, reflected. "The reaction was the same as the first visit of the Rolling Stones a few years earlier. We had heard that the Sex Pistols were a pretty wild group in regard to their interaction with the crowd, and that there might be problems. We had been given information that there'd been a near riot somewhere else where they'd played. The place they were going to be immediately prior to Memphis was Atlanta, so I sent a couple of people down there from our intelligence unit, just to see what we might expect."[11]

One of those packed off to the Great SouthEast Music Hall on a fact-finding mission by Chapman was the legal advisor for Memphis police department's detective division, Clyde Keenan. Keenan's brief was to spend the days leading up to the Pistols' U.S. debut liaising with officers from Atlanta's vice squad and then speak with the people from Warner Bros. that were accompanying the Sex Pistols and the band members themselves. "My primary concern was how incendiary the Sex Pistols might prove in terms of causing people to get violent," says Chapman. "But Clyde came back to Memphis, and reported that the content was not as outrageous as the hype would have us believe."

Somewhat ironically, it was the city officials themselves who would prove the cause of people getting violent, as Tom Graves explained. "The Taliesyn supposedly held around nine hundred people, but no one thought to mention that this was to be with festival seating where concertgoers are herded like cattle into an open room and made to stand without seating for hours. I later discovered that Buddy Chapman was already worried that the Sex Pistols might instigate some sort of riot, and along with the fire marshals, he declared the festival seating arrangement unsafe and had instructed the promoter to put seats in the room. This, however, meant that at least two hundred people holding tickets weren't going to be admitted inside."

Having been satisfied with Keenan's assessment that the Pistols' stage act wouldn't violate any Memphis state laws, Chapmen hadn't intended on going to the Taliesyn until receiving a call about the growing unrest outside owing to the fire marshals' decision to restrict admission. "What it amounted to was that they had, like, ten times as many people as could get in. They already had the ballroom full and there were a whole lotta people on the sidewalk—people who had tickets. It was grossly oversold!"

♪ ♪ ♪

Prior to his and Vivienne Westwood's taking over the lease at 430 King's Road, McLaren had studied film and photography at Goldsmiths, University of London. He'd abandoned the course midway through, but his fascination for moving pictures had never diminished. When the Sex Pistols had first started to gain momentum, McLaren had hired Cambridge graduate Julien Temple (who would of course go on to direct *The Great Rock 'n' Roll Swindle* and *The Filth and the Fury*) to document many of the Pistols shows. Temple had even accompanied the band to Ivanhoe's to film the Christmas Day show, yet McLaren hadn't thought to invite him to accompany the U.S. tour. The U.S. shows would be captured for posterity, however, thanks to another rookie filmmaker, Lech Kowalski.

The London-born Kowalski had relocated to the U.S. with his Polish refugee parents at the end of World War II. He'd been enrolled at New York's School of Visual Arts when he'd become enamored with the city's burgeoning punk scene. He'd been desperate to get in on the action surrounding the Pistols' U.S. tour but had no independent means of financing such an escapade. Just when it seemed he'd have to watch the tour from the sidelines, a mutual acquaintance put him in contact with the colorful Thomas King Forçade (born Kenneth Goodson).

Thirty-three-year-old Forçade was the founder of *High Times* magazine, which took its name from the MC5 song of the same name and advocated the legalization of marijuana. Forçade believed he and the Sex Pistols were kindred spirits. So much so that the December 1977 issue of *High Times* had featured an article on the Pistols titled "Stormhippies of the Seventies" and had featured Rotten on the cover. Kowalski's crew had distributed copies of the issue inside the Great SouthEast Music Hall.

Like Kowalski, Forçade was an aficionado of the New York punk scene. So much so that he helped finance *Punk* magazine. "Tom helped us out several times in very big ways, including advertisers and national distribution," *Punk*'s cartoonist and co-founder John Holmstrom explained. "Tom was our biggest fan, and a true punk rocker. Keep in mind that although Bob Marley, Blondie, and Johnny Rotten appeared on the front cover of *High Times*, you never saw the Allman Brothers, or the Grateful Dead, or any other hippie bands on the cover."[12] Forçade had launched *High Times* in 1974, the same year he'd been indicted over an alleged conspiracy to firebomb the 1972 Republican Convention in Miami. "Tom was arrested for 'attempted sabotage' because he was driving a truck that supposedly contained explosives," Holmstrom continued. "Tom was bat-shit crazy all right, but these so-called 'explosives' were actually smoke bombs which were to be used at 'Eat the Rich,' a Yippie rock concert. The charges were eventually dropped, but at the time he had to go into hiding. It was during his exile that he came up with the idea for *High Times*.

"Glenn O'Brien, who was working as an editor at *High Times* back then, claims he was the first person to tell Tom about *Punk* magazine. But since Tom lived near Bleecker Street, which was plastered with 'Watch Out! Punk Is Coming!' posters, I think he was already aware of us. One day in May 1976, Tom came storming into our office, sat down at my desk and said, 'I'm going to make you rich and famous!' It was Tom who arranged payment for the printing costs for Punk #6 ('The Legend of Nick Detroit,' our first feature-length photo comic). *High Times*' parent company, Trans-High Corporation, paid $2,000 for an 8-page 'mini *Punk Magazine*' that appeared in the February 1977 issue of *High Times*. He also gave us remnant advertising space whenever possible. However, this didn't stop Tom from bellowing, 'I gave you $2,000 worth of advertising space' whenever we ran out of money and the rent was due."

Forçade had launched *High Times* on a $20,000 shoestring, but such was the magazine's popularity that the circulation had doubled with each issue. By January 1978, *High Times* was selling some four million copies a month and grossing $5 million a year.

In exchange for Kowalski agreeing to re-edit a long-forgotten film titled *The Smugglers*, Forçade agreed to bankroll what would become *D.O.A.: A Right of Passage*.[13] Forçade's reputation was such, however, that upon discovering his involvement in Kowalski's movie project Warners had flatly refused to grant Kowalski and his film crew any access to the Pistols. Yet someone from the label must have been in cahoots with Forçade, or how else could Kowalski's crew have gained access at each venue?

"Tom Forçade was pretending to be a journalist, as I recall," says Rory Johnston. "My impression was that Noel Monk was dealing with Forçade, and yet his crew was being allowed to film the shows. I couldn't understand it. It didn't make any sense. It got to the point where I confronted Forçade in Tulsa. I said, 'What the fuck are you doing? I don't want to see you inside as you haven't got permission!' But he and his crew still managed to get inside somehow."

Punk was primarily championing the Ramones, Patti Smith, Blondie, and all the other leading lights on the burgeoning New York scene, but Holmstrom had got to hear of the Sex Pistols early on in their career and had been keeping a watchful eye on their subsequent rise to infamy. "We had a clipping service at *Punk*. We paid a small fee for each clipping and in return we received a 'tear sheet' from a newspaper or magazine article whenever 'punk' was mentioned. At first, the service was inexpensive as there were few mentions of punk rock in the media in 1976. By mid–1977, however, we couldn't afford the service anymore as we were getting huge packages with hundreds of news clips from all over the world. We were also trading mail subscriptions with *Sounds* and the *New Musical Express* in London, as well as fanzines, notably *Sniffin' Glue*, and *Ripped and Torn*. *Punk* was like 'Punk Central HQ' back then."

Mary Harron, who is perhaps better known for her work as a director and screenwriter on movies such as *I Shot Andy Warhol*, *American Psycho*, and *The Notorious Bettie Page*, was an early *Punk* contributor. In October '76, she'd flown to the UK to conduct an interview with Rotten backstage at Eric's in Liverpool where the Pistols were playing. (The interview appeared in *Punk* #8 in March 1977.)

"Mary told me she was planning to visit England," Holmstrom explained. "She had attended St. Anne's College, Oxford University, where she'd dated Tony Blair! When she asked me if there were any bands I would like her to interview while she was in England, I was ecstatic. I was so excited that *Punk* magazine was going to cover the English punk scene. Not much was happening in New York, or the rest of the U.S., by late 1976. I think Mary's interview with Johnny Rotten is the best we ever ran in *Punk* and maybe the best punk rock interview ever. He was honest and revealing, perhaps the only time you got an idea of what he was really like."

Harron's "scoop" would prove a double-edged sword for *Punk*, however. "The Pistols

"The problem is you!" Rotten, sporting the tartan suit Vivienne Westwood made especially for the U.S. tour, addresses the Taliesyn crowd while Vicious watches. One fan came away from the show sensing Vicious was "playing the clown to Rotten's psycho killer" (©Tom Graves).

seemed to turn against us after it was published," Holmstrom continued. "I never read another interview with Rotten that didn't seem manufactured, which is a shame. Rotten is an intelligent man, and his fans deserve to hear the truth from him."

Holmstrom was well aware of Forçade's bankrolling Kowalski's project, but hadn't expected to be handed a ringside seat on the Pistols' tour. "Tom called me on the afternoon of the Memphis concert, and from out of nowhere invited me to join the tour. He had already bought a plane ticket to Memphis, and had promised me a ticket on the door at the Taliesyn Ballroom. I frantically picked up the ticket, but the banks were closed by then. ATMs didn't exist yet, so there was no way for me to get any money. The few dollars I was able to scrape together would enable me to get a cab to JFK, and then from Memphis airport to the venue. After that I would be left with a couple of penny rolls, but I wasn't worried as Tom had told me that we would meet up after the show."

♪ ♪ ♪

Monk had booked the tour party into a Holiday Inn situated just off Interstate 55. The hotel was some distance from downtown Memphis, yet close to a major highway should the need to make a hasty getaway arise. Monk had no doubt spent a restless night en route to Memphis, as losing a Sex Pistol within three days of his taking charge of the band wasn't going to look too good on his CV. He was therefore mighty relieved when Glenn Allison arrived at the hotel with Vicious in tow. Satisfied that everything was back on track, Monk had placed Vicious in Tiberi's care before retiring to his room to grab a couple hours of sleep.

Tiberi, however, had no intention of playing babysitter and left Vicious to his own devices. "Sid had his private life, and it wasn't a case of me looking after him, shaking his willy, and putting it away again afterwards.[14]

"As I've already said, the Pistols were a professional band," Tiberi reflected. "Babysitting Sid, or any of the others, wasn't in my job description. My job, as I saw it, was to keep everyone focused—to 'keep the motor running,' if you like. But things got very disorientating because of the visas. And then there were the band's internal dynamics to consider. John and Malcolm were simply not communicating by this point. If anything, John was going out of his way to spoil Malcolm's plans. And while a huge finger of blame can be pointed at Sid, Steve was also going a bit off the rails. But what Monk says in his book about his rooming with Sid is absolute nonsense! Sid wouldn't have been seen with someone in a baseball cap—let alone room with them!"

Discovering Vicious had been allowed to go walkabout again wasn't the news Monk had expected when he made his way down to the Holiday Inn's reception area. Fearing what the reaction might be within the Warners hierarchy should they discover their $1 million surety had been put at risk for a second time within as many days, Monk called Ted Cohen, Warners' national director for special projects, at the Taliesyn Ballroom to give his version of events surrounding Vicious' latest powder act.

Cohen, of course, was experiencing problems of his own as the two hundred or so ticket-holders who had fallen foul of the fire marshals' decision to restrict the Taliesyn's capacity were becoming increasingly vociferous at their literally finding themselves left out in the cold. The beleaguered Cohen was still relating his concerns about the unrest flaring into a full-scale riot when the receptionist interrupted Monk to indicate he had an internal call waiting. Puzzled as to who could be calling, Monk hung off from Cohen and waited for the caller to come through. It took but a heartbeat to put a name to the southwestern drawl on the other end of the line—Tom Forçade. It seemed Forçade knew where Vicious might be located, and was hinting at a quid-pro-quo arrangement whereby he'd reveal the bassist's whereabouts in return for Kowalski and his crew being given full access to the Sex Pistols.[15]

Monk assumed that Forçade had Vicious with him; Vicious later showed up in the courtyard and was collected.

John Holmstrom says that "no one at Warners seemed to care about Sid's obvious addiction problem. The goal seemed to be 'whatever it takes' to survive the tour. It was sad to see." Monk once again had Vicious under wraps, but he couldn't risk any further mishaps where the latter was concerned and decided it prudent to trade places with Johnston and room with the bassist for the remainder of the tour.

♪ ♪ ♪

Tom Graves arrived at the Taliesyn early to ensure getting a good seat. Aside from himself, he'd also purchased tickets for his wife and best friend—both of whom he says were somewhat less excited than he on the drive to the Taliesyn. Graves' excitement would go into overdrive upon hearing a familiar tune emanating from within the ballroom as they pulled up outside. "As we arrived I heard the familiar sounds of 'Pretty Vacant' shaking the building; the Sex Pistols were inside doing a soundcheck. Not being able to yet enter from the front, I ran around back to try and catch a glimpse of them. A very small crowd had gathered, and suddenly people started shouting out to Sid and Johnny. But once they finished the soundcheck their security people hustled them out quickly and back onto the bus so that only a few people caught sight of them."

Jeff Golightly remembers arriving at the Taliesyn at almost the same time as the Pistols.

"They were in a MATA bus. MATA [Memphis Area Transit Authority] is our public transportation. The Sex Pistols were just sitting there watching out and enjoying the circus. It was quite a surreal sight."

The fire marshals' edict about the capacity restrictions quickly dampened Golightly's mood, however. "I was extremely pissed off! They said it was oversold, and were no longer letting anyone in to the building. I was mouthing off to a fire official when I was tapped on the back by the promoter, Bob Kelley. Bob asked to see my ticket and then took me around the back entrance. I entered through the kitchen into the ballroom. Bob did this with a lot of other people. However, he never took my ticket. I kept it, and years later sold it on eBay for $1,000. So I got to see the Sex Pistols, and got paid for keeping the ticket. 'Ever get the feeling you've been cheated?' Nope, not me!"

The support act in Memphis was Quo Jr. ("The Son of What's Happening"). "They were a local band composed of veteran rhythm and blues musicians," says Golightly. "I'd only heard of them as they were a black rock band, which was pretty rare for Memphis. I thought they were good. I ended up becoming friends with their guitarist, Harold Otis."

Bob Kelley had initially booked a local punk outfit called The Scruffs to open for the Pistols before deciding at the eleventh-hour to replace them with Quo Jr. The Scruffs' then-manager Henry G. Loeb (whose father had been serving as mayor of Memphis at the time of Martin Luther King's assassination a decade earlier) had booked his charges onto the bill via a verbal handshake with Kelly. "He [Kelley] had booked the Sex Pistols as some kind of novelty act. For Memphis, they were a pretty avant-garde crew. Then, the day of the gig, one of his [Kelley's] subordinates called me and said, 'Sorry, y'all are off the bill and this band Quo Jr., is going to play.' We were infuriated—it made for an unbelievably unpleasant morning and afternoon."[16]

Tom Graves had never heard of Quo Jr., until that night, but, as with Golightly, he would find them an amiable bunch as he subsequently befriended the band's charismatic front man, Roland Robinson. "Roland, who sadly passed in November 2004, was surprised at Quo Jr. being chosen as the warm up band. I don't think they actually met the Pistols that night, but Roland talked about it being a memorable and exciting evening. Quo Jr. had a song called 'We Can't Communicate,' which was pretty apt as the audience didn't know what to make of a black rock band. They got a very nasty and rude reception from a crowd that was totally amped-up for the Pistols.

"The crowd was entirely white, and seemingly didn't give a damn about the music, especially that of a black warm-up band. I have never felt such anticipation and electricity in a crowd before or since and it was both exhilarating and very frightening. The feeling was as if we'd been soaked in some inflammable juju and were waiting for the first spark to ignite us."

Stacy Hall was already familiar with Quo Jr., as the band had played at her high school prom. "They were just a typical black covers band … or so I thought at the time. I can't recall much about their performance at the Taliesyn, other than a black band being a super odd choice to play before a band like the Sex Pistols. I think they [Quo Jr.] were probably terrified, looking out onto a sea of asshole white kids itching to do some damage to whoever showed up on stage. I've since come to realize they were actually groundbreaking musicians.

"The venue was half-lit while Quo Jr. loaded onto the stage. There were no chairs that

I recall, and people milled around. It didn't even seem crowded, because the venue typically had lots more people for oversold shows. The event was oversold by a few hundred tickets. I think that was typical for most rock shows in Memphis back then, and folks would usually just squeeze in. But with the press attention this particular show was getting, the fire marshals were called in and the rules were enforced.

"Inside the hall, there was a lot of silly behavior from rednecks who were taking advantage of an opportunity to throw beer cups because they had heard that violence was part of the 'punk rocker' scene. I'd say the vast majority of the crowd had no insight into the aesthetics or philosophical underpinnings of the punk movement. Because the fire marshals had blocked the door, it was pretty comfortable. I remember the same Alice Cooper songs playing over and over the PA and thinking, 'Why Alice Cooper?' Perhaps that was an inside joke at our expense—that whoever was playing Cooper's records thought we wouldn't know the difference from old rock and this new musical experiment?"

The mood was turning ugly out in the street, but Tom Graves says was oblivious to the unfolding drama outside the Taliesyn until paying a visit to the bathroom. "It was before the Pistols came on, and you could hear the chief of police [Chapman] outside with a bullhorn. People were throwing things and breaking windows out. It was scary. This was going on outside and you didn't know if it would cause a riot inside. You just didn't know."

"Part of my issue with the bullhorn was to calm them down and say that this was not a police issue, it was a safety issue," Chapman explained. "That it wasn't a question of fire marshals being unreasonable, but that, and I remember telling them this over the bullhorn, there was literally no more room inside. You just couldn't get in there. I know that the locked-out ticket-holders wound up being confrontational with my officers, and I knew that there might end up being some arrests made. It was obviously a situation that could have precipitated into something that was out of control.

"When those ticket holders were told the venue was full they were naturally very upset and began to try to get in. People were screaming and throwing things. It was spilling over into the street. It wasn't like they were throwing bricks or things like that at the windows. What they were doing was pressing to get in, and the club had to go ahead and lock the doors. And in the course of all these kids pressing up against the windows, they shattered the glass."

One of the more-enduring myths surrounding the Memphis show is that a SWAT team was called in to quell the disturbance outside the Taliesyn Ballroom. Chapman, however, insists that the situation far from warranted such measures. "I never feared any real violence would occur. Some doors and windows were broken, but when the breakage occurred, we cleared the area with no real problems. I do not remember if there were any arrests, but I don't think there were. At worst, there were perhaps some 'confrontations.'"

John Floyd, who would go on to write for the *Memphis Flyer*, was only 12 at the time but was desperate to catch sight of the Pistols. "I had a friend who was a bit older than me. She had a car and she took me down there. I didn't have a ticket or anything, and it was complete mayhem. Some of the front windows were smashed through. When I got there, the Sex Pistols were already on but I just kind of wormed my way through one of the window areas."[17]

Reflecting on the events outside the Taliesyn some four decades on, Graves says that while a few "brickbats and stones were thrown through a few windows," it wasn't a riot. "The police presence plus the sleet and cold diminished anything serious. Had it been a hot August night, no telling what might have happened. A lot of people were very unhappy about being shut out of the ballroom. I'm just very glad I wasn't one of those people."

John Holmstrom was standing in the lobby fearing he was going to be "one of those people" left out in the cold. "When I got to the venue there were dozens of cop cars outside. It was surreal. I quickly discovered that a riot had just taken place because of bootleg ticket sales, and that there was no ticket left for me at the door. More importantly, as far as I was concerned, there was no sign of Tom Forçade. I asked to see someone connected with Warners, and just seconds before security kicked me out of the lobby Warners' rep Gary Kenton—God bless him!—appeared and let me into the venue. Ironically, it was only because of Sid going missing, and because of the bootleg ticket riot that led to the show being further delayed that I was able to catch the show."

♪ ♪ ♪

The Taliesyn Ballroom's acoustics were undoubtedly ill suited for staging a rock concert, but Tiberi's rudimentary soundboard skills ensured a cacophonous racket. "Something no one has mentioned previously about the show is that Johnny Rotten's voice was heavily reverbed during the opening number, 'God Save the Queen,' Graves explained "After the song ended he began to speak to the crowd, but all you could hear was echo. He gave a deadly look to someone off-stage who corrected the problem and we could then hear him speak. We could only understand him after they turned down his high reverb.

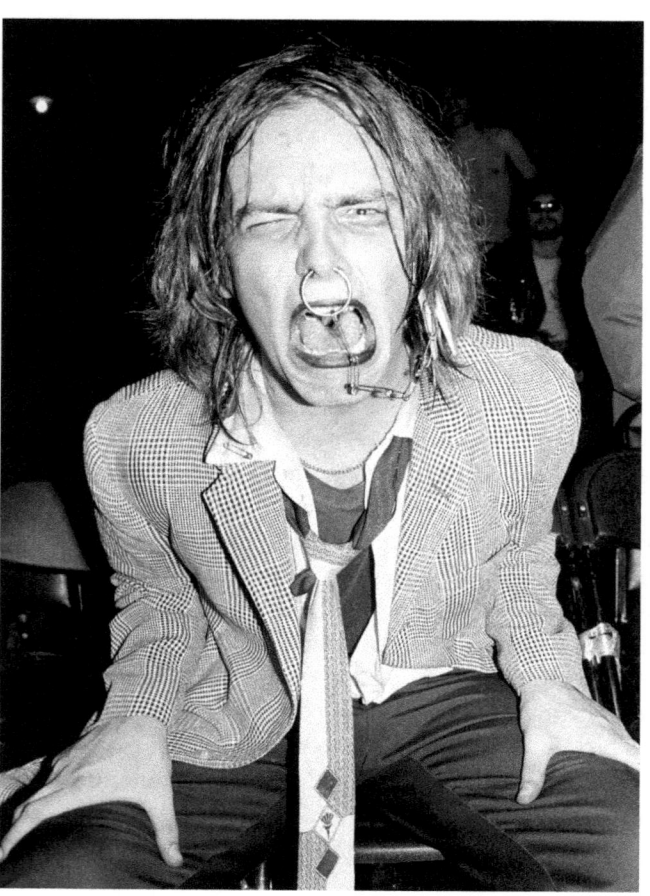

A fan striking a punk pose. Whether the hoop went through the septum Roberts can no longer remember (© Ebet Roberts).

"Johnny looked great in his blue/green plaid suit. Throughout the show he mimicked some of the Shakespearean mannerisms of Sir Laurence Olivier, particularly Richard III, hunchbacked, rocking back and forth as he sang dementedly; his eyes blazing like pilot lights on a stove in the spotlights. His voice was different ... an acquired taste. Almost no one in the crowd had heard the Sex Pistols' music, but Memphis always loved the Who so the power chords and thunder drumming was totally accepted. They had nowhere near the amplification firepower of the Who, but my God, when Steve Jones and Paul Cook thundered down I thought the Taliesyn Ballroom would fall to pieces.

"You couldn't buy alcohol at public concerts in Memphis back then, so all they had that night was Coke served in small cups with big fat chunks of ice. The ice was big enough to throw at the band, and I saw several pieces hit Johnny in the face causing him to wince. What none of us knew at the time was that Sid could not play bass guitar at all. His sound was so thick and muddy you could not distinguish notes; all you could hear was a huge, earth-swallowing throb. He was wonderful entertainment though, a character very much like the high-art wrestling characters we Memphians love. He had red markings all over his torso, but I was too far away to make out what they were."

It wasn't until reading a review of the show in the following day's newspaper that Graves discovered the markings in question had been self-inflicted. Such was Vicious' desperate state that he'd daubed "Gimme A Fix" across his chest with a felt-tip marker in the hope that someone in the crowd might answer his pitiable plea.

Roland Robinson had observed Vicious during the soundcheck and had been disturbed by what he'd seen. "Sid was totally out of his mind, man. I was sitting there after the soundcheck and he'd be grabbing and shaking me. He'd get up, walk around and pace, then sit back down and start doing it again. When he first came in and started talking, I turned to the other guys and said, 'You see this guy? That's the picture of a dead man.' He looked like somebody who had either just escaped death, or was about to see it very shortly. He had that pale look, like he was a shell that walked and talked like a man."[18]

Being a bass player himself, Robinson was naturally scathing of Vicious' questionable talent. "Steve and Paul were the real musicians in that band. You could unplug Sid and just the guitar player and the drummer had the energy level to keep that band going and Johnny Rotten had the energy level. Those three were the focal point and Sid was just the amusement."[19]

Stacy Hall was familiar with the set list as she'd managed to get her hands on an import version of *Never Mind the Bollocks* at her local music store. She'd discovered the Pistols purely by chance while idly flicking through the TV channels one evening after dinner. "I caught a news segment, perhaps *60 Minutes* or a similar network program that had a segment about a political music movement in England that was being broadly defined as 'punk rock.' I was transfixed: here was bullshit-free music with the same sense of urgency and bareness that I heard in the local garage bands and blues trios I had grown up listening to. I ended up doing my high school senior term on the sociological influences in Great Britain that led to the punk movement, and how it echoed the antihero of U.S. films on the Fifties. The paper got an 'A,' and it gave me an excuse to spend hours reading music rags.

"No one really knew what 'punk' meant in the context of an event, but my friends and I—thinking the Sex Pistols were an authentic distillation of the British underclass rebellion that I'd put forward in my high school paper—wanted to endorse this rebellion so we co-opted the uniform. We were garbed in torn T-shirts, tight trousers, and white pancake makeup. I think we were taking more influence from the 'droog' look of *Clockwork Orange*, actually. We made for a striking look, in any case."

Hall's dedication to detail from what she'd picked up in the UK music press saw her pierce her cheek with a safety pin (She can be seen in *D.O.A.: A Right of Passage*.) "It hurt like hell. And yeah, I took it out immediately after the show. However, we were among only 20–30 people whose attire reflected any knowledge of the UK punk scene. The rest of the crowd was in typical dress of the time for going to concerts: jeans, tube tops, baseball caps. So, obviously, the press focused attention on us."

Hall and her friends had taken up a position at the front of the stage so as to ensure the best possible view. "Rotten was absolutely mesmerizing. He absolutely owned the crowd. People were screaming obscenities at him—again, misinformed about what 'punk' was supposed to be. He just stood stock still, head slightly cocked, unblinking. Even when lumps of ice hit him, he just kinda flinched. To this day I don't think I've seen such a successful display of calculated, chilling charisma. I think Lydon is a brilliant showman, totally in command of his brand. Even back then, that was starkly clear.

"Sid played the clown to Rotten's psycho killer. He behaved exactly like a teenager who was given too many drugs and too much attention would be expected to act. Not sure why the obsession with spitting began, but soon the crowd was spitting on the band, and the band spat back. I was in the crossfire, so to speak. At one point Sid spit on me, and for years afterward I would joke how 'Sid spat on my cheek and I didn't wash it for months.' He had a lot of fresh cuts on his stomach that night. I do remember fresh blood, which I thought was rather glamorous.

"I thought it was a really incredible show. The Pistols were kind of desultory, though. If I were to look at that show now I'd say that they didn't have much enthusiasm, but at the time we just all bought the whole attitude as part of what was appropriate. A funny think happened after about the fourth song, though. The crowd kinda started drifting away from the stage. Remember, most had just showed up to see the spectacle. When the spectacle turned out to actually be just a medium-tight rock band that played super fast and loud with inaudible lyrics, people seemed to lose interest. Of course, the famous quote of Rotten's: 'I'm not here for your entertainment … you're here for mine,' could have also done the job of shutting off any remaining sympathies. As a result, space cleared out for the remainder of the set, and I think I even recall some folk pogoing."

Rotten, left, and Malcolm McLaren, right, sharing a joke. The bonhomie wasn't set to last, however. The person in the background is unidentified (© Ebet Roberts).

Three. Memphis

With the exception of "Belsen Was a Gas" being introduced to the set, the running order of the songs was pretty much identical to what the Pistols had played the previous night in Atlanta.

"Belsen" was mooted to be the Pistols' fifth single, set for a February release. Vicious had penned the darkly humorous lyrics prior to his joining the Pistols. Truth be told, it was a substandard ditty that should have been left alone, but such was the paucity of material that the band had been forced to incorporate the song into their set. "Belsen was a very poor song, at least by the Pistols' standards," says Tiberi. "I know John didn't like it, and didn't enjoy performing it. A lot has been said about Glen being the only one who could structure songs, but I disagree. I watched them working on 'Holidays' while we were in Sweden. And when we returned to London they went into the studio to work on the song proper."

Contrary to what is written elsewhere, it wasn't until the Taliesyn show that Rotten amended the lyric of "Anarchy in the UK" to "Anarchy in the USA," and unlike Atlanta, the Pistols returned for an encore, performing The Stooges' classic "No Fun."

Buddy Chapman had stayed behind, if only to see if the Pistols had warranted the near-riot. "To be honest with you, and this is my personal opinion, I thought the show itself was an anticlimax. Firstly, there was barely room to move in there, and, secondly, because both the group and the audience well, the group was definitely zoned out on something, and the audience, well, a lot of them were too. My tastes are very varied from classical, to country, to Rolling Stones, to Beatles, to Tina Turner, to Mannheim Steamroller ... and

Rotten, center, and Cook (striped shirt) making their way through Memphis International Airport flanked by Monk's security team (© Ebet Roberts).

most definitely not the Sex Pistols. It was probably as unnoteworthy a thing as ever happened in Memphis."

John Floyd thought the crowd's reaction to what they'd just witnessed was part anger and part bemusement. "Here's this horribly mangy, lousy, bad band onstage, and it was just a complete fuck you to the musical ethos of professionally trained musicians. That's probably the hostility that even as a goofy 12-year-old I could sense. I remember people walking past me and just saying, 'That was the biggest load of garbage I've ever heard. These guys are terrible!' I was only in there for about 20 minutes or so, but I remember when I left, walking across the street to my friend's car, just hearing so many people expressing so much rage. It was like nothing I'd ever experienced at a music event. It wasn't as simple as someone leaving a Rod Stewart concert and complaining because he'd fucked-off during 'Maggie May.' This was a group of people extremely upset at what they'd just seen."[20]

Walter Dawson, however, came away from the Taliesyn that night knowing he'd just witnessed a seismic shift. "Because of that show, a lot of people were drawn together who might not have found each other and it showed that there was a scene for that kind of music here in Memphis. The whole thing about the Sex Pistols was that they drew a line in the sand, and you had to decide which side you were on, which is what all good rock 'n' roll does anyway. Music that can piss off that many people!"[21]

Jeff Golightly was happy to step across Dawson's metaphorical line in the sand. "After seeing the Sex Pistols, I realized it wasn't all about being perfect and I thought, 'Fuckin' hell,

Jones, right, and band associate Boogie Tiberi chat on the drum riser after the show (© Ebet Roberts).

I can do that!'" Abandoning his acoustic in favor of an electric guitar, he formed his own band. "The Crime was considered 'punk' for Memphis! We were more new wave than punk, but we did a lot of Clash and Sex Pistols before we started to write our own material."

The Pistols kicked ass "as far as I was concerned," says Graves. "There was tension and electricity at the same time. You didn't know if the show was going to be totally great and historic—which it was—or if it was going to be a total riot disaster, which in a way it was too. It was this weird clash of everything. I've never been to a concert, as many as I've been to, that had the same feel. And I don't expect I ever will."

The pin hole in Stacy Hall's cheek would soon heal, but the memories from that night will stay with her forever. "I'm not a musician, and I barely understand the academics of musical structure. But I am an obsessive pop culture consumer. I am constantly appreciative of the opportunity I had growing up in Memphis where music and pop culture have such a strong, vital, symbiotic relationship. In 1975, I sat in 95-degree heat and watched Furry Lewis play for about twelve people at a crafts fair (I bought him some lemonade). In 1977, I watched the drugstore check-out lady in front of me break down and sob right in the middle of tallying purchases when the announcement came over the PA that Elvis had died. Six months later, I stood in a musty ballroom and watched the Sex Pistols wipe rock 'n' roll clean. How lucky am I?"

Four

San Antonio

Sex Pistols in Memphis
Officers of the Memphis, Tennessee Vice Squad attended the Sex Pistols' American debut performance in Atlanta on Thursday just to make certain that the band was not a threat to public decency of their city. The Pistols passed the test.
—*Sounds*, January 14, 1978

In an October 2012 interview with the *San Antonio Current* to commemorate the 35th anniversary of the Sex Pistols' show at Randy's Rodeo, John Lydon would lump much of the blame for the hostility the Sex Pistols endured during the '78 U.S. tour on those reporters who had "deliberately turned up just to write rubbish and create friction."[1] Lydon doesn't make any distinction, but he was referring to the British journalists who were following the tour as the U.S. media had by and large focused on the Pistols' musical merits. Bob Merlis certainly believes it was the British press contingent that posed the biggest threat in regard to the $1 million surety Warners had riding on the tour. "Those British reporters were far worse than any others I encountered on that tour. I was only at the opening show in Atlanta, and the final one at Winterland, but I saw enough to know those guys were always looking for ways to make trouble. I lost count of how many of them tried to bribe me to get backstage in Atlanta. I sold tickets—at face value—to the U.S. press, but I'd made the decision that I wouldn't sell to the British press. But they wouldn't take no for an answer. They literally kept shoving money into my hand!"

The UK tabloids had certainly looked upon the Pistols as maniacal manna from heaven. After reporting on the band's exploits for some fourteen months by that juncture, however, they had to conjure up ever-more lurid headlines in order to titillate their respective readerships. McLaren, of course, had done all he could to fan the flames and wasn't above lighting the touch paper himself on occasion. His credo was to create chaos whenever and wherever possible, and though there had been a distinct lack of chaos at either of the two shows played to date, he could rest assured of a more incendiary reaction in San Antonio.

Steve Jones had been living in LA for some twenty years when called upon by Stephen Colgrave and Chris Sullivan for his thoughts on the '78 U.S. tour. In that time he'd toured America extensively, either as a solo artist or with the reconstituted Sex Pistols, and still regarded San Antonio as the place where only the hardiest musicians had dared to tread. "[It's] bad now, but it was really weird back then."[2]

The 2,200-capacity Randy's Rodeo, at 1534 Bandera Road (State Highway 16), was a large Texas-style ballroom that proudly boasted being "the finest western dance hall and night club in San Antonio." Named in honor of its owner (Randy Sherwood), Randy's Rodeo had started out several years earlier as the Bandera Bowl, and with precious little else to do in the way of entertainment for teenagers living in the area, the bowling alley had proved something of a godsend. Inevitably, the makeover caused resentment among those same teenagers, but Don Strange, who ran a rib joint directly across from Randy's Rodeo, says that while the bowling alley was regarded as being state-of-the-art for its time, it was ultimately doomed to failure. "The bowling alley was built to be world-class, and it earned some national exposure. But the caliche-laden soil—along with the heat—caused the ground to shift, and the lanes never remained even. Hence, the bowling alley failed, setting the stage for Randy's Rodeo."[3]

Sherwood's decision was soon paying dividends as Randy's attracted all the leading lights of the country music scene. The makeover would also benefit the local community, as the build up in traffic forced the city planners into paving all the dirt roads within the surrounding area.

Rock music would be slow in coming to San Antonio, however, as Charlie's Quarter Place in neighboring Universal City held that particular franchise. Things only started to change when San Antonio's KISS-FM, which had started out with a show tunes format, switched to playing album-oriented rock (AOR), then encouraged its DJs to produce their own shows, with many of them bringing in albums from their collections. With KISS' playlist soon boasting nothing but rock and heavy metal, San Antonio was on its way to being known as the "Heavy Metal Capital of the World."

Today, Randy's Rodeo is a bingo parlor run by the Catholic Church, but San Antonio certainly hasn't forgotten the Sex Pistols or the anarchic events of January 1978. Aside from the *San Antonio Current* feature, January 2013 also saw the South Texas Popular Culture Center stage the "We're So Pretty: The Sex Pistols in San Antonio 1978" exhibition. The exhibition featured a plethora of photographs from the show, as well as the original Sex Pistols-at-Randy's PR package. *The Austin Chronicle* would also post a commemorative feature titled "Holiday in San Antonio: The Night the Sex Pistols Went Off at Randy's Rodeo." The feature was penned by one of the *Chronicle*'s senior staff writers, Margaret Moser, who was also at the show.

Moser was 24 back in January

"Sex Pistols in Texas tonight" (© Roberta Bayley).

1978 and was working for the long-defunct *Austin Sun*. She'd gone to Randy's with her boyfriend (and future husband), Ken Hoge, who was also working at the *Austin Sun*. (Hoge's photos from the show were among those on display at the "We're So Pretty" exhibition.) "As a fledgling rock journalist, I followed regional scenes, and was particularly interested in the New York, CBGB, and Max's scene," Moser revealed. "I worked at a bookstore to support my writing habit and devoured the *New Musical Express* and *Melody Maker* as they came in—often three weeks behind. I'd anticipated something equivalent from the Brits, though the path to punk was already well-trod with the likes of John Cale and Brian Eno.

"Ken and I drove down to Randy's together. Ken bought the tickets for $3 in advance at Joske's at Highland Mall. Joske's is like Marks & Spencer's in the UK, and the irony of buying tickets for the most 'fuck-you' band ever at a suburban mall was too rich. We'd bought *Never Mind the Bollocks* the day it came out at Inner Sanctum Records in Austin, and were howling at the thought of the Sex Pistols playing at Randy's Rodeo of all places!"[4]

"Margaret and I had been playing the album on high rotation because we liked it so much," Hoge adds. "I'm not sure when I first heard of the Sex Pistols, but I'd read about the punk scene and did not immediately identify with what seemed to me like a bunch of scary people. It took listening to the music for me to transcend the initial revulsion to the whole anarchy in dress and hairstyles and what seemed to me like, well, punks. You have to remember how revolutionary that attitude was. I still dressed like a hippy with long hair, you know. We gave each other the peace sign. That was 'hip.' Punk was not 'hip.' It wasn't the next 'big thing.' If anything, it was the anti-thing."[5]

Like everyone else with a taste for the wilder side of rock 'n' roll, Moser and Hoge knew the Pistols impeding date at Randy's Rodeo on their debut American tour was one of those seismic events that people would be talking about for years to come—an added twist coming with the show falling on what would have been Elvis Presley's 43rd birthday. Moser says that while their more senior colleagues at the paper made "enthusiastic noises" about the Pistols, they were accompanied by a "rather you go than me" attitude. Indeed, from the moment the U.S. tour was confirmed it seemed that the American media as a whole became instantly polarized as to whether the Pistols would live up to the hype or the emperor's new clothes were simply being held together by safety pins.

The *Austin Sun*'s then-music editor, Bill Bentley was one of those making "enthusiastic noises" about the Pistols, having read about the band in *Village Voice*. Bentley wasn't one for sitting behind a desk while the paper's junior staff went out into the trenches, however. "If something new was happening, I wanted to be there to see it in person. I knew punk was the new musical revolution, so when the San Antonio show was announced there was no doubt I'd go. We had a semblance of punk in Austin, but the Sex Pistols were the masters. I was 27 years old at the time, and knew enough to know that an event like this wouldn't come again!

"I sensed a true hatred for humanity coming from Johnny Rotten. I didn't like that. I still wanted to make peace, love, and understanding save the world. Hatred was for creeps, and Johnny Rotten played the role of 'King Creep.' But musically the Sex Pistols mattered, and I wanted to experience it in person—to be where real music is born."[6]

The bus that would ferry the Pistols and their entourage all the way through to San Francisco was state-of-the-art. Noel Monk says it was equipped with all the on-the-road necessities, including six bunks and plenty of legroom for those grueling all-night drives.[7]

Four. San Antonio

San Antonio awaits the Sex Pistols. Future Go-Go's member Kathy Valentine "couldn't believe the Sex Pistols were coming to San Antonio" (© Ken Hoge).

Instead of driving directly to San Antonio from Memphis, the tour party stopped off en route in Austin where they would stay overnight before then heading to the venue. Monk made the decision to set up a base camp in the Texas state capital (which, as the crow flies, lies some ninety miles north of San Antonio) owing to death threats the Pistols had supposedly received since arriving in the country. There was, of course, no way of knowing whether said threats were real or had been manufactured by McLaren, but with Warner Bros. having made a significant outlay on the Pistols, Monk couldn't afford to ignore the threats and thought it prudent to err on the side of caution. Rather than accompany his charges, McLaren had opted to remain in Memphis till later in the day before flying to San Antonio.

Rory Johnston says the decision to stay in Austin was reached simply because Austin was a college town and the Pistols could go sightseeing or whatever without fear of being attacked. "Warners had arranged some radio promotion, but after that was done the band were free to do what they wanted. We couldn't risk letting them loose in San Antonio, because, well, San Antonio was nuts at the time. Randy's Rodeo sold bottled beer at the show, which gives you some idea as to the mindset."

The Pistols had been in America for several days now, but it was surveying the Texarkana landscape flashing past the windows during the 650-mile drive from Memphis to Austin that introduced them to the real America. "Sid would sit next to me, and we'd look out the window," Lydon subsequently enthused. "We'd stare at that endless scenery and imagine John Wayne and the Indians. You wouldn't sleep. You wouldn't want to—it was so 'first time.'"[8]

Vicious poses for the camera while Rotten adjusts the mic stand and Jones checks his tuning. Local musician Jesse Sublett remembers the Pistols "hit the stage blasting like a pack of howling coyotes loose in a chicken pen: blowtorch guitar, machine gun drums, snarling vocals, sneering faces, bass rumble" (© Ken Hoge).

♪ ♪ ♪

Saturday, January 7, had been a designated rest day. The Broadway Plaza was situated in downtown Austin and within easy walking distance of the city's sights and delights, but Rotten—with his designated bodyguard Glenn Allison dutifully in tow—opted to spend his last free evening before four consecutive shows at the cinema watching Clint Eastwood's latest action movie, *The Gauntlet*. His fellow Sex Pistols, however, acted more in keeping with their hedonistic reputation and whiled away the hours at a massage parlor situated within walking distance of the hotel.⁹

John Holmstrom arrived at the Broadway Plaza that day with a rather interesting tale to tell. "After the show in Memphis ended, Joe Stevens, the New York photographer that was covering the tour for the *NME*, offered me a ride to the hotel where the Pistols were staying. I turned him down, as I was still expecting to meet up with Tom Forçade at some point. Big mistake! I didn't know Tom was banned from all performances, due to the rumors of his being a CIA/FBI agent. Total disinformation!

"It was Allen Ginsberg that accused Tom of being an FBI informant—a rumor that quickly spread around town. Ginsberg later regretted his actions, and apologized for starting this false and destructive rumor. Sometime during the late Eighties I ended up working at *High Times*. While I was there I set about putting together a definitive history of Forçade, and spoke to as many of his associates, co-workers, friends and relatives as possible to sort out the rumors about his being linked to either the FBI or CIA.

"Besides being a road manager for the MC5, Tom was also very prominent in the White Panthers. The White Panthers were a far-left, anti-racist, political collective. Look it up: they supported the Black Panthers' ten-point program as well as 'Total assault on the culture by any means necessary, including rock 'n' roll, dope, and fucking in the streets.' There are also statements against wearing underwear, and demanding 'Everything free for everyone!' Tell me, does this sound like your typical CIA/FBI guy?

"Anyways, Tom was again a no-show, and seeing as I didn't have any money I started walking to the airport. After a few miles I was exhausted and decided to hitchhike. I was immediately picked up by three pimps in a 1950s Cadillac. They tried to sell drugs to me. When I said I was dead broke they attacked me. I threw my suitcase at them, blocking their attempt to stab me with a switchblade knife, opened the car door and ran for my life! They drove around for a while looking for me, but I hid from every car that drove by.

"I wandered around a weird suburban ghetto area until, as if by magic, the airport appeared next to the road. I entered a hotel, where I met the filmmakers Tom had hired to document the tour. We did a short film interview with Don Snyder, a well-known hippie photographer that Tom had hired to work on the documentary. While the filmmakers bought a sandwich for me at the airport restaurant, I heard the whole crazy story of Forçade vs. Warner Bros. vs. the Sex Pistols. They let me sleep in a room they had rented.

"I could not wait to get home, but I'd lost my plane ticket during my near-mugging. The next morning I called the airline and prepared to return to New York. Instead, Forçade met with me in a stretch limousine and proceeded to reveal his plan about documenting the Sex Pistols tour, while explaining that I would produce a book and a *Punk* magazine cover story. To me, this made perfect sense seeing as the Sex Pistols had become the biggest entertainment story in the U.S. at the time." The *Punk* cover story would obviously require photographs, and so Forçade arranged for Holmstrom's colleague Roberta Bayley to join up with the tour. "I was at home one night when someone called me from *High Times* magazine and told me I had a ticket to San Antonio in the morning and to pack my bags," Bayley explained. "They wouldn't give me any details, but Holmstrom, who was already out on the tour, said to just do it.

"The Ramones were playing that night at the Palladium; I think the Runaways were opening, so of course I had to go. There was an 'after party' at Julian's Billiards next door. Richard Hell was there, Ivan Kral from Patti Smith's band, Joan Jett, Dee Dee Ramone, etc. I was freaking out because I was leaving first thing in the morning and I had no cash—this was way before cash machines. So David Johansen lent me $50. And yes, a first class ticket was waiting for me at JFK."[10] Upon her arrival at the Broadview Plaza, Bayley received another unexpected piece of news. It seemed Don Snyder had had second thoughts about working with Forçade, and Holmstrom had suggested Bayley be flown in to document the tour for *Punk*. "I don't remember anything about Don Snyder, but John knew the details much better than me," Bayley reflected. "But since I was contacted the night before, and flew down on the day of the show, if that was a factor then it must've been decided earlier. I just think Forçade realized John's story would need photos and I was a bargain. They didn't pay me anything!"

Like plenty of others on the Bowery scene, Bayley hadn't been impressed on learning the Pistols wouldn't be playing New York. "Of course we were all pretty pissed off about that, because most of us in New York could not afford to travel to any of the cities they were playing. I didn't even own a car! Bob Gruen and Joe Stevens, they were more professional and went down to the first gig in Atlanta. Because it was a subject that you could sell, there was a frenzy of interest. It was an 'event.' Bob and Joe liked what was going on and joined the circus." Coincidentally, renowned rock photographer Annie Leibovitz was on the same flight as Bayley, having been commissioned to cover the tour by *Rolling Stone*. "Annie was sitting behind me in first class. She said, 'Aren't you Roberta Bayley?' I was a little shocked that she knew who I was. I guess she was trying to figure out how I, a virtual nobody from *Punk* magazine, got into first class! Who was paying me? Here she was the big hotshot *Rolling Stone* photographer, so how could I be on the same plane? I was thinking the same thing."

Bayley was already acquainted with McLaren from her having temporarily helped out at 430 King's Road during the summer of 1973 (back when the shop was named Let It Rock). She'd relocated to London from her native California after dropping out of college. "I only worked at the shop for a couple of weekends. I remember showing up for my first Saturday at noon and no one was there! I guess I didn't realize things were that casual. I knew Malcolm and Vivienne because they used to come eat at this vegetarian restaurant I worked at called the Chelsea Nuthouse on Langton Street in World's End. Later, I met Gerry Goldstein who was a friend of Malcolm's, and Malcolm had hired him to work in the shop. But Gerry couldn't start right away because he was still working at a porno bookstore or something. So I offered to sit in until he could start."

Bayley and McLaren's paths would cross again while the latter was in New York with the Dolls. By this time, Bayley was working the door at CBGB. She'd taken to snapping pictures of the bands while they were onstage, which in turn had led to her working for *Punk*, and ultimately to her being commissioned to shoot the cover for The Ramones' eponymous debut album. Little could she have imagined as she'd watched McLaren's futile attempt to rejuvenate the ailing Dolls that he'd return to America within three years as the manager of the most talked about band on the planet—an accolade she herself felt worthy of the Pistols. "I bought all the singles, and I also had the album. I loved all of it—especially the beginning of 'Pretty Vacant.' The Pistols were a great band, they really were."

McLaren was still operating a limited access with the media policy, but thanks to Bayley's

Four. San Antonio 61

Several fans give the Pistols the finger, but all eyes are on the stage. Photographer Ken Hoge remembers how the mood inside Randy's went from "funny, to frightening, teetering on the edge of a riot" (© Roberta Bayley).

association with McLaren, Holmstrom was able to join them for dinner. His initial impression of the Pistols' manager was very telling. He thought McLaren's manner to be subtle to the point of being near imperceptible, and that while he appeared "a bit spaced" on occasion he was nonetheless the "most eloquent person I spoke with during the whole tour."

During the meal Holmstrom sat enthralled while McLaren unveiled his plan for the tour. Back in New York he'd been as curious as anyone else as to McLaren's reasoning for eschewing the North in favor of the South. Listening to McLaren waxing lyrical about how he believed the South would prove a receptive environment where the Sex Pistols' philosophy could take root and thrive had reminded Holmstrom of the late-night conversations he'd had with Forçade, and he immediately recognized the two mavericks had much in common.

♪ ♪ ♪

The ticket price for Randy's Rodeo was again set at $3.50, but those attending the show would get extra value for their money as there were two support acts on the bill. Ultra, the main support act, were more mainstream rock whereas The Vamps were more in keeping with what the crowd could expect from the Pistols as they had incorporated songs from the New York Dolls and The Stooges into their set.

The Vamps were able to grab the opening support slot thanks to the band's keyboardist Joe Pugliese working for Stone City Attractions, which was promoting both Texas dates. His older brother Frank was their singer. "Frank and I wanted the band to open the show and my co-workers at Stone City agreed to let us open," Pugliese explained. "Some guys in the band still had long hair, but we played punk and glam so we were a goods fit for the Sex Pistols. I already had a copy of their album. The owners of Stone City, Jack [Orbin] and Greg [Wilson], were hard rock enthusiasts and didn't necessarily understand the punk stuff. When they asked me about booking the Pistols for San Antonio and Dallas I urged them to book the shows. Only after they had booked the shows did they find out about the safety pins and anarchy. So I'm going to stress my personal taste in music as the reason those dates were booked."[11]

Sig McKenna Izbrand, who was living in nearby Olmos Park, was good friends with Joe Pugliese, and says it was through him that she first heard about the Pistols coming to San Antonio. "The phone rang. 'Hey, Sig. It's Joe. You won't believe who SCA have booked into Randy's Rodeo.' I was instinctively intrigued by the conspiratorial tone in his voice. San Antonio had a long-standing reputation as being the 'Heavy Metal Capital of the World' at the time, yet Joe knew that I had diverse musical tastes that extended far outside that genre. I couldn't imagine that he would be calling with such a sense of urgency to tell me that Judas Priest were coming to town. I waited expectantly for him to reveal his mysterious news. 'The Sex Pistols are coming,' he whispered into the phone. He could hardly contain himself while explaining that The Vamps would be on the bill. The Vamps had been steadily gaining traction on the local club scene, but going from that to opening for an international sensation overnight was a huge leap."[12]

It took Izbrand a moment or two to process Pugliese's news that the Pistols were set to play Randy's Rodeo, a venue she'd only thought of as a "country music dive." She was another that had been intrigued by Charles M. Young's *Rolling Stone* feature on the Pistols, and her immediate reaction had been to ponder why a band that was being hailed as a cultural phenomenon in Britain would be coming to San Antonio. "In my mind, scenarios didn't get any weirder—or better—than that. The more I thought about it, the more I liked the idea. I had not as yet heard *Never Mind the Bollocks*. I didn't even know what 'bollocks' were at the time, frankly. But the title alone seemed to be a warning that I should toss all my preconceived notions of what music should or could be."

The Pugliese brothers, and their fellow Vamp, Ed Wilson, were taking a break after setting up their gear in readiness for the soundcheck when the Pistols' tour bus pulled up outside Randy's. "I spoke to all the Sex Pistols and Malcolm McLaren when they arrived for soundcheck," says Joe Pugliese. "I remember their hanging out making small talk and joking around. Paul and Steve were perhaps the more accessible members, but Johnny autographed a promo photo for me. I recently found it again after not seeing it for many, many years."

Given the exaggerated tales about the Pistols that had been circulating in the local press—such as the *San Antonio Times*' decrying the band for "making obscene gestures at everything that moves, and telling teenagers to give up on their future"—Pugliese remembers thinking that other than Rotten and Vicious being a bit "weird," the Pistols were "just regular guys."

A dozen or so fans were loitering by the door, several of whom were clutching album covers for their heroes to sign. Once the autograph hunters had been catered for, Rotten, Jones, and Cook followed McLaren inside Randy's, while Vicious remained outside shooting the breeze with the Puglieses and Wilson. It soon became apparent, however, that the bassist had an ulterior motive behind his bonhomie, as Pugliese explained. Ed was wearing wraparound sunglasses, and Sid decided he'd like to borrow them for the show. Instead of asking though, he just grabbed the glasses off of Ed's face and said, 'I'm gonna need these.'"

Before heading inside the venue Vicious had promised to return the shades after the Pistols came off stage. In hindsight, it's difficult to see how Wilson could have objected. Joe Pugliese might have worked for Stone City Attractions, but a disparaging word from Vicious could still have seen The Vamps expunged from the bill. Despite Vicious' promise to Wilson, however, this was the last the guitarist would ever see of his sunglasses other than when the Pistols were on stage. "Frank and Ed joked about it for years," Pugliese reflected. "Frank loved to tease Ed in front of other people, asking him what happened to the sunglasses he lent to Sid."

The guys in Ultra would also find Vicious in an amiable mood. "Sid came into our dressing room wanting to try a Lone Star beer," the band's bassist Scott Stephens recalled. "Backstage they [the Pistols] were nice guys, but we heard them fighting among themselves that night. With the cowboys, rockers and punk guys all there, the whole thing was really volatile. We were asked to warm up for them in Dallas, too, but we bowed out. We felt like a square peg in a round hole."[13]

Vicious clowns around for the crowd. One reviewer would liken the bassist to a "kewpie doll in shock treatment." Vicious' playful mood would subsequently darken, however (© Ken Hoge).

Joe Pugliese says that while Randy's wasn't a sell-out, he reckons the Pistols drew a crowd of around 1200 or so. "There was big buzz about the show, but I'd say only half the audience were fans and knew of the Pistols' work. The other half was just curiosity seekers and people who were there for the spectacle. They only knew what they'd either read or heard about the Pistols, and had come to see the freak show ... colored hair, torn clothes, safety-pinned faces etc. That is what contributed to the tension in the room! Also, it seemed to me that some people came just to throw something at the Pistols because they thought it was part of the 'scene' that they'd read about."

The "safety-pinned faces" Pugliese saw that night were due to a quick-thinking local entrepreneur who'd had the foresight to cut the pins in the middle so as to give the appearance of the pins protruding through the flesh. He was selling the "Punk Pins" from a concession stand at a dollar apiece.

♪ ♪ ♪

The Vamps weren't the only local act intent on grabbing the opening slot, as musician and author Jesse Sublett III revealed. "My band, the Violators, tried to snag the opening slot for the Sex Pistols. We thought the local scene sucked big-time, with its cosmic cowboys and progressive rock geeks. We were rock 'n' roll terrorists, primed to strike. We were mostly a covers band. We had two or three originals, but the rest was pub rock and Sixties stuff. During rehearsal breaks, however, we'd play Stooges and Sex Pistols. But if you played Stones, Kinks, Who, etc., loud and a bit fast, then it was pretty much punk rock."[14]

The Violators' guitarist was Kathy Valentine, who would of course go on to find fame with The Go-Go's. She had only recently returned to her native Austin after a lengthy sojourn living in London where she'd joined the fledgling Girlschool after responding to the all-female band's ad in *Melody Maker*.

Valentine's time in Girlschool (who were going under the name Painted Lady at the time) would be brief, owing to her missing a gig through illness, but her head had already been turned in another musical direction. "This was when I figured out that punk was what was happening. While I was in London I saw Eddie and the Hot Rods, the Vibrators, Boomtown Rats, and Buzzcocks. I was back in Austin by October '77, and started the Violators with Marilyn [Dean] and Carla [Olsen]. We wanted the line-up to be all girls, but we couldn't find a bass player. So Jesse either offered, or we asked him."[15]

Valentine had brought back the stash of punk-related singles she'd amassed while in London, but Jesse Sublett is keen to stress that he and his circle of friends were already hip to what was happening in London before their friend's return. "We weren't ignorant hicks here, not our group of people. Today, people may say, 'Wow, there was no internet, how did you know about what was happening in the world of music or anything else?' We read *Trouser Press* and *Creem*, and the *NME*, for one thing. Those magazines kept up to date, and they wrote about cool stuff, not so much the mainstream old bands. And Inner Sanctum Records in Austin was the nerve center of the music scene. They had all the newest stuff and you found out about it before it came out. We bought the first Sex Pistols' singles as soon as they came out. I even had a 'God Save the Queen' T-shirt!"

Though living in Austin, Sublett didn't learn about the Pistols using the college town as a base camp until some time later. "There was a comment in a magazine called *Rumors* that always cracked me up. One of the Pistols, I think it was Steve Jones, said, 'We've been on your high street (referring to East Sixth Street, where a lot of bars were located and still are). We've been to six bars, and this town sucks.' They stopped at Rottles, which was an old mom and pop clothing store that sold mostly NOS (New/Old Stock). And a friend of mine worked at Old Pecan Street Cafe when they came in there. It was one of a smattering of trendy cafes on the street at that time. The street was just then starting to gentrify."

Randy's Rodeo was probably the last place in the whole of Texas in danger of being gentrified, but Kathy Valentine wasn't fazed by the choice of venue. "I was so excited to see the Pistols; I didn't care where they were playing. I couldn't believe they were coming anywhere near us!"

On hearing the Pistols would be playing San Antonio, Sublett says he thought the Violators stood a pretty good chance of getting the opening slot at Randy's. "We knew people, and we were pretty confident that we were the only punk band around. We knew the guys at Stone City Attractions, and we sent them a tape and photo. We thought we'd get the gig, but of course, our friend Joe Pugliese was working for SCA."

Valentine says she personally didn't think The Violators "anywhere near ready" to open for the Pistols, and as such, didn't concern herself with anything other than the headliners. "I don't remember paying any attention to the opening bands 'cos we were either outside hovering around the tour bus hoping to meet the Pistols, or socializing with people we knew from the scene. In fact, I met a cute punk that night and brought him back to Austin to be my boyfriend."

Aside from putting his own band forward, Joe Pugliese also played a part in getting Ultra the main support slot. "Their singer, Donjon Evans, was a good friend of mine so we put them on the bill. Ultra were a hard rock band with twin lead guitars. The punk fans didn't like them, but they were a great band."

Evans, who was working on his master of fine arts degree at the University of Texas, in San Antonio, at the time of the show, says he jumped at the chance for Ultra to play. "I was excited because I knew of the punk scene. My friends and I had already been to CBGBs, so I wanted to see the Sex Pistols. I was, however, a little apprehensive because we were a heavy metal band, and I was wondering how we would be received by a crowd that was there to experience punk. When I got to Randy's the tension in the air was so thick you literally could cut it with a knife. I met Annie Leibovitz, who was there for *Rolling Stone*. I asked her why all the reporters were there and she said, 'We're waiting for the big fight to erupt.' I asked her, 'What big fight?' She said, 'The clash between the punks of England and the rednecks of Texas!' I had to laugh. A young punk in a wheelchair with a pin through his cheek told her, 'That's not San Antonio's style, lady!'"[16]

Evans says he has no recollection of Ultra being offered the opening slot in Dallas. "I personally don't remember us ever being offered the Longhorn gig. I would, of course, taken it had it been offered. Maybe Sid said something about it while sharing a beer with the rest of the band. I was by the back door smoking a joint at the time. I would usually smoke one before going onstage back then to settle the nerves."

Izbrand had been born and raised in Texas, and yet says she had never rode a horse or owned a gun. Nor had she previously set foot inside a western honky-tonk bar, and was praying that the Randy's regulars wouldn't be comprised of "tobacco-spitting, Stetson-wearing, Lone Star Beer-drinking bronco busters."

Suspecting that Joe Pugliese was going to be too busy to spend any time with her, she co-opted a roommate to accompany her to Randy's. "We positioned ourselves close to the stage, and immediately begin killing time practicing the time-honored sport of people-watching. It really was as if the circus had come to town. People garbed in leather, with safety pins through their noses and ear lobes and cheeks. Clearly, those edgy characters surrounding us were not from our conservative city of San Antonio. Yet somehow, they had all heard the same clarion call from wherever it was they lived and had come to Randy's to see the Sex Pistols. There were so many photographers milling about, sporting an 'I am important' aura, and the kind of intense expressions on their faces reserved for those who are on a sacred mission."

Margaret Moser remembers being impressed by the Randy's crowd. "There was so much attitude to be seen that the audience was half the show. For many, this show was the first time to try out punk fashions and haircuts. People imagine the show with a crowd of mohawked and dyed-hair punks, but it wasn't. It was mostly longhaired San Antonio heavy metal fans. The 'punk look' hardly existed. Those in the crowd that did dress punk were in the minority."

♪ ♪ ♪

The Pistols had played to hostile audiences in the past, but they'd never experienced anything quite like the reception that greeted them at Randy's Rodeo. Jesse Sublett would describe it as a "punk baptism of Texas" as a storm of beer, bottles, food, spit, and other detritus rained down on the band as they launched into "God Save the Queen." "The Pistols hit the stage blasting like a pack of howling coyotes loose in a chicken pen: blowtorch guitar, machine gun drums, snarling vocals, sneering faces, bass rumble. They were half rock 'n' roll messiahs, half sideshow freaks. Johnny Rotten fomented chaos and rebellion; Steve Jones and Paul Cook anchored it with napalm-drenched Eddie Cochran riffs and a backbeat crackling like a nail gun. Sid Vicious spewed venom."[17]

Rotten was again wearing the new blue, green and red plaid tartan suit that Vivienne Westwood had made especially for the tour. He also sported a McLaren/Westwood T-shirt bearing a screen print depicting two gun-toting cowboys facing each other as though in conversation. It was an image that might have served as a hanging sign for Randy's Rodeo or indeed any bar or roadhouse in Texas. It is only when Rotten launched into his spasmodic stage act and his jacket flew open that the print is revealed in its entirety: the cowboys naked from the waist down (except for their boots), their flaccid penises almost touching.

The "Two Cowboys" shirt, as it was known, was drawn in the style of the Finnish fetish artist Touko Valio Laaksonen, who went under the pseudonym Tom of Finland. Three years earlier, McLaren and Westwood had found themselves in front of a London magistrate facing a charge of "exposing to public view an indecent exhibition" as a result of one their shop assistants (the aforementioned Alan Jones) being arrested in Piccadilly Circus while wearing the shirt. The arrest also resulted in a police visit to SEX and the removal of a selection of items including all the Two Cowboy shirts. McLaren and Westwood had received nothing more than petty fines and a slap on the wrist, but this was Texas. The audience had been searched for weapons at the door, but the low stage meant that Rotten could have been dragged into the crowd and pummeled senseless—or worse—before Monk or any of his team had time to react.

Izbrand was totally taken aback by the crowd's hostile reaction when the Pistols came onstage. "There'd been some fist fights during the Vamps' set, and I was overcome with a sense of foreboding as the time drew nearer for the Pistols to come out on stage. As if in some kind of coordinated effort, insults, obscenities and spit were flying spontaneously from all directions, volleying back and forth between the band and the audience. Things very quickly took a dark turn and being so close to the stage was no longer a desirable location. I felt trapped. My friend and I agreed that perhaps we should give up our prime location and move towards the back of the venue, where we could observe the show from a safe vantage point. The possibility that might be victimized by some rage-fueled maniac if we stayed put seemed very real. I couldn't directly witness the events that were unfolding about me, because I was fully engaged in the act of self-survival."

Valentine had also taken up position towards the front of the stage, but unlike Izbrand, says there was never any point when she feared for her safety. "I was maybe 10–15 feet from the front, but I wasn't afraid. It was all very exciting and a big adventure. They were the Sex Pistols! It was about being there, and being part of the spectacle. I knew all the songs by heart. The Violators were playing 'Pretty Vacant' in our set."

Ken Hoge was another caught up in the excitement. "For all I could tell, the violence was more play-acting than real—except for maybe when that full can of beer connected with Sid's head. It went from being funny, to frightening, teetering on the edge of a riot. But the Pistols egged us on, we rallied to the challenge, and that was what everyone was there to experience. Punk! Real live punk! I have always felt it was the first time I ever saw performance art. It wasn't just music. It was the crowd and the band participating together. I never saw anything like it. It was liberating! Everyone was having a blast."

Before fleeing to the back of the hall, Izbrand remembers witnessing an onstage altercation between Rotten and Jones. "Steve accidentally caught the bridge of his guitar to knock it out of tune during 'God Save the Queen.' I was close to the stage and could hear Rotten over the din. He really tore into Jones."

Jesse Sublett believes it would've been hard for any band to get a good sound at Randy's. "As you know from the haphazard tour date scheduling, the venues the Pistols played on that tour weren't chosen for their acoustics. I don't remember what sound company worked this show, but the sound wasn't good overall. It was kind of muffled, which was a little disappointing, really. Randy's was a former bowling alley with low ceilings. Even a little acoustic honky-tonk singer would've probably sounded like shit in there.

"Steve Jones broke a string early into the opening number. "For a while there—I'd guess at least a minute—the band sounded like shit, but they recovered before the song ended. Sid was a pretty terrible bass player, but that was the only time I remember that it affected their sound all that much. We really admired the fierce performance, basic the pile-driving rock sound, and Paul Cook really impressed us. We could see then that Cook and Jones were a hell of a rhythm section."

When penning his review of the show for the *Austin Sun*, Bill Bentley likened the Pistols' onstage sound akin to "dogs being slaughtered inside a big tin drum." "I wrote that because it really did sound like dogs being slaughtered in big tin drums," he says today. "The Pistols played in what was basically a bowling alley vibe! The sound was turned all the way up so the guitar shook the fillings out of my teeth, and the drums knee-kicked me in the cock. In hindsight, it was utter bliss sonically … even if it sounded like the end of the world had arrived."

"Bliss" isn't the word that springs to Margaret Moser's mind, however. "The Pistols sucked musically. Jones could play, but Vicious couldn't, so the overall sound was inept. Except for Rotten, who couldn't sing, but visually exploded onstage. He was the man in charge. He was like a cheerleader, reacting as well as causing reaction. It did seem he was getting what he wanted from the crowd response, and that would spur him to respond in kind. And it's possible the audience looked a little more threatening than in Atlanta or Memphis, therefore stoking his performance. It didn't necessarily feel stage-managed, but in hindsight, it seemed obvious that every performance was regarded as an opportunity for chaos. I kind of miss that element in bands today."

♪ ♪ ♪

The Pistols launching into another sonic assault. Punk cartoonist John Holmstrom says the Pistols' performance at Randy's was "the best rock 'n' roll show I've ever seen" (© Roberta Bayley).

The Pistols' reputation had once again preceded them, and officers from San Antonio Police Department were in attendance at Randy's. The day prior to the show, Captain James Depress went before the press to assure the public that he and his officers would be in attendance to ensure the Pistols wouldn't violate state obscenity laws concerning exposure and sexual conduct. As the drums were mounted upon a riser, Paul Cook had a panoramic view of his surroundings and remembers armed officers from various law enforcement agencies watching on from the sidelines. "[The] tour was so heavy with paranoia. Sometimes there were policemen with guns standing at the side of the stage while we were playing, two on each side. I got the feeling someone was going to get killed at any time; it was really heavy."[18]

Rory Johnston had also sensed the rapidly darkening mood. "So much stuff was being hurled at the stage that I ended up hiding behind the PA. I could see this sheriff standing a few feet from me get hit smack on the side of the head with a bottle. He was only a little guy, and the force of the bottle caused him to stagger back. He was in total shock and started reaching for his gun. I thought, 'He's going for his gun and he's looking at me!' When I saw him draw his gun, I dashed out over to the sound booth to warn Malcolm that someone was going to get killed. The booth was empty! I found Malcolm hiding outside. It was utter chaos, but I still think San Antonio the best rock 'n' roll show I've ever seen."

Tiberi, however, has a different take. "Randy's was an absolute farce! They [the Pistols] should never have played there. The soundboard was homemade! In fact, the whole tour was a travesty. In hindsight, we shouldn't have gone to America. We should have taken some time off, and then focused our energies on the forthcoming European tour. The Atlanta show was okay in terms of an opening show, and the shows in Memphis and Tulsa were passable, but none of those shows were good. John certainly didn't enjoy them, and neither did Paul. I kept saying to them that, 'We'd do better tomorrow,' but it didn't get any better.

"The Pistols had already achieved a lot. The album was recognized. They came in for criticism about how long they took to record the album, but that wasn't the band's fault. They had a lot on their plate during the summer of '77. I know I'm repeating myself, but the Pistols were a professional act. They didn't need a PA, fancy lighting, or even a stage to put on a tight show. They showed that in Sweden during the Scandinavian tour when they played in a youth club! So to be put in that situation like that…

"I don't know about Malcolm hiding outside at Randy's, but I would never have abandoned the soundboard while the band was onstage. The only thing I can think of that I must have gone down to the front to speak with Rory about something at the same time that he was making his way to the back."

Vicious' musical ability was again being called into question, but Randy's Rodeo is nonetheless the first occasion where he steals center-stage from Rotten. He'd been playfully cavorting about the stage like a "kewpie doll in shock treatment,"[19] when, taking offence to one of the hecklers at the front of the stage, he whipped off his bass and brought it crashing down into the crowd. The incident was captured in full "JFK Zapruder-esque glory" by Lech Kowalski's crew. According to Johnston, the arcing bass glanced off of Vicious' intended victim and struck Ted Cohen flush in the face. "I've no idea what Ted was thinking in going out front. Maybe he wanted to sample the Sex Pistols' experience?"

Holmstrom isn't afraid to admit to fearing for his life that night. "Randy's was the most hostile crowd I have ever been around. Roberta and I stood several rows back from the insanity—away the front of the stage because it was so violent. It wasn't like a mosh pit; it was more like a team of gangsters intent on killing their enemy. It was scary! I was kind of happy to hear later that Sid missed hitting his stupid tormentor with the guitar, and that he hit a Warners' executive instead. It seemed like poetic justice. But then the lights went out, and the crowd began to murmur. I think that if the lights had stayed off for any period of time, there would have been a riot. Fortunately the lights soon came back on, and the Pistols delivered the most desperate, crazed performance I have ever seen.

"It's difficult for performers to face down a hostile crowd, but the Pistols seemed to enjoy all the negativity. The crowd was throwing so many beer cans and so much debris at them, but they carried on playing! The Sex Pistols instantly gained my respect."

Roberta Bayley thought her days working at CBGB had prepared her for every unsavory occasion, but says Randy's was at another level entirely. "That San Antonio gig was really scary! There was a feeling of … menace isn't the right word. But there was a definite sense of violence. Dallas was also a little nuts: the head-butting, the blood, etc. In those cities there was the feeling that there were people who just came to cause trouble—not fans, just troublemakers."

"Bill [Bentley] and I had deliberately placed ourselves on Sid's side of the stage," says Moser. "I was gambling on Sid as the loose cannon. I couldn't really see or hear the heckling, but it was clear something was brewing. As Sid swung his bass at the guy, Bill put his arm in front of me and yelled, 'Step back, Margaret, this could get ugly!'"

"Seeing Vicious hit the guy with his bass felt like all hell was getting ready to break loose," Bentley added. "I hate fighting, so while it was extremely danger-inducing, it was also thrilling to see this type of mayhem on a music stage. I was a fan of wrestling when I was young, and this had the same adrenalin."

Hoge had been even closer to the action. "It was rather acrobatic how Sid, in one swift move, strode forward towards us while swinging the bass up over his shoulder and completing the swing around the other side with a swipe at the guy in front of me while holding the neck of the bass. I was so close that I could feel the breeze as the bass swept past my head. Sid was being constantly pelted with sloshed beer and empty cans and he was pretty cool with it. He kept urging the crowd with the finger, rubbing his crotch and making rude faces while occasionally trying to play his bass. But I saw him hit in the face with what was obviously a full can of beer and it both surprised and hurt him. He saw who threw it and it was game on. I didn't blame him; it crossed a line.

"I was scared my camera would get broken and fell back with the group of us standing by the guy who threw the can. I was determined to photograph the Pistols, though. It was everything I wished for. They came on determined to piss off us 'cowboys,' and they did. I am speaking of Johnny and Sid here, since Paul and Steve pretty much kept their heads down and just played. Johnny made sure we saw his T-shirt, which showed two naked cowboys standing dick to dick while one adjusted the other's neckerchief. I recognized the photo from a porn mag I saw somewhere and was shocked to see him wearing it. You could get a T-shirt of that? And someone would wear it … in a redneck bar in San Antonio?"

Rotten watches in bemusement as security bundle heckler Brian Faltin over to the exit. Roberta Bayley remembers the show at Randy's Rodeo as being really scary. "There was a feeling of … menace isn't the right word. But there was a definite sense of violence" (© Ken Hoge).

After the show McLaren was ecstatic, playfully asking which of the photographers had captured Vicious in mid-swing as such a snap would surely be adorning the front cover of newspapers around the globe. "Malcolm never approached me," says Bayley. "Maybe Joe or Bob, I don't know. Supposedly, Joe got the shot and Malcolm just said something like, '£10,000 shot, that one!' From where I was standing, it just seemed like a moment of confusion. As far as I know, Joe's photo was never published—if it even exists. Ironically, many years later, I realized that I got the shot—albeit from the back.

"Looking back on the tour, San Antonio was only 'scary' because it was an open floor gig with no seating in a small space. Also, there seemed to be quite a lot of audience members who were there to antagonize the band. So yes, I did not feel like pushing into the front of a crowd of drunken hooligans and took photos from the back. I still got the shot of Sid hitting the guy with his bass. Plus it was a good introduction to the situation, to see the overview. And then to meet the Pistols after the show, on the floor, and photograph them."

Vicious' intended victim was aspiring actor-musician Brian Faltin, who hailed from neighboring Comfort, and was enrolled at Schreiner University. Despite being arrested and placed in handcuffs, Faltin was released in time to re-enter Randy's to watch the remainder of the show. Speaking with the media after the show, Faltin said that he didn't like what the Pistols stood for and thought them nothing more than "sewer rats with guitars." However, when reflecting about the show in January 2003, the fifty-something rancher's opinion of the Pistols had mellowed somewhat. "[They] just rubbed me the wrong way. I was there as a protestation. In retrospect, I wish I'd never gone there that night. I stooped to their level by going there and acting that way. They were too extreme for me, but they probably did give music a kick in the pants."[20]

The scene inside Randy's once the Pistols had departed the stage resembled a garbage dump after Labor Day. Cook stands amid the detritus collected at the front of the stage (© Roberta Bayley).

Speaking about the incident after the show, an unrepentant Vicious said, "If someone gives me trouble and I have a weapon in my hand, I hit him. But all that happened tonight was that my strap fell off and that's the end of it."[21]

Vicious had two identical white Fender Precision bass guitars. Depending on which version you believe, he either accidentally left one in a taxi or gave it to the driver in lieu of payment shortly after returning to London. Steve

Jones bought the other bass—along with the "Sid" embossed leather strap Vicious had picked up in Baton Rouge during the U.S. tour—from Vicious' mum Anne Beverly in 1995 for $1,000. Jones claims to have since been offered $200,000, which if true, has proved a very shrewd bit of business.[22]

♪ ♪ ♪

The scene inside Randy's once the Sex Pistols had departed the stage had resembled a garbage dump after Labor Day as the floor at the front of the stage was a sea of empty beer and soft drink cans, discarded cigarette packets, and ticket stubs. Despite what had gone on before, after the show Rotten and Cook came out to mingle with those of the audience who had remained. "That was kind of part of the punk ethos," Bayley reflected. "That you weren't above the fans, they were your peers. You weren't a 'star.' The lights were up. Some fans had lingered, and John and Paul came out to talk to them. A lot of the British press was there, but I don't think that's why they came out. John answered their questions."

Nancy Gray, an aspiring local photographer who describes herself as being "just a kid with a hobby and a camera," had arrived at Randy's believing that the Pistols' tour might someday be a part of pop culture. "I was 18 and living on the outskirts—or boondocks as we call them—of San Antonio. I had a couple of friends who initially wanted to go but they backed out after hearing the 'sheriff's warnings' on TV. I didn't see the warnings myself, but the county sheriff's office had come on the TV over the weekend saying it was 'rumored' that there may be spit, blood, violence and perhaps homosexuals at Randy's. I was shocked at that remark!

"My thought was, as I made my way to Randy's in my '72 Chevy Impala, was that I couldn't not go. It was that important! And I ended up meeting with some photographer friends there anyway. It was well worth the drive. I had a Canon TX camera with a 100–300mm zoom lens, so got to take some really close shots of the band, and a couple of Johnny talking after the show. As soon as I got back to my apartment, I processed the photos right away."[23]

Bill Bentley had been forewarned that the Pistols wouldn't be speaking to the press

Jones, center, engaging the locals after the show (© Roberta Bayley).

either before or after the show, so had been heading for home on I-35 when Rotten and Cook emerged from the dressing room. "I was told 'No interviews allowed,' but to be honest, I didn't feel the pull to try and get backstage anyhow. In fact, I wanted to go hear some soul music in a Latino bar. I did, however, write a positive review of the show. It was positive because of how the world shifted that night. I didn't keep a copy, but I remember writing about the 'dangerous elements that reared their head and could have ended in murder.' I really do believe that if Johnny Rotten had called the Mexicans 'faggots,' and not the cowboys like he did, he would have been pulled off the stage and stabbed to death. Those were killing words for that audience."

Margaret Moser's abiding memory from after the show was seeing the Randy's regulars strolling in after the Pistols had left the stage. "They were real shit-kickers in their hats and boots. They looked horrified at the carnage inside. I'd never actually attended Randy's before. It was known as a hardcore country joint, the kind of place that didn't cotton to the hippie, cosmic cowboys, but to old school country music lovers who liked to dance.

However, as a writer, I had a fair amount of experience going into different types of clubs and sizing up the clientele. So it was easy to recognize the regulars sauntering in late by their bewildered expressions.

"There was this feeling of survival, as if we'd been through a significant joint experience. I guess we had. There were so many people there I'd never seen before but would come to be friends, or people that I ended up working with. It was that big of a catalyst. The Sex Pistols restored my faith in rock 'n' roll. I know now that they were just as manufactured as the Monkees, but they turned music upside down and put the music back in the hands of musicians."

Sig McKenna Izbrand also came away recognizing the enormity of the occasion. "There was a shared sense in the room that rock 'n' roll as we knew it was in the process of a genuine metamorphosis. It was both terrifying to contemplate and fascinating to behold. It was a pivotal time in

Rotten meets the press after the show. Ken Hoge couldn't believe Rotten would dare to wear the Two Cowboys T-shirt "in a redneck bar in San Antonio" (© Roberta Bayley).

our lives for many of us who were there. I don't think there were many casual attendees who just happened to stop at Randy's for a beer that night. We were hardcore music fans who had their ear to the ground and a sense that their world was about to change. As I was leaving Randy's a television reporter stopped me and asked if I would consent to be interviewed on-camera. 'Yes,' I said. 'Why did you come to see the Sex Pistols tonight?' he asked. 'Curiosity,' I replied. 'I wanted to find out what all this hype about them is about.... Don't you?'"

Jesse Sublett is somewhat rather more pragmatic with his evaluation, however. "My feelings were mixed at the time and they have since evolved. We didn't go to the show expecting, you know, a sea change or a life-changing experience. And afterward, we were excited, not blown away. It's not like we left saying, 'This is the best band we've ever seen,' but it was more of a feeling of, 'It's about time, we've been ready for this.' And it was the first real punk show in Texas."

Five

Baton Rouge

Sex Pistols Win S.A. "Shootout"
Pie-Guitar Fracas

The Sex Pistols—England's notorious punk rock band—had a "shootout" in San Antonio Sunday night—a pie in the face was exchanged for a whap with a bass guitar.

No one was injured in the fracas which erupted at Randy's Rodeo and the raucous concert resumed shortly after the incident.
—Ben King Jr., *San Antonio Express*, January 9, 1978

The Sex Pistols were set to play two shows in Texas. In terms of U.S. land mass, the Lone Star State is second only to Alaska, and as Tulsa lies just 260 miles north of Dallas in an ideal world Baton Rouge would have been slotted in after Memphis before then swinging eastwards to San Antonio and then onto Dallas. But of course, what appears straightforward in theory doesn't necessarily carry over into practice. "The itinerary wasn't perfect but you can't always do things in a straight line," Rory Johnston explained. "Sometimes you have to zigzag to get the right venues, dates etc. I'd been living in America for over a year by then, but my familiarity with the lay of the land was nowhere near as good as it is today. It meant more traveling time between venues of course, but I don't remember any grumbling about the routing ... at least not from our camp."

The Pistols had been on the road for seven days now, and their operating cheek-by-jowl within the close confines of a tour bus for a week had inevitably brought about a relaxed relationship with Monk's security team. This was evidenced when one of the team purchased a blow-up doll to serve as the tour mascot en route to Baton Rouge.

The on-the-road buddy-bonding didn't quite extend to Monk himself, however. This was perhaps only to be expected given that the Warners' surety buck literally did stop with him. Spending endless hours cooped up on a tour bus might have been driving the Pistols to distraction, but Monk had come to view the bus as a mobile sanctuary. He could even relax to a certain degree, because as long as the wheels were rolling, the Pistols—and Vicious in particular—couldn't get up to much in the way of mischief.

Monk had signed on knowing the Pistols' tour would be no run-of-the-mill rock 'n' roll excursion. Before going out on the road he'd playfully had a T-shirt made up bearing the slogan: "This Sure Ain't the Beach Boys Tour."

Vicious was a full-blown addict by the time of the U.S. tour, yet he wasn't the only Sex Pistol to have tried heroin. Ex-New York Doll Jerry Nolan would subsequently boast to his being "the guy to turn Johnny Rotten on to heroin"[1] during the Anarchy Tour while with The Heartbreakers. It wasn't until speaking with Barry Cain for the latter's excellent 2007 book, *77 Sulphate Strip*; that Lydon confessed to taking heroin "three or four times. I chased the dragon—and hated it."

Steve Jones had also furtively imbibed. The first occasion came in Paris on his 21st birthday while the Pistols were making their European debut. He'd also snorted it with Johnny Thunders at the Carnaby Street flat of Heartbreakers' manager Leee Black Childers. (Within a couple of years of the Pistols' demise Jones would also be a full-blown addict. Indeed, it wasn't until the late Eighties that he finally got himself clean).²

It wasn't only Warners' $1 million surety that was weighing heavily on Monk's shoulders of course, as keeping the four Sex Pistols out of harm's way was of equal importance to the label owing to its six-figure investment in the band. The Pistols had grown accustomed to dealing with hostility back in the UK. In the wake of the release of "God Save the Queen" Rotten had been set upon by machete-wielding thugs, while Cook was struck over the head with a crowbar. But as savage as these attacks were, they paled against staring down the barrel of a gun.

Being harried at every turn by the media was also proving problematic, as the last thing the Pistols wanted—especially after a lengthy all-night drive—was to fend off reporters desperate for a quote for the morning edition. Monk, of course, was well-versed in diversionary tactics. If having their driver, Charlie Jones, seek out an alternate route failed to shake off a tail, he could further beguile the news hounds by foregoing the pre-booked hotel and instead book the tour party into out-of-the-way motels.

To pass the time between the occasional pit and piss-stops, Rotten had Charlie Jones run the dub tapes that Tiberi had made up especially for the tour through the bus' built-in sound system—"deep grooves on the southern highways."³ It's always been assumed that Rotten's mate Don Letts had assembled the dub tapes for the tour. Indeed, Bob Gruen stated as much at the "Sex Pistols and America" talk he and Tiberi gave at the British Library in July 2016, only for Tiberi to halt him in his tracks by finally taking ownership.

While the Pistols were onstage at the Kingfish, a clip of the promo video for "God Save the Queen" was aired on CBS' *Variety '77—The Year In Entertainment*. From left, Cook, Vicious and Rotten (© Carlton Freeman).

♪ ♪ ♪

Baton Rouge has the honor of being Louisiana's state capital, but in musical terms the city is the poor relation of New Orleans; the recognized wellspring of jazz, Cajun, and, of course, the Delta blues. McLaren had visited New Orleans while en route back to New York with Syl Sylvain during the spring of '75, and had been completely enamored with both the city and its vibrant music scene. This, of course, begs the question why McLaren didn't insist on the Pistols playing New Orleans so that he might sample the Big Easy a second time.

Rory Johnston says he's pretty sure that Baton Rouge was the best option in terms of staging a Sex Pistols show in Louisiana. "It could have had something to do with keeping the band out of New Orleans, and therefore out of trouble. Like Austin, Baton Rouge was a college town, and therefore less of a risk. Or it might have been as simple as there not being a suitable gig at the time in New Orleans ... or a promoter willing to take it."

Baton Rouge's musical heritage might have paled in comparison to New Orleans, but during the mid-to-late Sixties it had nonetheless boasted a thriving live music scene—particularly the swamp blues as advocated by Slim Harpo and Lightnin' Slim, both of whom had proved inspirational to the Rolling Stones and The Kinks. By the mid–Seventies, however, the Red Stick was somewhat stuck in the mud in terms of live music.

As with the Great SouthEast Music Hall, the Kingfish Club was situated within a shopping mall. In this instance, the Southdowns Shopping Center at College and Perkins. The club was the brainchild of Robert Day, a proud Baton Rougean who'd returned home determined to put the profits he'd accrued from selling the lease on the restaurant he'd been running in Aspen, Colorado, to good use. Day had invited several like-minded local entrepreneurs—Danny Kertacy (pronounced "Courtesy"), Grady Smith, and Tommy Grand—to join him in the venture.[4]

Day's idea for the Kingfish was to cater for those acts that had outgrown playing bars but had yet to make the step up to headlining arenas. "It looked to us like there was a crying need for such a place," he explained. "When you looked around the country there were only a handful of places that were big enough to do almost anybody below, you know, the Rolling Stones and those stadium-size people. And even those groups sometimes like to go into small clubs just for the intimacy of it."[5]

The Kingfish boasted a stage area half again as large as any other music venue in Baton Rouge, a state-of-the-art 16-track recording facility, and could comfortably seat up to 1,000 people. Slide-guitar king Ry Cooder headlined the club's official opening in early October 1976.

The Kingfish was named in honor of Louisiana's most renowned politician, Senator Huey Pierce "The Kingfish" Long Jr. (1893–1935). (An image of the beaming Long also featured on the club's logo.) The colorful Long, who'd co-opted the nickname Kingfish from a leading character in the long-running radio show *Amos 'n' Andy*, had served Louisiana as governor and senator. (Long was assassinated by the son-in-law of a longtime political opponent. Such was his popularity in the Creole State that an estimated 200,000 people attended his funeral.)

Day might have believed Baton Rouge was in need of the Kingfish Club, but Tim Parrish, a professor of English in the MFA Program at Southern Connecticut State University, as well as being the renowned author of several highly acclaimed tomes including *Walking Blues: Making Americans from Emerson to Elvis* and *Red Stick Men: Stories*, wasn't immediately won over. "The Kingfish set-up had a dance floor in front of the stage surrounded on three sides with upper tiers of tables and a bar in the very back. Normally the dance floor had tables set up also, but it was cleared out and full of people. They'd removed all the front glass windows and installed angled wood strips in their place. It was unremarkable, un-rock 'n' roll and generic from the outside in every way. Prefab American drab, which, in hindsight, made it perfect for the invasion of the Sex Pistols. Later the building became a fitness place—gotta fucking love that!

"I was 20 years old, sporting a sagebrush afro, and listening to Led Zeppelin and Deep Purple when the Pistols rode into Baton Rouge. I knew very little about punks, but I carried suspicion and contempt for anybody I thought of as 'dressing up' because I equated that to being inauthentic. A friend, actually a high school friend's boyfriend, almost had to drag me to go to see Pistols for while I had a visceral sense that something exciting and liberating was happening, I wasn't ready to embrace it. I have to admit the Pistols were barely a blip on my screen. I became more aware once they were booked to play the Kingfish. Not only because my friend was so excited, but because the BR mainstream press was excited about it, and the police were setting off alarms that the end of civilization was coming with these skinny English boys as if they were the four horsemen. When my friend played *Never Mind the Bollocks* for me, I thought it was just 'dumb-fuck noise!' I thought the whole thing was bullshit. I was firmly ensconced in my working-class anger and, ironically, increasingly convoluted rock—not realizing the Pistols were bringing the real working-class anger."[6]

"The Kingfish was what we Americans call a 'strip center,'" says Greg Ellis, who was 19 at the time, and was working in the local record store Leisure Landing. "It was the corner storefront in an 'L-shaped' strip mall-type structure, set back from the road with a parking lot out front. Depending on the show, there would sometimes be tables and chairs on the floor in front of the stage. It was standing room only for the Pistols show. When the club opened in the fall of '76 it was the premier club in the state–national headline acts at least

Vicious' "Gimme A Fix" plea is plain for all to see (© Roberta Bayley).

three days of the week. It was modeled on clubs like the Bottom Line in New York City. It wasn't a 'punk' venue at all. I would say the management was down for the publicity, but probably didn't appreciate the Sex Pistols."[7]

Brad Orgeron was 21 in January 1978. He'd dropped out of school three years earlier to start a Dolls-esque glam band which, owing to his passion for MC5 and The Stooges, had recently morphed into more punkish mode as The Backstabbers. "The Kingfish was a pretty typical club of its day. It wasn't terribly big, but had a good room setup and sound system. It was located on the wrong side of the river from New Orleans, the side where I grew up. Their booking policy was eclectic, mixing punk, funk and mainstream rock bands, both touring and local. It was one of the premier places to secure a gig."[8]

♪ ♪ ♪

Baton Rouge may have been bereft of an alternate music scene, but the city's entertainment magazine *Gris Gris* was nevertheless hip to what was happening in London. Its August 31–September 5, 1977, issue not only reviewed "God Save the Queen" but also provided a brief history of the Pistols' career to date—going so far as proclaim the music lived up to the hype. The ongoing uncertainty as to the U.S. State Department's decision regarding the Pistols' U.S. visa applications meant that at the time of the magazine's January 2–8, 1978, issue going to press, *Gris Gris* was unable to confirm whether the tour would be going ahead. All it could state with any degree of certainty was that Danny Kertacy had spent much of Wednesday, January 5, on the phone with Warners trying to confirm the Kingfish date.

Kertacy had told *Gris Gris* that he remained confident the show would proceed as scheduled. He was, however, still hedging his bets as the magazine also carried a Kingfish flyer advertising legendary jazz pianist Mose Allison as an alternative booking should the date fall through.

The tour had been rubber-stamped by the time Gris *Gris'* follow-up issue hit the newsstands. Surprisingly, the magazine makes no mention of the U.S. State Department's eleventh-hour volte-face but did carry a Sex Pistols-related article detailing an approach by Warners to Jerry Lousteau, one of its main contributors. Lousteau, an established DJ at Baton Rouge's premier music radio station WIBR, claimed that Warners had called him offering free copies of *Never Mind the Bollocks* for what was termed "listener response contests."[9]

Lousteau was said to have been left scratching his head by the label's approach. It wasn't so much that he estimated probably only one out of every thousand of his listeners would have known anything about the Sex Pistols other than they were "capital-P.U.N.K.S.," but rather that he'd yet to take receipt of the albums. He'd also doubted that his program director would have allowed him to play the album on air. However, the albums did arrive and the program director hadn't raised any objections. The competition went ahead, but according to the article, the vast majority of those calling in thought it was "all some kind of a joke," which, Lousteau believed an infinitely more "interesting P.R. scam."[10]

Twenty-year-old Eddie Flowers, who'd recently relocated from Los Angeles to Jackson, Alabama, thought the Pistols far from being a joke, and was very much looking forward to the Kingfish date. "I first heard about the Pistols in '76 after seeing an article about one of their early live shows in the now long-defunct *Phonograph Record*. It featured a photo

The Pistols bringing "real working-class anger" to Baton Rouge (© Carlton Freeman).

of Johnny Rotten on his knees and sneering. I'd been a Stooges fan for years, so something clicked right away. I followed their records as they came out."[11]

Since the age of 14, Flowers had been writing for independent rock magazines, alternative papers, and fanzines. (His first published work was in a 1972 issue of *Teenage Wasteland Gazette*, a magazine run by a pre–Dictators Andy Shernoff.) "There was no original rock music scene in Baton Rouge back then, but my friend Russell Desmond edited a great fanzine called *Can't Buy a Thrill*. He had a few friends into music, but most of them were still suspicious of punk. I remember one guy at the Kingfish telling me, 'You should come back for Robert Palmer, so you can see something good instead of this stuff [the Pistols].' I told him I thought Robert Palmer 'sucked!'"

"There had been a thriving original local scene in the Sixties through to the mid–Seventies when my older brothers were carousing," Tim Parrish said. "The LSU Assembly Center catered for established acts such as the Stones and Led Zeppelin, but there were no places that would even think of having punk or alternative music. The scene wouldn't get cranked up until the summer of '78, but the Ramones played the Kingfish a month or so after the Pistols [February 22].

"The Ramones also paid a visit to Leisure Landing, the record store that was bringing in all the new music and aggressively pushing the music at anybody who came through the door. The main provocateurs were the store's manager, Jimmy Strickland, and Bill Mallory, who would soon be one of the founders of the amazing Shitdogs—the first 'outsider' band in Baton Rouge. The first time I went in Leisure Landing, Mallory screamed, 'Jeeesus mother-fucking Christ!' I almost hit the floor, not knowing that was simply his way of saying that a record was in the wrong bin."

Earl Reinhalter, who'd moved to Baton Rouge from his native Maryland the previous summer, believes the Pistols' Kingfish date might not have happened had it not been for Jimmy Strickland. "Danny Kertacy called the Leisure Landing record store and asked Jimmy if he should book the Sex Pistols. It was a different kind of music from what the club usually booked, so I guess he was just wondering what Jimmy thought of the idea. The Sex Pistols had gotten a bit of press, and the network news reports about their Atlanta debut weren't too promising. But they didn't play enough of the music on TV to give an idea of what the band sounded like. Catching a brief item in the local newspaper was the first I knew about the band coming to Baton Rouge."[12]

"Baton Rouge was a backwater and the trends moved so much slower then," Greg Ellis reflected. "Also, there was no place that sold the *NME* so it took a while for stuff to trickle down. I had heard both the Ramones and the Pistols' music but wasn't overly obsessed. I didn't even know the Pistols were coming to Baton Rouge as I was home in Oklahoma for the holidays. I knew they were in the States of course, but I only found out they were in town when I returned on the day of the show. I grabbed up one of the last remaining tickets, then went home and listened to *Never Mind the Bollocks* repeatedly to familiarize myself with all the songs."

Getty Freeman, who was working as a DJ at WSLU, the campus radio station at Louisiana State University, was also out of town visiting family when he heard a report on the Pistols' tour on the radio. On discovering the Pistols were en route to Baton Rouge he

Thanks to the local entertainment magazine, *Gris Gris*, Baton Rouge knew of the Sex Pistols in advance. Shown here are Rotten (left) and Jones (© Carlton Freeman).

packed his bag and grabbed the next available flight home. "They'd mentioned that tickets were still on sale, and I got the last three from a record shop on College Drive on my way home from the airport the night before the show. Score!"[13]

LSU student Carlton Freemen (no relation to Getty Freeman) was another who'd been away visiting with relations over the holidays but had fortunately returned to Baton Rouge earlier than intended. "I was good friends with Jimmy Rink, who owned the Record Rink, which was situated a few blocks from the Kingfish. Luckily, the Rink was one of the ticket outlets for the Kingfish and Jimmy had saved me a ticket on the off chance. He was always turning me on to new groups, and it was in his store that I first heard *Never Mind the Bollocks*. I didn't think much of it at the time, but found the 'hype' surrounding the Sex Pistols interesting. That was one of the reasons I attended the show. I went expecting it to be a 'spectacle,' but came away a big fan of the Pistols. I was somewhat surprised at what good musicians Steve Jones and Paul Cook turned out to be. Sid didn't seem to be much of a bass player and just was going through the motions. Rotten, however definitely had stage presence and knew how to work an audience."[14]

Twenty-five-year-old John Guarnieri was also a campus DJ. "I had my own punk show on Tulane University's WTUL. I was also head buyer at The Mushroom, the largest record store in the Southeast and also owned by Tulane University. We had a large college base and always carried import albums and singles, but by 1977 the UK singles market jumped up and we turned everyone on to the Pistols, Damned, Stranglers etc. I got to play all the import singles before anyone else. One of the perks from working at Mushroom was that record company types would come in offering free tickets. A guy from Warners swung by shortly after the holidays with comp tickets for the Pistols' Atlanta show, but I couldn't make that date."[15]

♪ ♪ ♪

Brad Orgeron still maintains that anyone dressed "remotely punkish" at the Kingfish show had to have traveled from New Orleans. "There really wasn't anything remotely punk-wise going on in Baton Rouge before the Pistols. There was definitely a scene in NOLA though, and by the time of the Pistols' show a few younger bands had also begun to appear. The crowd at the Kingfish was mostly made up of rubberneckers and jock-types looking for trouble. There was a bit fighting at the front, but that was typical of any other local show so I didn't pay too much attention."

Eddie Flowers remembers seeing "a handful of obvious punk-rockers" in the crowd. "I knew there was a smallish punk scene going on in New Orleans, so it figures those kids came from there. Most of the audience looked like college students. There were also a few frat-rat or jock types who spent their time throwing shit at the bands ... sometimes beer bottles."

"I don't know about any NOLA punks but I remember there were some New York punk-types there," says Getty Freemen. "They were bitching about having had to fly to such a shithole as Baton Rouge to see the Sex Pistols. I wanted to kick their asses. We might not have had any real punks in BR at that time, but we definitely had attitude—in spite of our long hair and redneck drawls!"

Tim Parrish remembers seeing what he describes as "safety-pinned, leather-wearing punks" in the audience. "The Kingfish dance pit swam with creatures like nothing I'd seen:

heavy unisex mascara, safety-pinned faces, and studded leather. They were so strange-looking that they overwhelmed my impression of the rest of the crowd. There was a charge in the air that night that I'd never felt at a show before—not even at the Stones' tour-opening show in Baton Rouge in '75. The charge wasn't dangerous, however, and I was still scoffing in order to feel superior and alienated and not drawn in. But there was definitely a tension between so many different types of people; people with different agendas for being there, and people sensing that something brand new and completely inexplicable for BR was about to materialize in front of us.

"Onstage several battered amps and a tiny drum kit squatted beneath meager lights. I shook my head and sneered. I'd seen the buffalo, rattlesnakes and ten-gallon hats of ZZ Top's World Wide Texas Tour fill the Sugar Bowl, a police riot when Lynyrd Skynyrd didn't show, Aerosmith tear up City Park Stadium twice in New Orleans, Zep and their lasers, the Stones and their inflatable penis. What was this lame shit supposed to be?"

Greg Ellis still maintains there were more journalists than punks in the crowd. "There were maybe thirty punkish types from New Orleans or wherever, but the journalists easily outnumbered them. It was a pretty diverse crowd, and I'd say there were maybe 500 people in there. You could probably fit another hundred or so, so it wasn't technically 'sold out.' I think they limited the capacity to make it a little less tight and volatile.

"I was so excited about seeing the Pistols that I honestly didn't pay much attention to anything that was going on. I wasn't aware of any frat/punk confrontations. I don't even recall much pushing and shoving going on. There were maybe a hundred or so frat types

Rotten carries on singing, but Vicious (left) and Jones have their eyes on someone in the crowd (© Roberta Bayley).

with dates in there, but they were gone by the end of the third song. I do remember seeing two punkish-looking girls fighting outside for a TV crew, but it looked a little too staged."

John Guarnieri also witnessed what he describes as "cursory punk rock type fighting." "The audience was egging the Pistols on to be more outrageous, and the band was very accommodating! I've since heard that the Kingfish drafted in guys from the LSU wrestling team. I don't recall seeing them, but if they were there then it's likely they were hired to watch the door and make sure things didn't get too out of hand."

♪ ♪ ♪

Before making his way over to the Kingfish, McLaren staged a meet-and-greet session with the local media in his hotel room at the Ramada Inn. At the conference he talked about plans for a Sex Pistols world tour, which would see the band follow up their stint of forthcoming shows in Finland and Scandinavia with a string of dates in Europe. A UK tour was being lined up for March, which would be followed up with a return to America for a second, more substantial tour. While playing nursemaid to the New York Dolls, McLaren had come up with the idea of their performing in front of a backdrop bearing the hammer and sickle. He now teasingly waved the red flag a second time by suggesting the possibility of a Sex Pistols show in Russia. Rory Johnston remembers McLaren holding "a press conference of sorts in his hotel room," but doesn't recall anything specific being discussed other than the potential tours/shows. "By that time, the tour was more or less a continuous press conference—almost like daily briefings to the traveling press corps."

By happenstance, the Kingfish date fell on the day the Sex Pistols made their debut prime-time American TV appearance on CBS' *Variety '77—The Year in Entertainment*. There was never any question of the Pistols performing live on the show, and segueing them into the show's sugary, self-congratulatory format may well have proved problematic for the producers had it not been for Prince Charles' attending a star-studded charity dinner in LA two months earlier. Standing before a screen bearing an image of the prince, Sada Thompson (best-known to American audiences for her role as Kate Lawrence in ABC's *Family*), revealed how Dean Martin had greeted the heir to the British throne as "Prince Chuck." As the studio audience laughed on cue, the image of Charles rotated to reveal a close-up of Rotten while the camera panned to Dionne Warwick.

For the benefit of the vast majority of the audience—both in the studio as well as the millions watching at home—Warwick provides a brief introduction to the "most controversial new act in music [whose] music is young, raw, and anti-establishment." She then goes on to explain how the Pistols had "got themselves banned from English television" before introducing the "song they can't sing in England" as the promo video to "God Save the Queen" appeared.

♪ ♪ ♪

The support act for the Kingfish show was a zydeco outfit called Rockin' Dopsie (pronounced "Doopsie") and the Twisters. Dopsie (born Alton Rubin) had been playing professionally since the late 1940s, but it was only in the last couple of years that he'd begun to achieve a wider recognition, releasing three albums through the Swedish label Sonet Records. (Zydeco, derived from the French "les haricots," is cited as being a "bubbling, melodic gumbo concocted from Cajun/Acadian music, Afro-Caribbean rhythms and melodies.")[16]

Gris Gris' assessment of the Twisters was that they were worthy of "warm[ing] up for Satan at the gates of Hell, and as likely as not to tear the place down before the Pistols get a chance to." However, there had been some last-minute confusion as to whether the Twisters would get the chance to tear the Kingfish down as Dopsie's rival, Nathan Abshire, had apparently also been in the running.[17]

A zydeco band might seem a strange choice as opening act, but from what Kevin Bourgeois remembers from his conversation with Mark O'Neil, the Kingfish's floor manager, the Twisters were booked because Rotten had wanted a support act that reflected the local culture. "It was at another concert at the Kingfish. They announced that the Sex Pistols were coming to the Kingfish, and at that moment I happened to see Mark coming past. I stopped him and asked how he'd got the Pistols to come to Baton Rouge. He told me their management had been looking for small industrial cities to play. To my mind this was 'big'! This was the Sex Pistols live on a limited tour of the U.S. and they were coming to BR!"[18]

Like quite a few of his friends, the 24-year-old Bourgeois had been discovering punk rock through regular visits to the Leisure Landing record store. He'd also started to dress differently. "The 'punk' clothing and haircuts were not a big part of the BR scene yet, so I took my cues from the Ramones' uniform: blue jeans, T-shirt and an old black leather motorcycle jacket; well worn, zippers in all the right places, the elbows starting to get holes in them."

Carlton Freeman says that while the crowd seemed to enjoy the Twisters, they were obviously there for the headliners. "I'd guess that most of the crowd were locals and were therefore very familiar with the zydeco/blues the Twisters played as there were many local bands doing the same thing. The crowd had heard it before and were patiently awaiting the punk spectacle that was to come. It was my first time to see them though, and I found their set to be good. I particularly thought the smallish washboard player was a hoot. He was quite energetic and bounced around the stage."

(Dopsie would die unexpectedly from heart failure aged 61 in August 1993, but his legacy lives on through his son, Rockin' Dopsie Jr.)

After a short break, during which the house sound system delivered what *Gris Gris* would describe as being a "mixture of Cajun music and cosmic cowboyisms," the Pistols took to the stage. Jones and Cook "dressed in functionally altered T-shirts and jeans," Vicious "sporting leather, bondage belt and padlock necklace," and "the crowning glory of British punkdom, Johnny Rotten, snarling and alone, in a tacky blue plaid suit, T-shirt and S&M accoutrements."[19]

As with Memphis, the Pistols were greeted with a hail of ice cubes and playful insults, consisting mostly of "Fuck you!" and "Fuck you, Johnny!" Rotten normally thrives on such badinage, but tonight he appeared subdued. While awaiting Jones to run through his prerequisite tune-up, Vicious ambled up to the mic and yelled, "We hope you all fuckin' hate us!" which served as a cue for another barrage of ice and insults. The crowd then fell eerily quiet, except for a lone voice calling for someone to "throw something at 'em!" as the Pistols launched into "God Save the Queen."

Twenty-one-year-old Cyril Ruth, who hailed from New Orleans, was seeing the Pistols for the third time on the tour. "I was already into the Dolls and the Stooges when I discovered the Ramones. I was also into British punk—the Pistols, the Clash, and the Damned, etc. A friend of mine got us advance tickets for the Atlanta show, which had so much media coverage it was more like a news event then a rock concert. Since it was the first time I was seeing the Pistols I thought they would play better then they did, but I was still filled with excitement at seeing an act that was new and fresh.

"As the Pistols were basically doing the same set every show, the shows kinda blend into one after so long. I can't remember much about the Memphis show, other than it was a cold night and they had a problem with fire marshals wanting to shut the show down because of there being too many people to fit in the place. We got in early or I don't think we would have of gotten in at all. There was a great punk band in New Orleans called The Normals, but I've since heard that Malcolm McLaren didn't want a punk band to open for the Pistols so the Kingfish booked Rockin' Dopsie and the Twisters. In the opening part of the *D.O.A.* movie there's a scene of a guy with green glasses and wearing a Normals shirt and people pulling his jacket open. One of those people is me!

"Malcolm didn't want the crowd to waste any energy on the opening band so that the crowd would be ready for the Pistols. It worked! The crowd went crazy for the Pistols from the first song, which I think was 'God Save the Queen.' As in all the shows, Sid really couldn't play well at all due to drugs or whatever? He kept yelling to the crowd to throw money. He was probably hoping for bills, but people just threw pennies and nickels at him. Since I was standing right in front of Sid in front of the stage I kept getting hit on the back of the head with coins."[20]

It wasn't only loose change reining down on the Pistols, as Gaylon Keeling boasts of hurling a whisky bottle at the stage. "I remember watching it fly through the air towards the stage, but not much about Johnny Rotten's reaction to it as I was pretty wasted. I was 28 at the time and living pretty loose bumming around the LSU campus, and so didn't care much about anything except for music, friends, and drugs. I really only went that night because all my friends did as punk music wasn't that high on my music list. I mean I liked it, but only because it was rock 'n' roll in its rawest state. However, I became a huge fan of the Sex Pistols after that night. They were original, and they were real. They were definitely an influence on the Baton Rouge music scene."[21]

Cook once again "battering his kit" into submission (© Carlton Freeman).

Tim Parrish was both "annihilated" and "changed" from the moment the Pistols came onstage. "I'd never heard or experienced anything like it. I subsequently wrote about the show, and it truly was an 'almost epiphany-like, sexual, almost spiritual experience.' Steve Jones's guitar was ripped 'like a dull meat saw,' and Paul Cook battered his kit relentless. Rotten keened unintelligible lyrics was a sound that I'd have never have called singing.

"It almost took my legs from under me—the most awful, beautiful anguish of broken machinery meeting human flesh. An orgasm at the center of a warehouse collapse, a miracle, every bit as powerful as the Southern Baptist preachers who'd been telling me I was going to hell since I was seven. A grin as big as sex spread across my face. I tossed my frizzy hair, banged my palms on my thighs, stared amazed at the meltdown spilling across the stage. Every rock-star pose, every fast-fingered guitarist's neck diddle, every tight-pants strut I'd ever witnessed was being bludgeoned obsolete right before my eyes. The Pistols were ugly and fun and not virtuosic at all—just honest, raw, dangerous and sick with attitude. It was like being hit by a huge wave and not caring that I was trapped underwater as I was rolled around. It changed the possibilities of my life and my orientation to music.

"I remember Johnny Rotten being in this little bar next to the Kingfish where we stopped for a drink before the show. He threw a sandwich and a waitress jumped on his ass, saying something to the effect of, 'I don't care what kind of Pistol you are, nobody throws a sandwich in my restaurant.' Rotten acted like this was the funniest thing he ever heard, but he straightened up. Then he went over and started goofily preening in the mirror. I was fascinated from that moment on because he was putting off a kind of energy and charisma that I'd never been around before. The Pistols really did bring an anarchic freedom and sense of artistic possibility to a lot of people who felt like outsiders. I didn't get into the scene in earnest for a couple more years [forming his first band, The Human Rayz, in 1982], but that show was a touchstone and source of pride for the people who were there. We all knew it was special, and that knowing helped cement a community."

When the Pistols took to the stage, Earl Reinhalter's initial impression was how "scrawny" they looked. "I was expecting something more scary. These are punks? The Kingfish, or somebody connected to the club, had hired some LSU wrestling team jocks as security. I remember thinking, 'This is really stupid.' Did they think we were going to rush the stage, like pre-teen girls at a Beatles concert?

"Hearing this music for the first time—I hadn't yet bought the album—I could definitely feel the power. The volume, in fact, was so intense that it was hard to hear the vocals ... at least from where I was. The club's in-house soundman 'Hollywood' [a.k.a Bill Bennett] later told me that the band blew a speaker in the P.A. I don't know if he meant in the main speaker cabinets or one of the monitor speakers.

"I stood stage right, directly in front of Sid throughout the show. On his bare chest was scrawled 'GIMME A FIX' in what looked like Magic Marker. Overall, I was impressed that these guys had unique stage names and visual styles. I think that if you want to be famous, your fans have to be able to be you for Halloween. Your look has to be that unique. And, indeed, not long after this show I attended a Mardi Gras party dressed as Sid Vicious. Being a musician myself, I never got the impression that Sid wasn't playing, or could not play. That's a myth! Perhaps by the end of the tour, he was too far gone with his drug addiction to perform. A friend who witnessed the San Francisco show told me that he was definitely not contributing to the music that night. But in Baton Rouge, he was.

"When the audience sang along with 'EMI,' it was my impression—on hearing this song for the first time—that this would be their big U.S. hit if they released it as a single. During the latter part of 'Submission' the band played the same two chords over and over, which I thought was a great artistic statement. I also liked the song where Johnny sounded like he was singing, 'I don't wanna be anything'—which I later realized of course was 'I wanna be anarchy.'"

Brad Orgeron also thought "EMI" one of the standout songs, but begs to differ on Reinhalter's opinion of Vicious' performance. "Sid just looked lost. He barely played, and when he did, well … it was usually another song. The Pistols sounded far thinner live than on the album, it just wasn't the same without Matlock's melodic bass. Jones and Cook managed to hold things together though. I was standing right in front of Steve about two rows deep. He pulled all the right guitar hero shapes he'd supposedly learned off Johnny Thunders, while Paul was steady as a rock. Johnny was his typical half-bored/half-hysterical self. I don't think 'musicality' was in the forefront, but it was still quite a spectacle. I'm guessing the energy at their UK shows was higher as they seemed to be on their last legs. The standout songs for me were 'Seventeen' and 'Problems,' but my most vivid memory from that night was watching Malcolm across on the other side of the stage, grinning through the whole thing. That said it all, really."

"It's hard to convey just how exciting and powerful the Pistols were," Greg Ellis adds, still mesmerized by the experience after four decades. "Sid did play, of course, just not all the time. It didn't matter though because Steve and Paul were so locked in with each other. Johnny is the single most charismatic front man I've ever seen—terrifying, disgusting and impossible to look away from. I've always felt Sid's onstage antics were simply because no one would look at him otherwise. Johnny, however, was a force. Simply amazing! He had a cold and blew snot everywhere. People threw money. He demanded bills."

Getty Freemen was equally appreciative of Jones and Cook's ability to keep things from going off the rails. "Steve's right hand was machine-like. He and Paul Cook were locked in, loud and impressive. They seemed like serious musicians. They brought the fire. Sid was … well, 'Sid.' He wasn't much good, but he managed to stay mostly in the pocket. What blew me away the most that night was my standing ten feet away from Rotten. We were flipping each other off all show. When it was all over I felt he and I could've been mates. My hair was long, his was spiked. We both had attitudes that were confrontational, but also loving to those who understood.

"The Sex Pistols were almost cartoonish to me. Sid seemed like a dick. Very menacing and 'Gimme A Fix' scrawled on that pale torso. I knew he'd be dead before long. My personal preference is the Ramones, but the angst-driven energy the Sex Pistols had both live and on record can't be denied."

John Guarnieri has a slightly different take on the Pistols' performance. "It was just noise and testosterone! But the beauty of it was that it was so simple that any kid could go out and pick up an instrument and start a band. So from that aspect, the Sex Pistols, McLaren, and all the other punk bands, launched the DIY generation! It was a revolutionary thumbs-down to corporate rock!

"Soon after the show I ended up driving Steve and Paul around the streets surrounding the Kingfish in my friend's Lincoln Continental. Steve and Paul were in the back smoking joints. I ran a red light, and was stopped by the BR police. I turned around and told Steve and Paul not to say a word. I thought if the cops heard an English accent, they may have realized it was the Pistols. It would have made great press, but we would have been in jail! Alas, I can't recall any topics of conversation, but I can't imagine it was much other than stuff relating to the show and the tour. It was immediately after the gig and we were probably too drunk or stoned!"

The Pistols once again ended with "Anarchy in the U.S.A." before returning for an encore ("Liar"). Rotten and Vicious remained onstage to gather up the surfeit of dollar bills and coins. Earl Reinhalter says that while Vicious was hunched down to gather up his share of the booty, a woman jumped up and grabbed his sunglasses. "The girl somehow managed to get through the line of LSU wrestling team goons that were standing between the audience and the stage security. I think it was the same girl that I saw earlier wearing an army field jacket that had stuff written on it, including 'NEW WAVE.' This was the first time I ever saw that phrase. On the bootleg of the show, you can hear Sid asking for his shades back, and that's what he was whining about."

Getty Freeman, however, has an alternate version of events. "During the show there was a guy standing close to Sid's side of the stage with some cool sunglasses on. At one point, Sid reached down, grabbed them off the guy and put them on. A few minutes later, he took them off again and set them on top of his amp. I saw the guy motioning to one of the stagehands standing close to the amp to get them back for him and he did. A minute or so after that, Sid noticed and said, 'Hey, who got my shades?' So the guy handed them back to Sid again."

Eddie Flowers was impressed by how great the Pistols had sounded live in spite of "the obvious lack of guitar overdubs like the records" coupled with Vicious' rudimentary playing. "We recognized 'Belsen Was a Gas' as a new song we'd read about, and later talked about how it sounded like a step down from songs on the album. Being rabid Stooges fans we also cheered for 'No Fun.'"

Flowers' pleas for "Steppin' Stone" can be heard on bootleg recordings between "Belsen Was a Gas" and "Submission." His pleas, alas, went unheeded as the Pistols hadn't played the Monkees classic since the Anarchy Tour.

Cyril Ruth would go one better than Guarnieri as he ended up talking with three of his new musical heroes after the show. "I got talking to Steve, Paul, and Sid. I think Johnny had got back on the tour bus by then. Since I was meeting the Sex Pistols for the first time I wanted to know everything about the band, as well as everything about the punk scene in England. I was from New Orleans, which is far from London so I figured they could tell me what was going on over there. Of the three, Paul was the coolest to talk to. He told me stuff like the band's falling out with A&M Records.

"Steve and Sid pretty much just wanted to drink beer and hook up with girls for sex— a few groupies were hanging around them. Sid asked me about drugs, and about the chances of my getting him some drugs. But I wasn't into the drug scene, so couldn't help him. I just knew he would be dead within three years after meeting him. He talked a lot. He said how he hated Queen, and was making fun of Freddie Mercury. He also poked fun at the Clash. If you've seen the photo of Sid with his pants down and holding his balls, I was standing right there when that picture was taken."

Roberta Bailey, who took said photo, had been chatting with Vicious at the time. "He was sitting on the bar. All of a sudden, he said, 'Well, take a look at this!' and jumped off the bar, pulled his pants down, and grabbed his crotch! He was just taking the piss. It was a funny moment."

Kevin Bourgeois also has special reason to remember his encounter with Vicious

The *Baton Rouge Advocate*'s Smiley Anders came away from the Kingfish thinking the Pistols' style wasn't all that hard to take—even if the band themselves looked like "the leftovers from a four-day wake." Shown here are Vicious (left) and Rotten (© Roberta Bayley).

immediately after the show. "Everyone was milling about the bar area. I turned around and saw Sid standing right behind me. He was hanging on to some young woman I didn't recognize. He asked me if he could have my leather jacket. Like an idiot, I said, 'You've already got one.' If I'd have been thinking straight, I could have asked him to trade my jacket for his—then I would have really had a story to tell the grandkids. Instead, I asked him why people had been throwing ice at him during the show. Sid mumbled something I couldn't decipher before disappearing into the crowd. Pretty lame, huh?"

♪ ♪ ♪

The *Advocate*'s resident music pundit, Smiley Anders, was at the Kingfish to review the show for the paper's readership. "As I recall, I started the review ("Sex Pistols' Rock Style Not at All Hard to Take") by saying how they turned out to be more musical than they were violent, that they looked like 'the leftovers from a four-day wake' ... or something along those lines. From what I remember, they'd gotten a lot of press here in Baton Rouge, and the audience, college kids or slightly older folks, were ready to party with them. A Warners press officer [Heidi Robinson] had said something about the Sex Pistols being a 'people's band,' and their wanting to play to people at 'grass roots' level. Well, they got that here, all right.

"I might have been the only sober person in the room—and that includes the band! They were a scruffy lot, and Sid either came onstage without a jacket or took it off soon after they started playing. To my mind, Rotten's anarchic lyrics sounded like Herman's Hermits gone mad, but they played a hard-driving—if primitive—rock that wasn't really all that hard to take. Sure, they were rude and crude, but, hell, I grew up with rhythm and blues. It didn't shock me or anything. In fact, it was kinda fun. It seemed like kids playing rock again ... like throwback rock 'n' roll. A reminder that this thing we called rock 'n' roll had virtually come full circle."[22]

The Advocate's sister paper, the *State Times*, decreed that the Pistols had been given the "most enthusiastic reception they've received so far on their limited first American tour" from the Kingfish crowd. And that the "disgusting and grotesque behavior" that had generated overwhelming publicity and propelled the Pistols to fame had failed to materialize. Floor manager Mark O'Neil said how he'd found the Pistols "a lot tamer" than he'd anticipated. "We had reports of the band getting into a fight in San Antonio, and about fights breaking out in the audience in Memphis, but we had no incidents here that I know of."[23]

Speaking with the same paper, Heidi Robinson said that there had been more people at the Kingfish show that were into the Pistols compared with the other cities visited thus far. She then confided how the Pistols were "attempting to be on their best behavior because they had hopes of expanding the limited tour into a full blown U.S. tour."[24]

Smiley Anders was leaving the Kingfish—"hurrying to file the review before deadline"—when he was stopped by a French film crew. "These guys were in leather jackets and turtlenecks, smoking cigarettes, all looking like [French New Wave actor] Jean-Paul Belmondo. They asked me how I liked the Sex Pistols, and I gave them my impression pretty much as it appeared in the following morning's *Advocate*. I don't know if I ever made it on French TV, or in a documentary, or whatever they were doing. Of course, by leaving early I missed the legendary event: Sid receiving a sex act—some said simulated—from a drunken female fan as he continued to play."

The incident Anders refers to supposedly occurred during "New York." Noel Monk describes Vicious' amorous admirer as being a "five-feet-three-inch 160-pound package of bulging spandex"[25] that had somehow evaded the attention of Glenn Allison and the rest of his security team to get so far as undoing Vicious' jeans and pulling them halfway down before being forcibly restrained.

Somewhat amazingly, the incident appears to have largely gone unnoticed by the vast majority of those at the front of the stage. Greg Ellis, however, says he remembers it vividly. "Sid and the girl had been interacting. He motioned her up, undid those nasty-looking black pants of his and let her have at it. It lasted maybe twenty seconds before the security guy broke it up. They moved two other huge guys in front of Sid to prevent the woman from getting back up there. After the show, I saw Sid at the bar with the same woman. My friend Billy was tending the bar that night and he later assured me that the woman finished what she started."

"It definitely did happen, but it was a 'simulated' blow job since Sid never dropped his pants," say Carlton Freeman, who was standing next to the sound desk some fifteen feet or so back from the stage. "She was a slightly heavy-set girl. She was standing right at the edge of the stage and she grabbed Sid's bondage belt as he came to the edge. Since the stage was only a few feet high, it placed his crotch about face level for her. She hung onto the bondage belt, and he ground his crotch into her face for a minute or so with a big grin on his face and his bass guitar off to the side to keep from hitting her in the head. Not sure why I don't have a photo of it, but in those days I shot limited rolls of film due to the expense and my poor boy student budget, so I imagine I was out of film by that time."

John Holmstrom missed the incident, but remembers hearing how Vicious had "gotten a blow-job in the men's room from a pretty good-looking skank" after the Pistols had come off stage. Something was obviously in the air, but it could have simply been due to *Deep Throat* playing at the Regina Theatre out on Plank Road as part of a Gerard Damiano double bill (the other movie being *The Devil in Miss Jones*).

Holmstrom also remembers seeing Rotten sat on the stage gleefully counting his takings for the evening. "He got fifteen dollars, and said something about the Pistols being 'starving Biafrans.' I ignored him, went backstage, and started stealing Pistols posters off the wall. One of the owners spotted me. He took me through to his office and said I could help myself to a bunch of other posters so long as I left his Stevie Nicks poster alone."

The *Punk* cartoonist wasn't the only one to depart the Kingfish with gifts courtesy of the club's owners, as the Sex Pistols were presented with commemorative T-shirts.

The grey shirts (with black trim) bore the Kingfish and Sex Pistols logos with a Dennis Morris photograph from the "God Save the Queen" promo video shoot at the Marquee Club. Rotten and Jones were subsequently snapped while wearing the shirts on the tour, and if one were to come up for auction today it surely would command a reserve as high as any Westwood/McLaren creation.

"I'm pretty sure they were for the band only, but Malcolm might have got one also," says Rory Johnston. "I certainly don't remember being given one. And if I did get one, it's long gone now. It's at times like this that I really wish I'd been more careful with the tons of Pistols-related stuff I was given back then!"

Holmstrom and Bayley were given a ride back to the Ramada Inn on the tour bus— the only occasion they were invited to do so during the tour. "Roberta had called for a cab, but it failed to arrive. Whether it was because we were calling from the Kingfish where the Pistols were playing, I couldn't say. Malcolm ran into us standing there and offered us a ride on the tour bus. The most unusual thing was that Roberta, a beautiful young woman, was on a bus filled with horny men yet no one else seemed to notice.

"The bus itself was very comfortable. It was kinda crowded, but there were bunk beds, cushioned chairs, and built-in tables. We were sat in the back with Steve and Sid, with the security goons eyeing us suspiciously. Monk had already warned me that I couldn't write about anything that happened either on the bus or at the hotel. And Roberta wasn't to take any pictures." Rotten disappeared inside and up to his room the moment the bus came to a halt, but Vicious was still in an amorous mood. He teasingly demanded "a portion" from Roberta, and on being refused he started a play-fight. "Sid started slapping her, promising not to kick her," says Holmstrom. "Then Roberta began to win the fight, so he kicked her hand. Vicious may have been drunk, but he could see that he'd hurt Roberta. He was distraught that he offered her a free punch."

"We just started mock fighting," Bayley explained. "Sid actually kicked my thumb and broke the nail! Then he was very sorry and began apologizing profusely. He always seemed like a sweet guy to me. He just had gotten lost."

While Bayley tended to her broken nail, Vicious turned his attentions towards Holmstrom. "Sid came over and gave me an exhibition of his fighting skill. He started throwing punches, faster and faster, missing my face by mere fractions of an inch.... Then he punched me."

Vicious was again racked with remorse and offered Holmstrom a free shot, but the latter thought it prudent to put discretion before valor. "I felt threatened by the 'bodyguards' throughout the entire tour. I think they were looking for the flimsiest excuse to beat the shit out of me. I saw them kicking the shit out of people outside the Kingfish. They also threatened the English reporters with violence. It was fun for them. I was terrified whenever they came near me."

Six

Dallas

> They said no one could be more bizarre than Alice Cooper, or more destructive than Kiss ... they have not seen the Sex Pistols. Tuesday night, Stone City Attractions presents live, the Sex Pistols. Banned in their own home country, England's Sex Pistols, denied admittance to the United States, the Sex Pistols bring the new wave to the Metroplex this Tuesday night, in the Longhorn Ballroom. They said it couldn't happen, but it happens Tuesday night: the Sex Pistols live.
>
> —KZMP radio ad

While Ted Jaffe was locking horns with the U.S. State Department over the Sex Pistols' visa applications, his opposite number at Warner Bros. Television would in all likelihood been occupied with dotting the i's and crossing the t's on the distribution deal for a new five-part miniseries centering around a fictitious feuding Texan oil family. As with the Pistols, *Dallas* was set to feature an irascible, yet mesmerizing character with the initials "J.R." Warners were equally determined to establish the non-Stetson wearing JR a household name throughout America. As soon as Jaffe had worked his magic with the visas, Ted Cohen fired off communiqués to the heads of the WEA (Warner Elektra Atlantic) record stores in each of the seven cities the Pistols were set to visit on the tour.

In the letters—dated Friday, December 30, 1977, and carbon-copied to Bob Regehr, Bob Merlis, and Rory Johnston among others—Cohen stated that as Warners were in the process of attempting to "firmly establish Punk/New wave music as a viable and saleable commodity" in the U.S., it was therefore imperative that each appearance was "supported to the fullest extent possible." As the heads of the targeted WEA stores might not have known much about the Sex Pistols other than perhaps their name, he went on to explain how the "ground-breakers of a new musical turf [were] eliciting a response from audiences not seen since the early days of the Rolling Stones."

Cohen ended his missive by assuring the respective heads that with their cooperation the Pistols could be a major act for Warners, before then urging them to take full advantage of the various merchandising aids that were being shipped to the respective stores to maximize publicity.

The Longhorn Ballroom, located at 216 Corinth Street, was as unfamiliar setting for a rock 'n' roll show as Randy's Rodeo. It was built in the early 1950s, supposedly to the specifications of O.L. (Ocie Lee) Nelms—a colorful Dallas tycoon who had amassed a multimillion-dollar fortune from a candy and tobacco business that he'd built up from scratch. "With fiberglass Indians, teepees and cactus out front and a giant Longhorn bull beckoning under a sign, the exterior was pure Texas kitsch." The ballroom's interior was similarly tawdry, with huge stuffed Longhorn heads, wagon wheel light fixtures, steer skulls and murals of cowboys adorning the walls. The bar, which ran the entire length of the building and said to be the largest anywhere in the Southwest, was embedded with some 1700 silver dollars.[1]

The ballroom had started out as the Bob Wills' Ranch House, and the legendary western swing bandleader and his Texas Playboys had entertained discerning Dallasites on a nightly basis. However, owing to a combination of ill health and the questionable character of various business partners, Wills was forced into giving up the lease at the end of 1958. The lease was taken over by Dewey Groom, an established country singer who'd first made his name on local radio back in the 1920s when he was known as the Mabank Flash (in reference to his Van Zandt County origins).[2]

"Nelms owned the land and built the club for Bob, but Bob finished it out inside to resemble a California western-type theme and atmosphere," Groom's daughter, Saran Knight, explained. "I don't mean to say that Bob actually did the work on it, but that it was his request to have it fancy inside. There's two conflicting stories about what happened to the club after Bob left. I remember my parents telling me that the club sat vacant for a while, and then Jack Ruby opened it up and he and Dad were partners. The agreement was that all of the door money was Dad's, and the bar receipt went to Jack. After a year or two they had a falling out, which is a whole other story in itself! And then the club sat vacant because Dad moved out and went and opened up his own place in downtown Dallas on Main Street. Jack later went on to open up the Carousel club on Elm Street in Dallas and the rest, as they say, is history. The Longhorn sat vacant again and then Mr. Nelms approached my dad and they originally agreed to a ten-year lease. Dad moved his band

The Pistols' tour bus after Lamar St. John's graffiti makeover (© Roberta Bayley).

back in there in October 1968 and renamed it the 'Longhorn Ranch,' which later evolved into the Longhorn Ballroom."³

The Longhorn Ballroom was a family run affair as Saran worked the bar and her older brother Doug was responsible for booking the acts. "We were closed on a Monday and Tuesday, so we would rent out the club, mostly to black entertainers such as Al Green, B.B. King, Bobby B. Bland, and so on. Aerosmith also shot a commercial there. I'd already done business with Jack Orbin from Stone City Attractions, and he called one day to say he wanted me to hold a date for him but wasn't sure as to who the act would be yet. Jack was a real nice guy, and good to do business with. About a month before the show he called and told me it was the Sex Pistols. No big deal, it was just another band, albeit one with a strange name. I did try to cancel after what we seen on the news, but it was too late. Jack assured us we would have no problem, however, and we didn't. They [the Pistols] were an odd bunch, but real friendly—especially Johnny Rotten. I got the blame for all of it, even though I really didn't do anything. I still tell people it was just a publicity stunt."⁴

"I was working the bar the night of the Sex Pistols show," says Saran, who was 20 at the time. "We only sold draft beer in plastic cups that night due to fear of people either cutting themselves or others with a bottle or a can. I was working so hard that I never really got to watch the show, but Lord, I know it was the first time that I had seen so many strangely dressed young people in one place in my life."

♪ ♪ ♪

The tour bus arrived at the Longhorn Ballroom midafternoon after yet another grueling all night drive. The John Wayne scenery that had captivated Rotten and Vicious during their first foray into Texas had lost much of its allure. The tour was entering its second week, and the onboard relationships were proving as barbed as the prickly pear cacti dotting the lunar-esque landscape, the early ambience having all but disintegrated. So much so, in fact, that Jones and Cook had cajoled McLaren into letting them fly to Dallas with him, along with McLaren's secretary/personal assistant Sophie Richmond, Boogie Tiberi, and Rory Johnston.

Most bands are forced to endure love/hate relationships to survive the constant pressure-cooker environment of touring, recording, and writing, but the Pistols' internal wrangling was perhaps more fraught than the norm. Vicious' induction to the Sex Pistols had brought about a unification of sorts. Rotten had always felt that Jones and Cook had acted as a block vote whenever it came to discussing band policy, and bringing in Vicious had brought about a balance in power. "Steve and Paul just wanted groupies and fame. Glen wanted nice songs. Getting Sid in was to kind of change that situation somewhat. But Sid went straight into being the worst kind of rock 'n' roll idiot you could ever hope to have a nightmare about. It backfired on me. But it was still tolerable."⁵

Matlock's main grievance at the time of his departure from the Pistols was the meteor-sized chip Rotten had nurturing on his shoulder in the wake of the band's appearance on *Today*. The UK media's fixation with Rotten was, of course, only to be expected. Jones might have been responsible for turning the air blue, but "Johnny Rotten" was a tabloid editor's wet dream. The U.S. media had proved equally fascinated with Rotten, but the singer now found himself having to vie for the center of spotlight with Vicious.

For their part, Jones and Cook had shrugged off Rotten's being the center of the media's fixation on the Pistols. They'd also shrugged off Vicious' questionable musical talent when Rotten had forwarded—and seconded—the motion to have him replace Matlock. They were understandably less thrilled—as indeed was Rotten—at the constant mollycoddling Vicious was being afforded by McLaren owing to his spiraling drug dependency, but had been willing to hold their tongue for the greater good. They had also come to begrudgingly accept the trials and tribulations of the previous year having rendered the Pistols to little more than a traveling circus. What they were struggling to accept, however, was the clown savant dismissing them as little more than sidemen on occasion.

Jones says that while Rotten and Vicious looked great together on stage, and that the media frenzy surrounding the band had ensured plenty of column inches in newspapers around the globe, he was slowly coming to rue his not questioning the folly of bringing the latter into the line-up. "Teaching Vicious where to put his fingers on the fret-board so he could make some attempt at playing live was a total pain in the arse. I hadn't minded being second fiddle to John, but now I was playing third fiddle to this fucking idiot!"[6]

John Holmstrom would find himself privy to McLaren's musings on the internecine strife that was slowly but surely eroding the Pistols from within. Holmstrom had collared McLaren for an interview, but much to his chagrin, *Rolling Stone*'s Charles M. Young was purposely loitering within eavesdropping distance.

"Malcolm expressed the fear that the Sex Pistols would not face any competition, that the band would become self-congratulatory and complacent. He thought their role was to inspire competition and help other bands: To create a cultural revolution! We saw this play out when he wanted every punk rock band in the San Francisco area to open for the Sex Pistols, which would mean something like a ten-hour open stage. He wasn't able to pull this off because of resistance from Bill Graham. But Malcolm's attitude was contrary to the way the music industry did business at the time where bands at the top of the bill routinely screwed over bands below them in refusing to allow them to use the main PA system, the lighting, etc.

"We had a great conversation, and I became an instant fan and supporter of Malcolm. He was a genius! And although the Pistols were an amazing punk rock band, I doubt they would have become infamous worldwide without his ideas and actions. The weirdest thing about the Pistols is that although Malcolm manufactured 'The World's Most Important Punk Rock Band,' most of it was accidental. You know, the apocryphal story that Vivienne told Malcolm that this guy 'John' would be the perfect front man for the band, and how Malcolm thought that Lydon was that 'John' when in fact it was Sid. Well, you can't make this stuff up. At the end of it I think you must respect Malcolm for choosing the band members, as all five of them were why the Sex Pistols were what they were—one of the greatest rock 'n' roll bands of all time."

Holmstrom would surprisingly end up getting more than he'd been anticipating when McLaren compared the problems he'd faced dealing with David Johanson's ego to the ongoing problems he was now experiencing with Rotten. "I think Malcolm was worried at this point that Rotten had contracted LSD—'Lead Singer's Disease.' Rotten wasn't acting like a diva—he *was* a diva! This happens to so many people who front a rock band. They receive so much adulation that their brain gets warped. But to be fair, I think that while Rotten, and the other members of the band, were getting treated like rock stars, they were receiving a small daily allowance and were not receiving much in the way of royalties. Kind of the classic 'too much, too soon' thing the Dolls went through. Press clipping don't always mean your band is making money. The Pistols were on national TV in the U.S. while they were on tour, but their record was only charting around #114 on the sales charts."

Holmstrom was aware of the grumblings in the Pistols' camp about the preferential treatment Rotten was perceived to be getting from Bob Regehr and his Warners team, but says to his mind Rotten was getting the opposite of preferential treatment. "Rotten and Sid were stuck on the bus, while Paul and Steve got plane tickets. Rotten and Sid seemed to enjoy the bus, and I think they could have taken a plane from Tulsa to San Francisco if they had really wanted. And I heard they had a fun time in Los Angeles on their way to the show in San Francisco.

"As for Charles Young, he was a good guy and a good writer, but the way he stood behind us as I spoke with Malcolm was creepy. Especially since *Rolling Stone* was so anti-punk rock to the hilt! People ask now, 'Why didn't the Ramones become successful in the 1970s?' A big part of that was Jann Wenner's *RS* rag, which was as powerful as MTV in the late 1970s. *Rolling Stone* published a classic hatchet job on *Punk* magazine in 1977. They also dissed the Ramones, dismissed the Sex Pistols, and wrote about punk rock as if it was a fungus instead of the future of rock 'n' roll. In England, the weekly music papers had all supported punk rock as it was seen as a natural progression, the next stage of evolution in rock 'n' roll. So, punk rock became a huge movement in England. If it was controversial, it helped to sell papers and kept the UK music industry running at full-speed.

"But getting back to Charles' snooping on what I thought was a private conversation between me and Malcolm. I discussed this with Charles many years later. He said it was

Cook (rear) and Jones amuse themselves outside the Longhorn Ballroom while waiting for Rotten and Vicious to arrive (© Roberta Bayley).

fair game since we were all hanging out in the same place, but I still disagree. This was not a press conference, not a situation where he should have been sneaking up on us and taking notes. At least he could have asked permission. I also called *Rolling Stone* out, but you can imagine how that went."

♪ ♪ ♪

The Sex Pistols' calendar was booked up until the spring, and Warners, of course, were already making noises about a more extensive U.S. tour in the summer. McLaren, however, was harboring serious doubts for the coming year; that unless a band emerged to challenge the Pistols, they might not survive another twelve months with no one to compete against other than themselves.

McLaren had shrugged off Holmstrom's poser as to whether the Pistols' potency might have been watered down by the media's "stupid coverage," saying that as far as he was concerned it didn't matter what happened to the Pistols as the album would serve as the band's epitaph so long as they didn't "turn into entertainment."[7]

The paradox of his fearing the Pistols were in danger of becoming just another a staid rock act when it was the band's ongoing success that had filled Glitterbest's bulging coffers, as well as the cash register at Seditionaries, wouldn't have been lost on McLaren. But he must also have been harboring doubts about his own immediate future. He'd gained something of a reputation for subverting the music industry, yet the more established the Pistols became—especially now that they were signed to Warners—the less opportunity he would have for conjuring up mischief.

Another of McLaren's concerns regarding the Pistols' longevity that was aired during his chat with Holmstrom was the risk that a prolonged career might result in "Anarchy in the UK" and "God Save the Queen" becoming clichéd. Of course, given that all twelve tracks on *Never Mind the Bollocks* had featured in the Pistols' set list for eighteen months or so, it could be argued that the album itself was in danger of becoming passé.

McLaren thrived on controversy, and Virgin's decision to release "Belsen Was a Gas," as the Pistols' fifth UK single was sure to cause outrage within the UK media. Rotten, however, was intent on attacking the ultimate sacred totem—religion. It could be argued that Rotten had already dipped his toe into unholy waters in proclaiming himself an "Antichrist" in the opening couplet to "Anarchy in the UK." Unbeknown to the rest of the Pistols or McLaren, he'd been furtively working up a lyric for a new song he'd tentatively titled "Sod in Heaven." ("Sod In Heaven"—retitled "Religion"—would subsequently feature on PiL's debut album, *Public Image: First Issue*).

Rotten had revealed the new lyric to his fellow Pistols while en route to San Antonio, but the response hadn't been what he'd been expecting. "I wrote 'Religion' during the [U.S.] tour and Malcolm said, 'Ooh no, that's bad for the image, can't do things like that. I wanted to get them away from three chord rock 'n' roll into something more spicy. But they wanted to do what Malcolm wanted them to do. He would give this, 'Waay, we're all mates and he's the odd one.'"[8]

♪ ♪ ♪

Following the madness of Randy's Rodeo, the Pistols had every right to be apprehensive about returning to Texas. Sid was especially hesitant. "They killed Kennedy here and everybody had warned us that the people are crazy," he told the *Evening Standard*'s John Blake prior to going on stage. "I think there's a real danger that this is the town where I am going to be blown away." Roberta Bayley was also forced to suffer the bassist's morbid mantra. "Sid was sitting on the bar at the Longhorn Ballroom. He said something like, 'I want to be like Iggy. I want to die before I'm thirty.' I had to explain that Iggy was past thirty and still alive!"

Bayley herself was no stranger to heroin and the drug's inherent dangers from her relationship with Richard Hell, and readily identified with Vicious' need to keep his drug demons at bay with whatever came to hand. However, while she sympathized with the bassist to a certain extent, she could see that he was fast becoming a victim of his own creation. "Sid was a nice guy, but he got caught up in this whole punk thing. He was acting out, doing what he thought he was supposed to be doing."

Thanks to Tom Forçade's seemingly bottomless pockets, Bayley was able to travel from show to show in style. As with Charles M. Young, she and Holmstrom had arrived in Dallas on the same flight as McLaren's traveling party. While Holmstrom had been interviewing McLaren, Bayley had gone walkabout with Jones and Cook. If the duo were harboring any grievances towards Rotten and Vicious, they kept their broodings to themselves. "We didn't talk about anything like that. I gave them copies of several issues of *Punk* magazine to read, and we took some photos. I think they were quite enjoying the tour once they got off the bus. America. Airplanes. Nice hotels. Good shows, good fan response, journalists everywhere. What's not to like? We were all just in the moment, as you are when you're in your twenties."

When the tour bus had pulled up, Vicious had no sooner stepped into the Longhorn Ballroom when he was besieged by a clutch of LA punkettes who had driven all the way from California to see the Pistols. One of these was Gabi Berlin. "I was 20 years old and studying photojournalism in college. I was into Iggy Pop, Brian Eno, Roxy Music, and Bowie, of course. I first heard the Sex Pistols on Rodney Bingenheimer's radio show. I'm pretty sure 'Holidays in the Sun' was the song he was playing. I remember I had to pull over the car and start screaming and dancing.

"Our favorite hangout was the Masque in central Hollywood, which was situated beneath the now-legendary Pussycat porno theatre on Santa Monica Blvd. We were there one night, and Hellin [Killer, a.k.a Helena Roessler, who would subsequently earn a place in punk folklore by moving in with Vicious and Spungen at their Pindock Mews hideaway later in the year] had heard about the Sex Pistols tour, and was tearing around the place trying to get people together to go to Dallas. I was used to doing road trips, and was one of the few people in our group that had a car: a little blue VW Super Beetle."[9]

"Yes, it was my idea to go," says Killer. "I was not one to take 'no,' or even 'it's impossible' for an answer! So when I realized the Pistols weren't coming to LA, I started asking everyone we knew that had a car—and let me say, there were not many of us with cars at the time. Gabi had a VW Bug, and thankfully she said 'Yes!' You must realize this was just a couple days before the show, so there was no preparation here, ha-ha. I really don't remember how we all fit into that car! I don't think we took any luggage, just the clothes on our backs.

"My real name was 'Ross,' but not even my friends knew that. I'd been 'Hellin Killer' from like 1976 onwards. It was a pre-punk name given to me by a friend's boyfriend. He thought of me as 'the killer,' which means I was I tough little cookie back then. Still am, I guess."[10]

Six. Dallas

LA comes to Dallas. Pistols' fans Lamar St. John, second from left, Mary Rat, and future Gun Club member Terry Graham line up in the Longhorn Ballroom's foyer for Roberta Bayley. Graham's younger brother, left, is sporting the T-shirt Hellin Killer made for him (© Roberta Bayley).

Berlin had needed no second bidding. "I rushed home, begged gas money from a friend, and went back to the Masque. Hellin, Trudie [Arguelles], and a couple of other of our girlfriends were ready to go. I remember we waited for 'Dad.' That's Terry Baghdad [born Terry Graham], who was later in Gun Club. And there was another girl named Lamar who I think was from San Francisco. We barely had enough money for our gas there, and on the way home we had to duck into a truck stop, fill the tank, and rush off. That was back when you had to go in to pay. I don't know how we got away with that. I think that was Terry's idea."

Lamar St. John did indeed hail from San Francisco. "I discovered punk rock while working as a hair model at the Vidal Sassoon Academy in Frisco. My friend Vickie lived in a grand Victorian-style house with roommates that she moved to California with from the East Coast. They had a house-warming party and we invited a punk or two that I'd met at Sassoon's. Most of the teachers there were English and very 'avant-garde'; all 'high style and edgy.' My hair was died like a peacock. Well, a whole bunch of punks descended on the party. Vickie's roommates were so angry that they asked her to move out after that. And that's when we got our apartment together in North Beach. Our apartment was just up the street from the Mabuhay Gardens. We'd walk down to the Mab many nights, and we got to know the doorman, who began to let us in for free. We saw a lot of shows and got to know lots of people. That's where I met the LA girls: Gabi, Trudi, Hellin and a couple of others. We started hanging out whenever they came up to San Francisco. This was around October/November '77

"It was around that time that Vickie and I got evicted from our cool little apartment. We moved into another apartment on the corner of Haight-Ashbury. It was above a record store so we could make all the noise in the world! I think I flew down to LA in either November or early December and moved into the Plunger Pit for a while."[11]

"The 'Plunger Pit' was the name Hellin, Trudie, Mary Rat and another girl whose name I forget gave to the apartment where they were living," says Berlin. "It was a total mess! It was truly an amazing place with posters, artwork, and crazy stuff hanging everywhere. Kids would hang out there before gigs to get dolled up and party afterwards. You could devote a whole book to the whole Plunger mythology."

"Ah yes, the Plunger Pit," Killer chuckles. "Trudie, Mary [Rat], and I had just returned from our first trip to New York in the summer of '77. I'd recently received some money—about $2000—in compensation from an accident I was involved in, so decided to rent an apartment in Hollywood. I found a place behind Circus of Books on Santa Monica Boulevard in West Hollywood. John Doe and Exene Cervenka [bassist and lead singer with LA punk band X], lived in the building, as well as the guys from Zolar X [LA glam rock outfit]. They lived upstairs so for something like $200 a month, so I spoke to the building manager—a Polish guy—who said we could move in.

"Well that place quickly became the center of a lot of parties and gatherings as well as a crash pad for any out-of-towners and bands passing through. The punk scene in LA at this point was just amazing, small enough so that almost everyone knew each other. It was also just big enough so that every band that was ever gonna be someone or not was coming through town and playing at one place or another. We met everyone and made friends with them all. We had met a lot of the New York bands in the summer, and so when they came to town we already knew them. It was a small, intimate and friendly scene at that time.

"Anyways, I think what we had going was we had been hanging out and going to see bands in LA for a few years already. Trudie, Mary, and I were kinda a little gang of cute young girls that were always out and about and befriended everyone without ever becoming groupies. At least I never had sex with anyone back then! Ha-ha! Maybe I really missed out looking back on it. Oh well. We were fans; we loved the music, and the people that were coming into this tribe. We all had something in common, it seemed."

St. John doesn't remember ever being at the Masque, but says the idea to drive to Dallas to see Pistols could have very well spawned there. "I hadn't really heard of the Pistols until I was living at the Plunger Pit. Hellin was a very persuasive person, though. She had either a tarantula or a snake named Sid. She was a huge fan of the London punk scene and the Sex Pistols, but absolutely in love with Sid.

"What I remember most about the Dallas trip was that Hellin had most of the money for gas and food and wouldn't spend any on the way from California to Texas. She said she would pay on the way back, so the rest of us paid for the gas and food. There were five or six of us crammed into Gabi's Volkswagen Bug. Gabi was still in college, and was relatively 'normal looking' compared to the rest of us. I was driving at one point in Texas and got pulled over for speeding and given a ticket. I can't remember if I had my license or not, but the ticket was $200. The sheriff told us that we had to pay it ASAP in town, that there was a roadblock on the other side of town, and we wouldn't be able to get through it unless we paid the fine. So we went to the police station, and I had to call my dad who I didn't really talk to and hadn't seen in many years. I told him my situation and I think he wired the money to the station. We had to listen to the old fuddy-duddies talk about seeing the Sex Pistols on some TV show the night before. I told them that's where we were on our way to. We went on our way after the ticket was paid, and 'surprise surprise' there was no roadblock or cops on the other side of town."

"What I remember is getting pulled over somewhere in the middle of nowhere in Texas," says Killer. "I also recall that the cops were checking all of us for ID and I had none. But somehow in the confusion, and since there were so many of us, they missed me! If they hadn't, I believe I would have been detained and that would have been the end of my trip. As for the money, I really don't know why Lamar thinks I had any. If I did, it was probably only $40 or so. But I think we all had about that amount with us. I probably was holding on to it since we obviously needed to return to LA. And yes, I did have a snake named after Sid; he was my red-tail boa constructor. It was Trudie that had the tarantula."

Terry Graham had grown up in Oak Cliff, Dallas, and his family still lived there. "We got to the house around midnight," St. John continues. "His mother had left a whole table of food for us as well as bedding. It was a welcome sight! We arrived at the Longhorn some time the next afternoon. We had Terry's little brother with us. He was probably only 13 or 14 at the time. He was wearing a T-shirt that Hellin had made that had 'Sid' bleached out and some zippers sewn in. We were there when the Pistols showed up. I don't remember the interaction lasting real long, but I do remember how Sid was enamored with Terry's brother's shirt. He said something like, 'Look, you got my shirt on and I don't even have a shirt!' That sealed the deal for the kid—no going back to shitty rock music after that!"

"Lamar is right, Terry's little brother did go with us," Killer reflected. "So did his mom. I recall putting a safety pin through her pierced ear, and we did mess up a T-shirt for Terry's brother. I had a pair of jeans, combat boots and a black Seditionaries parachute jacket that I had borrowed from Terry. It seems that's all I wore the whole time we were in Dallas, ha-ha! We were so happy to be the only ones on the guest-list for the Pistols! I wish I had thought to keep that list, but then I was never much of one for saving souvenirs, or keeping journals or diaries, so some things have started to fade a bit over the more recent years. Terry's parents were totally amazing! They were so nice."

Berlin says they were waiting in the Longhorn's lobby when the Pistols arrived. "I feel foolish now, but then it was total hero worship. Sid walked up all skinny and cute like a puppy dog. He fell instantly in love with Trudie like everyone always did. He was absolutely floored. He just begged and begged her to be with him. He just wouldn't leave her alone! [Trudie, however, was dating K.K., a.k.a Keith Barrett, drummer with LA act The Screamers.] … The guys were crazy about Hellin too, of course, but she could be terrifying to be around. She scared me on occasion! Hellin was as equally amazing as Trudie, and she was available. She loved Sid so fiercely! And Sid did end up really loving Hellin a lot. I had never seen Hellin go after a guy so full on, so I was surprised. But her heart was no longer her own. She just fell so hard for Sid. I was so surprised, because she was such a loner.

"Anyways, Sid took Trudie's hand, pulled her into a corner and just kept begging her to go with him. But there was nothing doing. Trudie liked Sid, but she had no intention of cheating on KK. Soon after Sid got a hold of a bottle of alcohol, a *big* bottle, and started drinking. I'm pretty sure it was because he was just devastated that he couldn't have Trudie. It probably had never happened to him before.

"Sid asked if we'd bought tickets, and when we said we had he became outraged. There was a little old lady in the ticket booth, and he stalked over and demanded she refund our money. She was terrified! I clearly remember her cowering in her booth. She didn't say a word, just gave us our money back. Then Sid put us all on the guest list for the rest of the tour."

Killer, though "really foggy" about the drive over to the Longhorn, says she distinctly recalls the ticket situation. "We got to the Longhorn sometime in the afternoon—around 2–3 p.m. There was a woman at the ticket window, and we went over and bought our tickets for the show. It was shortly after that, that the Pistols' bus arrived in the parking lot. That was so exciting! I remember Sid coming off of the bus. He saw us standing there, and immediately came over to greet us. He seemed truly happy to see some punk kids. It was weird as I sensed very quickly that Sid wanted to just hang out with us. He was just a big punk kid himself. We told him that we had just bought our tickets, and that's when he said that we were going to be his guests.

"I walked over to the ticket window with Sid, and watched him arguing with the woman to give us our money back because we were his guests and we were to be in the guest list. She tried to say no, but he was not taking that for an answer. So she did return our money, and Sid put us on the list. Right after that I recall seeing Rory and Malcolm and went over to say hello to them. I knew them from when Malcolm came over to LA. They were like totally surprised to see me there. Inside we saw Bob Gruen. We knew Bob from our trip to New York the summer before. I felt pretty comfortable with all of them there."

Doug Groom is adamant that this didn't happen, however. "Sid had no way of doing that without my knowledge. And I wouldn't have let him do it anyway. Those people could have come in through the back door, but not the front. As I recall, I put one of Sid's girlfriends in jail after we closed. I was giving an interview, and she ran by and spit on me! My security guards chased her down, and I told them to 'send her to jail!'"

Lamar St. John backs Groom up to some extent as she recalls being put on the guest list for Winterland, but not for Dallas. "When the Pistols found out we'd driven all the way from LA they were really flattered and offered us backstage passes for Winterland. I don't remember getting a pass in Dallas though. It could have happened, but I still have my ticket stub for the show so I'm guessing I paid to get in. I don't remember Sid making any particular play for Trudie. She was a looker, though, so I don't doubt it happening."

Arguelles, however, backs up Berlin and Killer's version of events. "Malcolm let us in as I recall. He was great. Hearing we were a bunch of poor kids that had come all the way from LA to see the Sex Pistols, he said, 'You can get in for free. No problem.' It was a done deal. We had been talking to Sid, and Sid thought we should get in free. He then asked Malcolm to take care of getting us in. Malcolm agreed and took care of it. He was happy to let us in for free. We were in love with both of them for being such gents. Aside from the press, we were the only ones put on the guest list. We were also the only girls with Sid that day. And I don't remember any Longhorn managers."[12]

Berlin says that after the soundcheck she and her pals kidnapped Vicious and went driving around the surrounding streets. "We didn't have any particular place to go, so we just drove around to keep the heater on. It was too cold to stop. I still have a color slide somewhere of Hellin lying on top of Sid in the back to keep him warm. Hellin was in love! We drove around for a while until someone—probably Dad—said we should take him back to the hotel. I don't remember how we knew where the hotel was, but we found it."

Killer says that prior to the soundcheck she and Arguelles went off to buy a bottle of vodka. "We had to find a special liquor store 'cos in Texas you gotta buy liquor in special licensed stores. I recall Malcolm mentioning that they were having a hard time with Sid, that he had been trying to score drugs everywhere, and that they were trying to keep him from doing it! So Malcolm asked if I could try and keep Sid from doing that. Well, I hated heroin and would never try it. Trudie also hated it, so we were fine with that. That's why we went to buy the liquor. When we got back to the club, I was trying to hang out with Sid pretty much. I wasn't really too interested in hanging out with the rest of the Pistols. John seemed to have a really shitty attitude as far as I could see. I gotta say at this point that I already felt like Sid and I had hit it off. He was so easy to talk to, and to hang out with. He was kinda silly, and maybe not too bright, but so much fun and easy to be around. I was so happy to have met him!

"We hung around for the soundcheck and soon after that the crew got the band together to go back to the hotel. And that's when we stole Sid. We drove around for a bit, and then went to drink the vodka we'd bought and shared it with Sid out on the train tracks. Then we drove Sid back to the hotel. And I think that might be when we tagged the bus."

When the kidnapping posse arrived at the Pistols' hotel Berlin was half-expecting a roasting from McLaren for having driven off with his bass player so was astonished when the latter invited them to dinner. "I remember it as being an incredibly huge room with an amazing long table with everyone from Malcolm and the band to the roadies sitting around it. It was such a generous offer. And we were so hungry. In those days we were always starving because most of us had left home and were constantly scrounging for food. There was a lemon in net for the fish dishes, but Johnny didn't know that it was to allow you to squeeze the lemon without getting the seeds on the food and he tried to unwrap it. Everyone jeered at him. I don't know why that memory stays with me. Maybe because of the contradiction: seedy punk rock band on tour eating at a very fancy dinner party.

"Johnny was so cute. After the dinner we followed him up to his room to continue the party, but someone, maybe Noel, said he could only have two people in his room. Even though Noel had to protect the guys from us, he did it very skillfully. He was so friendly towards us. We never got a single bad vibe from him. Johnny got kind of angry and stared daggers at Noel, but then he looked at us for a long time and picked Mary and me!

"We hung out in Johnny's room until show time. He didn't try anything on like most guys would have done. He just lay on his bed and seemed so regal. Just so polite and sweet. He asked if we had any weed, and I had like a shopping bag full of weed that a friend had entrusted to me when he checked himself into the mental hospital. Johnny's face lit up. They didn't have smoke detectors in rooms back then. We smoked and talked about random things. He especially wanted to know everything about our lives in LA."

"Not everyone was party to the 'kidnapping,'" says St. John. "It was Gabi, Hellin, me, and maybe Terry. I'm pretty sure it was just a case of us driving Sid to the hotel where the Pistols were staying instead of him riding back on the tour bus. The Warners' security guy whose job it was to keep Sid relatively 'clean' and out of trouble was pissed about this, but

I kind of recall that he gave us his 'blessing' to take him. We found the hotel because it was the only one with a tour bus was parked outside. Things get foggy here, but I remember having a bite to eat with Malcolm, Johnny, Steve, and maybe Rory. Steve was just a total putz while Johnny was a sarcastic wiseass! I believe we were bantering back and forth about something. Afterwards we went up to the rooms and the awful security guy from earlier—who quickly became my nemesis—took the same elevator as I did. I remember him threatening me, showing me his brass knuckledusters.

"I'm assuming Hellin and maybe Trudie were with Sid, but I ended up in Paul and Steve's room. I found Steve totally gross, so I didn't hang around long. I do remember finding a shoebox full of weed though. Maybe I took some? Maybe we smoked some? I got myself a Sex Pistols baggage tag also. I wandered back downstairs and drove to a store to get the paint that I used to spray-paint the Pistols' tour bus. Yup, that was me. No more hiding for them!"

Having wrapped up his interview with McLaren, John Holmstrom had gone outside to find Bayley and witnessed the LA posse's arrival. "These LA groupies pulled up in the lot in a little VW Bug. It was like a clown car with all these people emerging this tiny, little automobile. We got talking to them, and discovered they had driven all the way from LA to see the Pistols. There weren't a lot of people dressing in punk rock fashions at the shows back then, but these girls were dressed to the hilt. They definitely got everyone's attention. Gruen got an amazing photo of them with Paul Cook that we published in *Punk* #14."

♪ ♪ ♪

Local act The Nervebreakers would be supporting the Pistols in Dallas. When reviewing the Pistols' performance, the *Dallas Observer* observed that punk rock was "still con-

Local act The Nervebreakers supported the Sex Pistols in Dallas. The ripped shirt singer T. Tex Edwards is wearing is the one he wore at the Longhorn Ballroom. The guitarst is Barry Kooda, the drummer Carl Giesecke (© Mike Haskin).

sidered an imported phenomenon" and had praised the five-piece Nervebreakers for "putting a Texas spin on this new kind of noise."

The Nervebreakers' front man, Thom Edwards (a.k.a T. Tex Edwards), had grown up listening to his older brother's Elvis and Chuck Berry records before moving onto Alice Cooper and The Stooges. "I worked at a Discount Records store after graduating high school, and got into many various styles of music there. I remember going into work one day and one of my co-workers threw down the first New York Dolls album, sneering derisively, 'Here's something you'll probably like' ... and they were right. I did! I later attended all three nights when the Dolls played in Dallas at Gertie's in '74. Soon after that, the Nervebreakers got together. We played a type of proto-punk music—Flamin' Groovies, Velvets' covers etc.—so when punk came along that was a part of how we sounded, so we went with it. Our lead guitarist, Mike [Haskins], started ordering imports of the UK punk releases to sell at Peaches Records where he was working at the time, so we had 'New Rose' by the Damned, 'Spiral Scratch' by Buzzcocks, and 'Anarchy in the UK' when they first came out."[13]

The Nervebreakers' rhythm guitarist, Barry Kooda (born Barry Huebner), says that while Haskins and Edwards' knowledge of new trends had kept him abreast of new and interesting music, his introduction to what was happening in London literally came about by accident. "At that time, Thom and I were working as delivery drivers for a beauty supply company. One day I ripped the crotch in my jeans. Not being able to find a needle and thread, I bought a package of safety pins and closed the hole with several pins. Since they came fifty to a pack, I stuck the rest in my pants and shirt and when Thom saw 'em, he said, 'Punk rock!' When I asked him what he was talking about, he said that the punk rock kids in England wore a lot of safety pins and told me about the Sex Pistols. Later, when the Runaways were in Dallas for a week, they borrowed our practice place and Joan Jett had a handmade Johnny Rotten badge with an old button and a photo of Johnny she'd covered with clear tape. I asked if she could play 'Anarchy in the UK' ... and she could.

"When it was learned that the largely unknown Sex Pistols were to include a Dallas show in their whirlwind U.S. tour, our bass player Clarke [Blacker] cut through the red tape by calling the tour promoters and offering us up as the perfect opening act. The promoters, not knowing much about either band, agreed and the date was set. Clarke had already decided to give up the bass so that he could manage the band instead, so the Pistols show was his swansong performance."[14]

"The local radio stations were running call-in shows where people could get on the air and say why they thought the Sex Pistols shouldn't be allowed to play in Dallas," says Blacker. "The small local punk scene was abuzz, but that was a pretty small bunch. The atmosphere around Dallas was absolutely poisonous. I was surprised by the hatred that came largely from mainstream rock fans, not just towards the Sex Pistols, but to the new music in general. I found it confusing and pretentious, like their music was somehow better than that of the new scene that was coming. In retrospect, I guess it must have threatened them somehow."[15]

Jim Parrett had moved to Dallas from his native Toronto the day prior to the Pistols' show. Parrett lived and breathed music. Between 1971 and 1976—during which time he graduated from Ottawa's Carleton University with a BA degree, he'd founded and edited his own fanzine, *Denim Delinquent*. He'd also penned articles for *Cheap Thrills*, a professional Canadian music magazine that would subsequently morph into *Stagelife*.

"'*Stagelife* was a follow up to *Cheap Thrills*, a rock publication put out by Mike Cohl's Concert Productions International," Parrett explained. "During the *Cheap Thrills* days I was offered the editor job because of my 'zine' experience. I had to turn it down due to financial reasons. To my chagrin, a folkie was hired, they changed the name to *Stagelife*, and it became more a pop mag after that. Luckily, Jeffrey Morgan from *Creem* took over the zine and that's why I was allowed to write about the Sex Pistols. *Cheap Thrills/Stagelife* had some pretty strong writers, including Morgan and Grammy-winning Rob Bowman, not to mention *Crash 'n' Burn* founder/punk poet Ralph Alfonso."[16]

The Longhorn Ballroom review would, however, be Parrett's last article for *Stagelife*. "I was 26, had a young family, and was feeling too old to write crazy stuff about rock 'n' roll bands. I certainly felt too old in the young crowd at the Pistols show."

Parrett had happened upon a copy of *Never Mind the Bollocks* in a Toronto store shortly after the album's release. "I'd read about the Pistols in the British music press and loved the cover so I picked it up. My mind was blown. Not only was it a great-sounding record, but the attitude was fresh and exciting. Punk was still new, rough and wild. I didn't expect Chris Thomas' magnificent guitar sound on that album to sound as good as it still does. No other 'punk' album ever came close to the sonics of that album. It spoiled the rest of punk for me because bands thought a good sound was establishment or something. It's unfortunate so many punk records sound so purposely shitty, because the music itself was extraordinary.

"There wasn't much going on in Dallas except perhaps for the Nervebreakers. Coming fresh from Toronto's vibrant Crash 'n' Burn scene, Dallas' punk scene seemed dead to me. However, the Pistols' show soon changed everything as bands like Control and the Earthworms started popping up. There was a sense of novelty about the show—the Pistols' very British point-of-view/London debauchery placed smack dab in Dallas' country music palace. You couldn't get a more ill-fitting match. Since I'd only arrived in Dallas the day before the show, all I knew was that my culture shock going from Canada to Texas; the Pistols coming to the Longhorn made for an out-of-body experience.

"Knowing that the Pistols were playing in my new home city, I contacted Virgin and organized an interview with the band after the show. However, I waited at the show and no one showed—much to the chagrin of the understandably harried Virgin rep. I should have stuck around just a few minutes longer as the band did make its way out onto the Longhorn floor. Man, that would have been a fun and perhaps contentious interview!"

Lannie Flowers (no relation to Eddie) had been counting down the days since learning the Pistols were coming to Dallas. "I would not have missed that show for the world at that point. I was 19 and living in Kennedale, a small town outside of Dallas. I'd loved music from early on and started my first band when I was 12. I grew up listening to the Beatles, Stones, Kinks, etc., but by 15 I began looking for different music. I started reading about the whole New York Scene with CBGBs. I'd always loved the Dolls, so that was where I was at that point musically. My local record store sold copies of *NME* and *Melody Maker*, so I really picked up on the English scene. I started reading about the Pistols and got 'Anarchy in the UK' from a special import shop. Loved it right away, got all of the 45s, and the album when it finally came out.

"I can't remember where I bought my ticket, but I know I had it in advance of the show as I would have been too afraid that I might somehow miss it. I went with one of the guys from my band. I was wearing an Iggy and the Stooges T-shirt that I'd bought through *Trouser Press*. Unfortunately, no one was impressed."[17]

♪ ♪ ♪

Thom Edwards had also been counting down the days to what was the Nervebreakers' most high-profile show to date. Yet come the day of the show, it was as if the fates were conspiring against him as he burning up with a hundred-degree fever. He was struggling to talk, let alone sing, but the rest of the band were in a similar state. "We were all nursing the flu and colds and kinda dragging ass," Mike Haskin explained. "Tex had a bloody nose from constantly blowing it, and one punk mag that reviewed our performance noted the blood, thinking it was a 'punk act' sorta thing."[18]

When the Nervebreakers arrived at the Longhorn, the Pistols were being interviewed by a KXAS-TV news crew. "The Pistols hadn't yet conducted their soundcheck, so we had to wait," Haskins continued. "Well, we waited, and waited … and waited. We waited at the bar for something like four hours while the Pistols clowned around in their stage gear. Sid Vicious had borrowed Steve Jones' guitar and played this one poorly played lick over and over for what seemed an eternity. Maybe three-quarters of an hour! Of course, after this bullshit there was no time for us to soundcheck. We turned in a pretty good performance, all things considered."

The already fractious atmosphere became even more fraught when Kooda got into an altercation with Vicious. "Sid and I had a minor altercation over his desire for my spiked wristband. I offered a trade for his studded wristband, which it seemed, was actually a dog collar. Sid said, 'No, I stole this off a dog … can't get much lower than that, eh? Stealin' from a dog?' To which I replied, 'Well, was it pregnant? That would be *really* low.' Sid indicated that he would like to have me kick his skinny British butt by throwing several mock punches in my face while saying, 'Come on, Come on.' I was about to eagerly oblige when Bob [Childress, who was set to replace Blacker on bass in The Nervebreakers] stopped me and said it probably wouldn't be a good idea to kick the crap out of the headliners' bassist before you play.' It was a tiff, but no punches were thrown as cooler heads prevailed."

Childress had brought along a portable tape-recorder, primarily to record the Nervebreakers' performance, but thought he might as well take advantage of the situation. "I set the recorder down—while simultaneously pressing the record button—during the Pistols soundcheck. Johnny made a lot of fun of Texans and cowboys, but they did sound good in the one or two songs they played before they quit. I've circulated the tape a little bit amongst friends, but it's never shown up on any record or CD officially so far as I'm aware. I watched the Barry/Sid encounter pretty close up. They had an argument over the bracelet Barry was wearing. Sid wanted it for free. I've also heard they tried to load our amps on to their bus. And Annie Leibovitz had her camera, and thus her film, stolen so I guess that was another altercation of sorts."[19]

"We were introduced onstage by a friend of Tex's," says Haslett. "He excitedly described us as being—amongst other things—'The best fucking punk band in Texas.' When the Sex Pistols took the stage, Rotten was moved to one-up us by introducing the Pistols as 'The best fucking band in the world!' The *High Times* magazine reviewer obviously didn't actually catch our set, but that didn't stop him from writing his review. He said that we were all wearing 'fake as hell Nazi helmets.' Barry wore his own U.S. army helmet, from his stint in the army, but no other helmets were in sight. The reviewer also mentioned some made up song titles 'No Bull,' 'Lone Star Anarchist' etc. We are still planning on writing songs with those titles, but haven't got around to it yet."

One song that definitely featured in the set was "My Girlfriend Is a Rock," which subsequently appeared on The Nervebreakers' debut EP, *Politics*, later in the year.

At some point during the set, Kooda brought some unexpectedly levity to the proceedings by attempting to play his guitar with a fish that had landed at his feet. "At an earlier Nervebreakers show, members of local punk band Dot Vaeth brought along a frozen whole fish," Haslett explained. "They threw the fish at Barry onstage. Not to be outdone, Barry began playing his guitar with the now-thawing fish, pounding his strings with it. Then he began chewing on the fish and throwing pieces back into the audience. Did I mention we got plenty of free beer that night? Anyway, a good time was had by all. In fact, it was such a good time that the Dot Vaeth guys brought another fish along with them to the Pistols show. Brilliant, really! *Rolling Stone* magazine featured a picture of Barry with the fish!"

"When Barry took a bite out of the fish, it seemed like the whole audience stood up with a camera to take the picture," says Childress, who was watching from the side of stage. "The Nervebreakers were well received by the audience and almost all feel they blew the Pistols performance off the stage. They ended—as usual—with their version of 'I Wanna Be Your Dog' by the Stooges. Johnny Rotten was standing next to me, visibly enjoying the performance. The Pistols, of course, their own Stooges' set-closer in 'No Fun.'"

John Holmstrom says his and Roberta Bayley's schedules were so "crazy" that he doesn't remember seeing any of the opening acts on the tour. "We definitely missed the support act in Dallas as we were late arriving back at the Longhorn Ballroom. We were late because we got stuck in the presidential suite in the most expensive hotel in town with Tom Forçade. Tom was having a meltdown. He threw a gold bar at Roberta."

"As I remember it, John and I went over to Tom Forçade's hotel," Bayley explained. "Tom always stayed at a different hotel than the Pistols, who were staying in inexpensive digs like The Rodeway Inn. He was in the presidential suite, and he was in bed shirtless when we arrived. I remember he had pierced nipples. He might've had on a cowboy hat. Anyway, basically I was putting all of John's and my own expenses on my American Express card. As I say, I'd left New York with only $50 cash which David Johansen lent me, the total was getting up in the thousands, and I was getting worried. I expressed my concern, and that was when Tom reached for a gold bar and threw it across the room at me saying something like, 'If you're worried about money, take this!' I didn't pick up the gold bar, but I guess that was Tom's way of saying, 'Don't worry.' So John and I left for the Pistols show. Someone told me later those gold bars were actually fakes!"

When penning his Pistols review for *Stagelife* in the immediate aftermath of the show, Jim Parrett mentioned how Dewey Groom had watched grim-faced as "an army of 2,000 weirdoes, punk look-alikes, and wild cowboys file into his ballroom."[20]

"The wild cowboys and curiosity seekers probably outnumbered the rockers by ten to one," Parrett reflected. "I worked my way up to the front during the show; the closer I got the wilder it got. The Pistols were not the loudest band I've ever heard, so people were getting as close to the action as they could to witness the atrocities. It was an historic night as any savvy rock and roller would have instantly known, but the audience was

Vicious' LA fan club getting up close and personal with their hero while Cook watches (© Roberta Bayley).

really mostly there because of the notoriety of the band. People were too disoriented for any real reaction. It was the oddest atmosphere I've even encountered at a concert, that's for sure."

Killer and her friends would have considered being included among Parrett's "2,000 weirdoes" as a badge of honor. "Well, like any fans going to see their favorite band in the world for the first time we made our way to the front of the stage through a densely packed crowd of the strangest bunch of people you can imagine. It was Texas after all, and the place was full of 'cowboy lookin' people—hats and all! But there were also a lot of kids trying their hand at the punk look, and either had handmade T-shirts with stuff written on them, or some make up or just anything to try to look 'punk' or just 'weird.' It was great! As for the cowboys, well they were there to see what all the fuss was about and it was pretty great. A really big turnout, if you ask me!"

The Longhorn's "plastic cup policy" was enough to ensure the Texan baptism the Pistols received was nowhere near as extreme as the reception they'd received in San Antonio, but a steady barrage of plastic cups and beer started reining down on the stage from the moment Vicious shouted out the "1–2–3–4" intro to "God Save the Queen."

The ballroom's interior layout wasn't all that dissimilar to that of Randy's Rodeo, and the low ceilings again played havoc with the sound. One reason for this was that the Longhorn's acoustics were unsuited for raucous rock 'n' roll. Indeed, when O.L. Nelms had commissioned an architect to put his ideas for the ranch house onto paper Jim Marshall had been renowned only for his drumming. McLaren and Tiberi's return to soundboard duty was undoubtedly another underlying factor.

Mike Haslett thought the Pistols' sound "awful" owing to the PA being extremely distorted. "McLaren and some other guy from their entourage were at the mixing board, and as a result the musical performance was pathetic. At that time, I was a huge Sex Pistols fan and so was left very disappointed. Vicious' bass playing was alternately lame, atrocious, and non-existent. This left it up to Jones and Cook to carry the music, sounding like a two-man version of the Ramones. Rotten was hoarse, distorted, and whining. Yes, I'm aware that some people might feel that a criticism of the musical qualities of a Sex Pistols live performance in 1978 is irrelevant and missing the point. However, let me say that I was a great fan of the album."

With little sign of the beer barrage letting up, the Pistols ploughed straight into "I Wanna Be Me." As the song came to a close, Rotten—having discarded his jacket to reveal a salacious salmon-pink "Fuck Your Mother" herringbone bondage top with a motif that left little to the imagination—sarcastically enquired if there were "anymore free gifts."

Vicious had once again discarded his leather jacket. Though faded, the crudely daubed "Gimme A Fix" was still evident for all to see, however. He was in boisterous mood owing to his LA fan club having taken up position directly in front of him. He was clearly reveling in the attention. So much so, that Rotten was forced to ask his "indulgence" so they might continue with the set. Vicious' concentration proved short-lived, however, and he was soon nursing a bloodied nose.

Blood-bonding: LA punkette Hellin Killer says she accidentally head-butted Vicious while he was leaning in to speak with her, hence the bloody face (© Roberta Bayley).

John Holmstrom could see the blood oozing from Vicious' nose, but says he was standing too far from the stage to see the cause of his injury. "During the show it was impossible to get close to the stage, it was pure insanity. Anyone who's been to a lot of live shows will know how it gets sometimes; that no matter how hard you try to get to the front, the crowd is too dense to penetrate. Also, like I said, we got there late."

Barry Kooda was watching the Pistols from the wings. "From what I saw, a fan shoved Sid's mic stand towards him, and the microphone either bust his nose or split his lip. He definitely used this to full theatrical advantage. The legend has grown a lot since then. Johnny and Sid were way into being the caricature of punkers with Sid signing an autograph for a fan and snorting, 'How do ya spell "Vicious"?'

"Paul and Steve were great guys and just wanted to play and talk music. Johnny played the audience brilliantly, and Sid bled and spit a lot. I think we played better than them that night, but of course I am sorta biased. Since the local TV stations needed a clip to play on the ten o'clock news, we got lots of air time. And seeing the Pistols on TV absolutely got a lot more people starting bands. Some good, most bad, but they all had something they wanted to say."

Killer has either heard or read all the varying theories as to how Vicious came by his injury. "After pushing my way to the front of the stage right in front of Sid, I placed myself firmly in the edge of the stage hanging on to the corral fence that was in front of the stage. It made for a great place for a short person like me to hang on to. I can't tell you how excited I was. Back then smoking was allowed everywhere. I had a cigarette in my hand and was jumping up onto the stage to share it with Sid. Holding it for him so he could lean over to get a drag every few bars!

"Well, this was great and felt special. There I was sharing my smoke with Sid Vicious, and him smiling down at me. I'm sure you've seen the footage of that show. It was packed, and I was crushed up front there. We were having the time of our lives ... at least, I know I was! As I said, I had been hanging onto that fence rail so I could kinda sit on the front of the stage and reach up to Sid. I got knocked off at some point, so I grabbed the rail to pull myself back up just as Sid leaned over to say something to me. And as fate would have it, I head-butted him square on the nose with the top of my head! Bob [Gruen] got a good record of what happened after that on film, ha-ha. I looked up and blood was pouring down Sid's face, and he, of course, loved that! Couldn't have planned something like that if you tried! After that, Sid leaned over and kissed me on the mouth and we were both covered in his blood. I was in love, ha-ha! I mean, really, how romantic is that? It was sealed that we would be friends ... and lovers! Although at the time, I guess I didn't know any of that. We were just a couple of punk kids having a great time in our lives."

"Sid leaned over as Hellin jumped up," says Berlin. "She bumped his nose and suddenly there was blood everywhere! Next thing I know, we were getting crushed and Sid was yelling for a security guard to get Hellin out of there. She was tiny and kind of fragile whereas I was tough from years of horses and swimming in the ocean so I just held my ground."

Vicious was just as concerned for Trudie Arguelles. "Sid saw that I was getting squished. He stopped playing and insisted the roadies help him pull me up onstage. I got to sit onstage for the rest of the set."

"What happened was that we'd hatched a plan to rush the stage during a particular song," St. John adds. "I forget which song it was now, but when the Pistols began to play the song we started scrambling up onto the stage. The mean roadie started threatening us—me in particular—what he would do if we got onto the stage. Those security guys were complete fucking assholes! My perception of them was mean, no tolerance American idiots! It seemed they hated the whole punk thing! I'm pretty sure we made it onto the stage anyway, and this made Sid happy. In the melee that followed Sid either bashed himself in the nose with his bass, or maybe Hellin hit him. Maybe I hit him? It was definitely one of us because he later said to me, 'Any bird who hits me is a bird I like.' I think 'bird' was the word he used."

After the show there was plenty of speculation as to how Vicious had come by his facial injury. Jim Parrett remembers explanations circulating among his journalistic peers that Vicious had either been punched in the face by one of the "LA nubiles," or had caught his face on a mic stand. "People were buzzing all around me about the blood, but nobody seemed to know what was going on. It was mayhem—except for Malcolm McLaren who looked all too comfortable in his delight. I was about five people back, standing somewhere between Rotten and Jones for most of the show. People were jumping around, pretending they were punks, so there was a rush of activity offstage as well as on. Recently watching the YouTube of the show, I was reminded of a girl in a striped dress climbing on her cowboy boyfriend's shoulders in front of me and me yelling my ass off for her to get out of the way. I thought I was going to be in for a fight!"

After the show St. John ended up getting evicted for helping herself to the tip jars on the bar. "I was totally broke after paying for the food and gas, so I took to stealing the tip jars off of the bar once we got inside the Longhorn. I got thrown out by security. Sid let me back in through the backdoor, but I got thrown out again. At this point I was pretty drunk, because aside from stealing the money I was also stealing beers. I wasn't what you'd call a pretty girly girl punk.

"There was a point when I was out in the parking lot lying in the dirt really, really drunk. A couple of guys from a film crew were trying to interview me, and I think someone had called the cops. The crew had the camera lights on me when the cops came over. Those guys totally saved me from being taken in. They told the cops that I was with them, and that they would look after me. I later discovered they were the crew that made *D.O.A.* I'm in the movie. I'm the one in the leather jacket rolling around in the dirt saying how 'Punks want to care, but we can't and that's why we carry chains in our pockets,' or something like that. The same footage is in *The Filth and the Fury*."

"It was kinda hairy while the Pistols were playing," says Bayley. "I know I've been quoted elsewhere as saying that I was worried for my personal safety. I didn't mean that I was worried for my life! I just meant that I didn't want to be pushed around, manhandled, or have somebody rip the sleeve off my cashmere sweater as some asshole bouncer did the first time I saw the Clash. I've been in the trenches, and seen many a crazed out of control concert—the Beatles three times, and the Stooges, for instance—so I can honestly say I didn't sense any real threat of violence at the Pistols shows—just a fear of drunken assholes or overly enthusiastic security guards. I was a slight young woman of 27, and did not enjoy being shoved around."

Vicious had in fact been caught in the face by his microphone as a result of a full beer can (in a near repeat of what occurred at Randy's Rodeo two nights earlier) sailing through the air and smacking against the stand as he leaned in to speak into his mic. His stumbling back towards his amp with blood gushing from his nose had brought Glenn Allison and the rest of Monk's security team scurrying across. Vicious, however, hurriedly assured Monk that everything was okay before darting towards the mic. "I think you busted my nose open again, ain't that good, eh?" he beamed, playfully smearing the free-flowing blood across his face and chest.

Rotten was not amused; his face set with a rictus grin as he watched the latest episode of the unfolding Sid Vicious soap opera. Jones was also clearly tiring of the "living circus," and as Cook beat out the staccato intro to "Holidays in the Sun," the guitarist summoned Vicious over to his side of the stage to administer an away-from-the-microphone reprimand.

With a chastened Vicious keeping to the script, the remainder of the set was completed without too much interruption. Rotten had earlier berated the crowd for staring instead of dancing, and during the middle eight in "Problems" he playfully showed off his own moves with a bit of reggae skanking.

The set was once again brought to a rambunctious finale with "Anarchy in the U.S.A." Unlike their previous visit to Texas, however, the Pistols returned to the stage for an encore of "No Fun."

After the encore, Rotten, Jones, and Cook headed for the dressing room, but Vicious remained onstage to check on his female friends from LA. Glenn Allison tried easing him away, but Vicious foolishly wriggled free to make another grab for Hellin Killer. This time Allison yanked him away rather more firmly. After being given a stern lecture from Monk, the bassist sheepishly allowed himself to be led off in the direction of the dressing room.

Vicious did end up getting his girl, however. According to St. John, the bassist also saw to it that Killer traveled home in style. "Hellin got herself flown back to LA by the Pistols. Great for Hellin, but she still had our road trip home finances! On the way home I had us stop in El Paso. It was nighttime as I recall, and I went across the border to get Sid a bottle of Mescal. I knew that if the Pistols had have crossed over, the border authorities probably wouldn't have allowed them back Stateside!

"The rest of the trip back to California was uneventful. When we arrived back in LA we sort of splintered off. I drove back up to San Francisco with Jane Wiedlin, who was later in the Go-Go's, and some other friends. Jane was also at the Winterland show. The weekend of the Winterland show a bunch of other people descended on our apartment on Haight and Ashbury—much to Vickie's surprise. It was an electric time."

"Malcolm did buy me a ticket back to LA," says Killer, "but I already knew Malcolm and Rory from prior meetings in LA, and Malcolm wouldn't have left me stranded in Texas. I only stayed behind because Sid asked me to. I took a big risk not knowing what would happen, but at the same time knowing that I wanted to stay with him. We hit it off immediately when we met, and I was of course fairly obsessed with him. It was going to be my first time to actually have sex with a guy. And what better guy could I hope for! So yes I stayed and took my chances. I was really, really shy and inexperienced in that part of my life. And like I said, we got along and I was having so much fun! Sid asked Trudie to stay as well, but she was always more rational than I. She said we had to go back to LA, or who knew what would happen to us. I think maybe she was also seeing KK by then, and Sid wasn't really the guy she was interested in anyhow. That's all just my opinion by the way.

"After the show everyone was getting kicked out but Sid told security we were with him and I recall Trudie and I went backstage and we were hanging out with him drinking and just talking. I remember someone I thought to be Boogie, but who knows now, telling us to keep an eye on Sid. Sid wanted to go with us to go back to the hotel with him, but the answer from security was 'No.' Instead, Malcolm said that I should come on the bus with them to get Sid to comply. To make a long story shorter, Trudie and I got on the bus and we went back to the band's hotel. Trudie and I went with Sid up to his room."

At some point Killer and Arguelles accompanied Vicious to Rotten's room, and Killer can still remember the frosty reception. "John just seemed frustrated with the whole thing—just irritated and angry—whereas Sid was having what seemed like a great time. Maybe that wasn't really true. Anyways, John was being pretty shitty to Sid so Sid asked Trudie and me to go back to his room. When we got there he asked us to stay with him, but Trudie said she was going back to Terry's mom's house because we were heading back to LA the next morning. I just stood there with Sid practically begging that I stay, and that's when I decided to stay no matter the consequences! You see here I was with Sid Vicious, and him asking me to stay. All I could think was, 'This isn't ever going to happen again!' So I told Trudie I was staying, and I did! What happened next was something I had never done before! I totally had the greatest time with the one guy I seemed to have been waiting for my whole life, ha-ha! Yep, we definitely had fun in that room! It was crazy because till then the idea of having sex was kinda scary to me. It just had never really happened ... at least not with a guy! So we, of course, did more than I can remember, and it was exciting and so much fun. I guess if I had known more about sex, or been more experienced, it might not have been the experience it was for me. We got along so well, and I was totally at ease with him.

"Afterwards, I remember we had to ask security if we could go out to get something to eat. At this point it was about 4 am? I was told that I was responsible for getting Sid back in time to get ready for them to leave for Tulsa. It's weird that they even let him go with me, but they did. We went downstairs and got a cab and Sid asked the driver where we could get a breakfast. I also remember the driver having a lapel pin that said, 'Jesus loves me.' Sid took a liking to the pin, and asked the driver if he could have it. The driver was very hesitant looking at the state of us and how we looked so Sid said, 'So you're sayin' Jesus doesn't love me?' So the driver thought about it a bit and gave Sid the pin. Sid was so happy! We went to a small all-night coffee shop and we both ordered steak and eggs (bloody and runny). That night I gave Sid a ring I had. It was a silver cobra, and if you look at photos I always know the before Sid or after Sid because he wore that ring till he died I guess ... he couldn't ever get it off. We sat talking for ages and we got to know each other a bit better. When we returned to the hotel Sid wanted to call Nancy and tell her about meeting me. I was terrified, and it seemed like 'Why?' But Sid called her, and told her how great I was and that she'd like me. We slept a couple hours, and when we woke up there I was in Texas without any idea what I was going to do. That's when Sid called Malcolm, and Malcolm arranged a flight back to LA for me. They dropped me off at the airport and Malcolm gave me some cash for a cab when I landed at LAX. That was the night Sid and I became friends. When I got back to LA I can't really say what my friends thought, except for Pleasant [Gehman] probably thinking it was about time, ha-ha. To be honest, I'm not even sure I said too much about it. I was too busy trying to hitch a ride up to San Francisco."

Jim Parrett cites the encore as being the highlight of the evening. "The show was pretty ramshackle. It was at once terrible and wonderful. But 'No Fun' seemed to fire them up, and it's *the* Sex Pistols moment that lasts with me to this day. Sid didn't sound like he was even plugged in—let alone playing along with the band. Rotten was in command and most eyes were glued on him. Jones was shockingly sloppy, but he pulled it together. He was pissed at Vicious for most of the night, but as the night wore on he seemed to find his groove. When the band started taunting the crowd, the atmosphere got even wilder but hardly dangerous. Punk may have been for real in London, but in Dallas it was still too new to react. People were like 'punk zombies' for much of the show. In reflection, the show was more an event than a music concert. It was history."

The local media didn't appear to share Parrett's assessment of the Longhorn show being history in the making, however. "There wasn't much press to be honest. I did get together with a *Dallas Morning News* photographer who supplied me with some wonderful shots, but my editor—out of cheapness—passed on them except for one 'icon-sized' shot. I remember the *DMN* guy ripping me a new one when he saw the published article, but I was just as pissed as he was. In fact, I'm still puzzled as to why such a momentous event wasn't covered with more of an eye on cultural history being made."

In his *Rolling Stone* feature, Charles M. Young had admitted to his being impressed with Vicious when he'd interviewed the band the previous August. The ensuing six months had, however—to his mind at least—seen the "most charming and spontaneous Sex Pistol" succumb to "Hey-look-at-me-I'm-a-star syndrome."[21]

Young had also been present backstage when Vicious had received another stern dressing down at the hands of Jones for his supposedly forgetting the key to "Pretty Vacant." While speaking with Rotten, the singer had held up his beer in mock toast to "Phase One of our attack on America."[22]

The attack was set to continue in Oklahoma the following evening. As with Gene Pitney, the Sex Pistols were only 24 hours from Tulsa.

Seven

Tulsa

Girl fan punches Vicious on nose
Dallas—Johnny Rotten and Sid Vicious were both punched in the face by girl fans as the Sex Pistols performed today deep in the heart of Texas.
Blood poured from Vicious' face as he was hit on the nose.
Instead of stopping the show the bass player rubbed blood over his face and chest so that he looked like a demented cannibal.
—John Blake, *Evening Standard*, January 12, 1978

Contrary to newspaper reports, Vicious was the only Sex Pistol who spilled blood onstage in Dallas, but Rotten was feeling the worse for wear as the tour progressed. He'd been suffering with flu almost from the moment he'd stepped off the plane at JFK, and the tour bus's air-conditioning was playing havoc with his sinuses. "Since it was the first time I had ever been to America, I didn't realize I was straining myself night after night with a totally dehydrated throat. I was ripping the back of my tonsils out."[1] Despite his discomfort, Rotten felt it would be churlish to bemoan a sore throat when Vicious was suffering the harrowing agonies of heroin withdrawal. Sleep deprivation is one of the major effects of undergoing "cold turkey." More often than not the bassist's discomfort was such that he took to sitting up front with driver Charlie—if only to keep each other company during the lengthy overnight drives.

Bob Gruen would join them on occasion. When Jones pulled into a truck stop for gas en route to Tulsa, the photographer suggested he and Vicious stretch their legs and grab a bite to eat in the diner. Everybody else on board appeared to be sleeping, and though Monk had apparently given strict instructions that no one was to leave the bus without his say-so, Gruen couldn't foresee any problems as the diner was all but deserted at that hour. He and Vicious had no sooner reached the counter, however, when the bleary-eyed Monk came bursting through the door demanding to know what was going on. Having been assured by Gruen that he would keep a watchful eye on Vicious, Monk begrudgingly returned to the bus.

Gruen and Vicious sat minding their own business when a guy whom Gruen described as a "huge cowboy" came in with his family and sat down at an adjoining table. The cowboy had obviously recognized Vicious from either the newspapers or television and insisted he and Gruen join him and his family at their table. Gruen's antennae were twitching, but as the conversation centered round the tour, he relaxed back into his meal. He was taking a bite of his hamburger when the cowboy suddenly put on a show of machismo bravado for his wife and kids. "He said, 'so you're "Vicious" huh? Well, can you do this?' He then stubbed his cigarette out in the palm of his hand."[2] Vicious continued eating his steak and eggs for several moments before nonchalantly slicing the blade of his knife across his extended palm. He then resumed eating while blood seeped from the wound and ran down his wrist and onto the eggs. The cowboy had seen enough. Without waiting for his order, he gathered up his family and hurried them out the door.

Gruen's on-the-road buddy-bonding with Vicious had flourished to the point that he didn't put up much of an argument when the bassist "borrowed" his biker boots on permanent loan. "They were good, heavy American motorcycle boots with a steel toe. I'd bought them off of Johnny Thunders. Sid loved them. I'd fallen asleep on the bus and left my boots sitting on the floor next to me. Sid picked them up and started walking around in them. Joe Stevens told me that Sid held a knife to my throat while I was asleep and said, 'If I killed him, can I keep his boots?'"

"Sid didn't really mean it, I suppose, because he didn't stab me. When I woke up he was wearing my boots. He said, 'Do you mind if I wear them for a bit? You can wear mine if you like.' They were army surplus, and had seen better days. But what choice did I have? When we reached San Francisco the first thing Sid did was buy me an identical pair of engineering boots. I've still got both pairs."[3]

♪ ♪ ♪

Located at 423 North Main Street, Tulsa, Cain's Ballroom is the sole remaining venue from the Sex Pistols' '78 U.S. tour staging live music. Local entrepreneur W. Tate Brady (one of Tulsa's founding fathers) had the two-story structure built in 1924 to house his cars, but sold the lease six years later to Madison W. "Daddy" Cain.

Cain was so keen to establish his Dance Academy that he offered dance lessons at 10 cents so the locals would know their way around the ballroom's newly installed maple, spring-loaded dance floor at evening jamborees. Coincidentally, Bob Wills' Texas Cowboys would make their live debut at Cain's on New Year's Eve 1935. Wills would be invited back so often that Cain's quickly became known as "the home of Bob Wills."[4] Country stalwarts such as Gene Autry and Hank Williams and Western swing musician Tex Williams, would help keep Cain's on the map, but when Daddy Cain refused to keep up with the times by shunning the "devil's music," as rock 'n' roll was known in the Bible Belt, his dancehall fell out of favor and into disrepair.

Cain's would remain closed for several years until a Bob Wills enthusiast took ownership in 1972. Time, however, had moved on and within a few years Cain's was again in financial straits. Indeed, the ballroom might have closed for good had renowned Tulsa-based concert promoter Larry Shaeffer not stepped in. "I'd been fascinated by the musical history of Cain's ever since I was a kid. I'd overheard stories about the 'Cain's Academy' from relatives that had gone there to dance to the music of Bob Wills and the Texas Playboys. Wills was a legend in Tulsa, and very often a topic of conversation, so I guess I must have absorbed all that oral history."[5]

Shaeffer had started out playing steel guitar, but as with many of his peers he'd been inspired to switch to electric guitar on seeing The Beatles' debut on *The Ed Sullivan Show* in February 1964. He and some like-minded friends got together to form The Undertakers. As with everywhere else in America, sock hops and teen dances were popping up all over northeastern Oklahoma, and the five-piece combo were soon pulling in crowds wherever they went.

"It was during that time that I knew I had to be involved in the music business in some form," Schaeffer explained. "When I was discharged from the Army in 1971, I'd previously received my degree in sociology from the University of Tulsa, but found my interests were only really related to live music, recording, and especially the concert industry, of which I knew practically nothing about. I first formed a booking agency, booking local bands in bars, dances, and parties. I started putting enough money together to bring in an occasional national act.

"By 1976 I was doing pretty well and brought Peter Frampton to Tulsa during his *Frampton Comes Alive* period. Cain's came up for sale at about the same time for $60,000, and so I bought it with the proceeds from the Frampton show. It represented a trophy to my success, and soon became a historical and sentimental journey for the next 25 years of my life."

Schaeffer was looking to take every interesting act he could find for Cain's, and a friend of his tipped him the wink about the Sex Pistols. "John Foutz of Honest John's Records had the most popular record store in Tulsa. He was always the first to know the cutting edge of music, and all the new artists. It was early in 1977 that he told me about a brash new band over in London, and I liked what I heard. To my mind, the Sex Pistols were a fresh change from the typical, stale rock bands at that time. They were loud, rude, and played music that was completely unapologetic. When I heard 'God Save the Queen' for the first time a chill ran up my spine. I was most definitely '*in!*' My agent, Jorge Quevedo, was with Premier Talent, the agency that was putting the Sex Pistols' tour together. I also had something of a reputation with Warner Bros. by then. I also knew Noel Monk very well as he'd been through Cain's previously with other acts. Noel was very sharp, and good to work with."

Schaeffer was excited at the prospect of meeting the band whose music had set his spine a tingling, but hadn't expected to find them waiting for him when he arrived for work that wintry Wednesday morning. "On the day of the show I pulled into my office and was surprised to see the Pistols' tour bus was already parked out front. It was about 9:30 a.m., I guess. I unlocked my office, and very soon after there was what seemed like a whole entourage flowing in and out of my office and the ballroom. We'd received a Warner Bros. press kit in advance of the show. There were plenty of stock photos of the band, so I knew who was who. I wasn't surprised to find they weren't the 'two-headed monsters' the U.S. press would have us believe. Sid and Johnny were both polite to me, as were all the others. It was all quite cordial. In fact, I enjoyed all the commotion they brought throughout the day."

Another who was on hand to witness the Pistols' early arrival at Cain's was Richard Galbraith, then a budding photographer looking to make a name for himself. "I took the day off from my job working for an auto supply store. I just wanted to get there early as it's around a two-hour drive from Enid, where I still live today. My friend Bob came with me. I think we left Enid around six a.m., and got to Cain's around eight. I guess the bus pulled in about an hour later. Cain's had three office areas, and we normally waited in the first one with the outside entry door. I heard a knock and opened the door to find the Pistols standing there. Everyone was fairly quiet and just hung out.

"Steve Jones went in the next room to check out Larry's guitars. I guess we were a bit afraid to say anything after hearing some of the stories about cameras getting banged up. I'm not sure why now, but for some reason I wasn't allowed to snap any pictures while we were sitting around. Bob told me later that Sid had been checking out the jacket I was wearing—a crushed velvet-type thing. It had studs on the back in the shape of a cross.... I wish we could have traded jackets now."[6]

It was a four- to five-hour drive from Dallas to Tulsa, and Shaeffer had been in the promotion game long enough to suspect the Pistols' early appearance might be due to something untoward having occurred the previous evening. His suspicions were soon justified. "There was talk of some trouble they'd had the night before in Dallas. Apparently there was some hostility built up between the band and the overly aggressive photographers. There was some pushing and punching going on between Johnny and one of the jerk photographers that ended in a fight. Threats were apparently made against the band and so they decided to leave for Tulsa. That would explain their being at the ballroom so early that morning, waiting for me to let them in."

Rotten had supposedly gotten into an altercation with someone belonging to Tom Forçade's film crew, and an expensive Bolex camera had apparently been damaged in the fracas. McLaren had ordered an immediate evacuation so as to avoid any legal repercussions should Forçade report the breakage.

Noel Monk would subsequently identify the Bolex-bashing culprit as Ted Cohen. On the day of the Cain's show he'd supposedly received a call from Forçade demanding $10,000 in recompense to replace the Bolex. Forçade had then supposedly issued a threat as to what would happen to Cohen should his demand go unheeded. Knowing there was little likelihood of Warners reimbursing Forçade for the camera given that his crew was filming the shows illicitly, Monk called Cohen advising him to skip Tulsa and instead head straight for San Francisco for the tour's curtain-closer.[7]

(Monk's worries about the incident was such that he'd given instruction that the bus drive directly to Cain's Ballroom without first checking in at their hotel.)

Rory Johnston confirms there being a "scuffle" backstage and a camera being broken. "Forçade and his crew were becoming increasingly intrusive. Initially they'd been playing the 'journalist' role to disguise what they were really doing, but we were catching on.

"The scuffle occurred because the band were becoming increasingly pissed off at having Forçade's cameramen in their face the whole time—especially Rotten, who bore the brunt of it. Sid was in his own space by then, so I doubt it affected him as much. And, of course, this was pretty much par for the course for them in the UK. I think that by the time we got to the Longhorn, and definitely by Cain's, I didn't become aware of Forçade's intentions until the tour was underway. He may have attempted to contact Malcolm about his documentary, but Malcolm would probably have refused anyway. Once I had been made aware, I had Forçade and his crew banned from the remainder of the shows but they still tried to get in. I think it was difficult for security to pinpoint who was who, as there was local and other press around too."

"It wouldn't have been too difficult for Kowalski's crew to get inside any of the venues," says Tiberi. "All they had to do was bribe one of the staff operating the doors. And Lech would probably agree that furtively filming the shows made for a better film. I don't know if Forçade made any approach to Malcolm, but Malcolm would have turned him down. Malcolm's number one priority at that time was keeping Warners interested in the *Swindle*, and he couldn't have any usurpers ruining things. Malcolm didn't invite Julien Temple over to document the tour because Julien would have wanted crediting as director, and there was only ever going to be one director: Malcolm. It was only because of the court case with John, and the official receivers being called in that Malcolm handed the film over to Julien. He wanted to remove himself from the film entirely, but he obviously couldn't do that."

Johnston had arranged with Warners to film one of the shows. "Warners were funding the shoot as they'd decided they wanted a document of the tour. We wanted to get the wildest show from the remaining dates, and Dallas was the obvious choice. I arranged for a multi-camera shoot at the Longhorn show. We did line cuts on the spot, and edited that with the remote camera footage after the tour. I don't think the crew we hired had much experience in shooting a rock 'n' roll show. They were probably more likely a sports crew. I remember having to help the director doing the line cut, giving pointers on what to watch for.

"I'm not sure why Warners sat on the footage for so long [*Sex Pistols: Live at the Longhorn* wasn't released on VHS till January 2000], though I think they did license parts of it over the years. I sat in on the first round of editing, but have never seen the final version. As I was only involved with the initial editing stages I can only surmise the opening six songs are missing from the DVD because of the sound quality. It wasn't an ideal situation, and it was sort of thrown together at the last minute."

Don Broughton was part of the Sundance Productions crew that Warners brought in to record the show. He is in complete agreement with Johnston's assessment that the project was rushed, but is adamant that they didn't require any assistance from Johnston or anyone else within the Pistols' camp. "We might not have had any experience in shooting a rock 'n' roll show, but I can assure you Sundance was a highly polished professional outfit with a score of credits under our belt. And we certainly didn't need any outside help!"

Broughton, who'd grown up in Bromley, Kent (now part of Greater London), had started out as a junior reporter with the *NME*, while his blues band Bobby Sherwood and the Foresters had operated on the same early Sixties circuit as the Rolling Stones. They'd also toured Germany, and had hung out with The Beatles in Hamburg during the time John, Paul, and George were in the process of poaching Ringo from Rory Storm and the Hurricanes. Broughton had then branched out into production, primarily working with The Zombies, who scored several transatlantic hits during the mid-to-late-Sixties. On relocating to Dallas in 1976, he'd joined Sundance as a boom operator; his subsequent film credits include *Robocop*, *Wired*, and *Freejack*.

He was also familiar with the Pistols. "Malcolm and I knew each other, and he approached me to produce some demos for the Sex Pistols. I'm not sure of the time frame, but it would have had to have been during the spring of '76 just before I relocated to Dallas. He invited me to come and see the band play somewhere. I went out of curiosity and came away again thinking, 'What a bunch of crap!' I was involved in music, and to my mind the Pistols had no musicality whatsoever! The Damned and the Clash were equally bad, but the Clash got better by staying together.

"It was a strange evening at the Longhorn. We were all thinking why is a band like the Sex Pistols playing here? I mean, the Longhorn was a country bar! Like I said, we didn't need any help because Sundance was a professional outfit—unlike the Pistols, I might add. I had the misfortune of operating the sound, and they were horrible, truly horrible. Worse than the night I saw them in London. I didn't bother reacquainting myself with Malcolm. In fact, I don't even remember seeing him that night. I certainly didn't want to talk to the band. What would have been the point? We had nothing in common. I just did my end of the job, packed up and went home. I have copies of all the films I've been involved in, but I don't have a copy of the Pistols show. I don't want one. I didn't even know it was out there. I'll take your word for it that some of the songs are missing, but it can't have been because of 'poor sound quality'—each song was as awful as the last!

"I got that the Pistols were angry young men making a statement, but there was no music to it; it was all just crash, crash, bang, bang! And that Sid guy was something else! I mean, everyone in music did drugs back in the Sixties, but nothing hard. I had no idea

The Sex Pistols arrived in Tulsa during a snowstorm (© Robert Galbraith).

what Sid was on that night, but I knew it was something pretty heavy. When that beer can or bottle hit him in the face he was so far gone that he didn't feel a damn thing! He kept right on playing. Of course, that's not saying much as he couldn't play the bass to save his life!"

Despite the cordiality, Schaeffer says that as the morning wore on he'd felt his job title gradually transitioning from promoter to babysitter. "Regardless of what we'd read about them in the newspapers, they were just a bunch of young kids, very kinetic at all times. It was a cold day, and snow was falling. But they quickly forgot about the snow—and pretty much everything else—on finding a case of Heineken that had been stashed in my office.

"Throughout the day the activity in and out seemed never-ending. By noon we had moved the bus to the rear of Cain's near the load-in doors. They did not have a lot of gear though—a small drum kit, and a couple of amplifiers—but it was obviously enough for them to do their show. The soundcheck started around three or four p.m. as I remember. It actually was not too loud at all. When they had finished everybody eventually migrated to the single narrow dressing room behind the stage. And yes, at some point in the afternoon Sid did punch a fist-sized hole in the wall that created an accidental view into the women's restroom. If I'd have witnessed the offense, I would have punched him! By then, I had come to realize that Cain's had a sacred aura. That portion of the wall has since been framed and hangs in the front office of the Ballroom." (Vicious was reportedly trying out the knuckle-dusters Lamar St. John mentions belonging to one of Monk's security team.)

Shaeffer had originally set the ticket price at $2.50, but on the day of the show upped the price to $3.50. This wasn't to bring the ticket price in line with the previous shows to date, however, but rather in response to a plea from McLaren. "I didn't know anything about the ticket price being set at other shows, I decided on a $2.50 ticket simply to entice people through the door. The reason we upped it to $3.50 was due to Malcolm calling en route to Tulsa bemoaning that they were 'burning up their money on the road and needed more money.' There was no time to order a fresh batch of tickets by then of course, so I took a magic marker and simply changed the two to a three."

♪ ♪ ♪

Tulsa is famed for the Tulsa Sound, a loose amalgam of country, rockabilly, blues, and jazz. When asked to explain the genre's origins its most renowned originator, the late John "J.J." Cale, once decried it as simply being the sound he'd accidentally hit upon while struggling to master the blues.[8] Using the same analogy, punk rock could be said to be the consequence of similar musical limitations. Larry Schaeffer might have been concerned about getting people through the door, but the Pistols weren't without their champions in Tulsa.

Greg Sewell, who was 25 and working as a machinist in a local factory while also going to school part-time, says he'd "gravitated towards punk" after gaining a musical education from the Velvet Underground and The Stooges. "I first got wind of what was happening in London after reading some blurb in *Rolling Stone* talking about a band of misfits being disrespectful to their queen. My curiosity led to my purchasing 'God Save the Queen' and a couple of other Sex Pistols' singles on import.

"At the time of the Pistols' U.S. tour the Tulsa Sound was dominating the scene. There were a few clubs in town featuring mostly cover bands, while The Magicians Theater was where you could see Clapton, Petty, Harrison, and other rock royalty hanging out. I didn't have anything against those kinda places, but their clientele were very snobby and extremely hostile towards punk rock. I remember the local media being up in arms about the Sex Pistols' visit. My friends and I were all pretty excited about it, however. I couldn't believe a band of their stature would be coming through this fucking piss-ant burg."[9]

Tom Dutton was another who couldn't quite believe the Pistols were coming to Tulsa. "I was excited because this was a very rare chance to see the new British band that was making a lot of people upset in their homeland. Just what this was all about, my friends and I had to find out. Being very die-hard rock 'n' roll fans we just had to explore this new music that was causing such turmoil. We were ready for a new adventure, but didn't know what we were looking for—we found it in the Sex Pistols!

"I was 20 years old and in my fourth semester of college at NEO A&M junior college in Miami, Oklahoma, studying graphic art. I'd bought three albums on a trip to Springfield [Missouri] one weekend the previous November—they were the three records that would define me and my taste in music for the next decade: the Ramones' debut, the Jam's *In the City*, and *Never Mind the Bollocks*. I played *Bollocks* so loud in my dorm room so everyone within earshot would hear it. A couple of my buddies were also into the Pistols and they would come down to my room, and we would listen to it over and over. Man, we *loved* that album. The guy who lived directly above me wasn't quite so enamored with the Sex Pistols, however. In fact, he became so enraged that he'd jump up and down on his floor yelling at me to turn it down. I never did.

"Within a few weeks of buying the album it was announced that the Pistols would be touring America. And lucky for us, we had a date in my hometown, Tulsa. OK! Obviously, we weren't going to pass on an opportunity like this! On the day of the show we decided we would take Route 66 to Tulsa instead of the turnpike, but as we were driving into Tulsa we ran into a heavy snowstorm. This, of course, didn't deter us in our mission. It was dangerous driving on those icy roads, but we kept on going."[10]

Much of Oklahoma lies in what is euphemistically known as Tornado Ally. The region is prone to severe weather—particularly in January, when the temperature barely creeps above freezing. It was just the Pistols' luck that the region was experiencing one of the worst snowstorms in recent memory.

Twenty-three-year-old Vernon Gowdy III was another who refused to be put off by the bad weather. He'd developed a passion for photography some three years earlier while attending the University of Oklahoma, where he was majoring in microbiology. "I'd gotten into photography around 1975, but didn't start shooting concerts until the following year. I was desperate to land a job as a staff photographer for the college newspaper, *The Oklahoma University Daily*. I submitted a couple of photos for publication that I'd taken at Linda Ronstadt and Rod Stewart concerts during the fall of 1977. After applying for the position of staff photographer for the spring semester for '78, I was finally accepted. My first assignment was to photograph the Sex Pistols at Cain's Ballroom, but I also wanted some shots of the band for my portfolio.

"The *OU Daily* wasn't just a small 'fly-by-night' newspaper; it was an award-winning daily with a 15,000 circulation. It had a sports editor, entertainment editor, cartoonist, staff photographers, the works! It was also a very liberal newspaper, with writers like John Liebrand, who knew all the bands like Buzzcocks, the Germs, the Ramones, etc. John was very familiar with all the bands that were being labeled 'punk rock' so to speak. The entertainment editor, Bill Crum, was also very cool, and didn't hesitate to publish stories and photos about the punk scene.

"I was already aware of the Sex Pistols, and had a copy of *Never Mind the Bollocks*. I might have gotten my copy from the local college record store, as John was a big fan of the Pistols. I really liked 'Anarchy in the U.K.' The sound was so different than I what I had been listening to in the past. I played that album many times. I was not familiar with the music scene in Tulsa at that time, but I knew that punk rock was gaining ground on the OU campus."[11]

Gowdy lived in Norman, which was a two-hour drive from Tulsa in perfect weather conditions. Yet despite repeated severe weather warnings in the media, he and four friends piled into his '75 Silver Camaro and set off for Tulsa. "The roads were hazardous, and the weather crews were telling residents to stay home and not drive but I was determined to go to the show and get some great photos. It was typical college student mentality, but I wasn't going to let a little blizzard stop me. It took almost five hours to get from Norman to Tulsa, but we made it. It was my first visit to Cain's Ballroom. Back then Cain's was on the bad part of town close to the highway—the rough area, you might say."

Ellis Widner was working as a freelance writer at the *Tulsa Tribune* in January 1978. "I assigned myself to the Sex Pistols show; that was my job. The *Tribune*'s news side sent a reporter and a photographer to handle other parts of the story, but I focused on the performance. I was 32 at the time. My favorite act was Talking Heads—I saw them play twice at Cain's in the late-Seventies—but I was aware of Pistols, about their rise being a reflection and manifestation of the political, social and economic unrest in England at the time.

"The Sex Pistols were social protest and rage; part real, part poseur. I appreciated the band as a reflection of its time and place. However, I just didn't think they were that relevant to American audiences. A song like 'God Save the Queen,' for example, was—apart from its energy and rage—absolutely meaningless to an American audience. Its ability to arouse action, tap into unrest and make a political statement was lost on most of the kids who came to see them. Americans responded to the band because of their energy, something lacking in much of American rock at the time. No one Stateside was pushing the boundaries.

"Cain's was famed for its stunning variety of musicians it brought to Tulsa. Schaeffer was a brilliant promoter. He bought Cain's before I knew him, but I was quickly impressed by his passion for the building's history, his preservation of the building, and his passion for music. I never thought of Cain's as being on the wrong side of town, though it was. Had it had been on what people considered the right side of town, it probably would have been torn down before Larry bought it."[12]

Twenty-nine-year-old future *Search and Destroy* contributor Annette Weatherman had returned to her native Springfield in October 1977 following a nine-month sojourn in London where she'd immersed herself in all aspects of punk: the music, the culture, and its politics. Upon her return to Springfield, she'd quickly set about turning her friends onto the records, articles, and attitude that she'd brought back with her. She'd also befriended the Pistols while in England, and was hoping to meet up with them again if the chance arose. "I definitely wasn't going to miss the chance to see the Pistols while they were in America, and cajoled four of my friends to accompany me to Tulsa. Behind the wheel of my car was Lou Whitney, bass player for legendary bar band The Morells. Our fellow passengers were Morells guitarist D. Clinton Thompson, Maralie Whitney, formerly of Morells, and Jim Wunderle, a popular front man for several local bands.

"Springfield and Tulsa were similar in country and cowboy culture; rural cities smack dab in the middle of America run by Christians and conservatives and good ol' country boys who all voted straight Republican. For those of us who were more liberal, rock music was a blessed relief from our pious, Bible Belt society. Both cities had zealous local rock scenes, which, while mostly underground, had some small influence against the smothering status quo. In short, rock music was essential to our lives. Prior to punk, the brilliant Seventies era had appeared to be on the wane, there was nothing comparable taking its place. There was no new Hendrix or Cream or Steppenwolf or Deep Purple or any of the early metal that had showed great promise for the future. Today we know there were Iggy and the New York Dolls, but back then, where information moved slowly, the splashes in NYC made hardly a ripple in the vast hinterland between America's seaboards.

"At the time the Pistols played Tulsa, I would say only one in ten of those who were at Cain's had actually heard punk music. The reputation of punk preceded the experience—and what a reputation that was! People were up in arms about punk rock. Violent, disgusting, dangerous—our media conveyed it as the scourge of the earth. Never mind that most of the news was exaggerated, even incorrect. It's a known fact now that the Pistols didn't vomit at airports or beat people up, but that's exactly the image Americans had of them, and most concert-goers were literally physically afraid of the band during that tour. Most of the crowd at Cain's were there out of curiosity, but a significant number were cowboys and rednecks that had come to find out if there was any reason to beat up the Pistols. Had there been, these rubes would have been more than happy to oblige. They took the role of America's 'protectors' seriously. They already hated the Pistols. They came to jeer, make trouble, and yeah, fight if the fightin' was good."[13]

♪ ♪ ♪

The Pistols arrived at Cain's Ballroom with a sense of déjà vu hanging on the freezing night air. During the Anarchy tour, McLaren had been forced to book an eleventh-hour alternate show at a cinema in the sleepy south Wales market town of Caerphilly to replace the original tour date in nearby Cardiff. The local council had tried to stop the show from going ahead. When their petition failed, a local vicar staged a protest in the car park directly facing the cinema. Directly opposite the entrance to Cain's some thirty or so teachers and students from the American Christian College—led by minister Donald B. Sanders—were gathered in front of a flatbed truck upon which a banner was unfurled proclaiming "Life Is 'Rotten' Without God's *Only* Begotten *Jesus!!!*" The "Jesus People," as they were calling themselves, handed out leaflets to those entering Cain's proclaiming the "Johnny Rotten" lurking within each of them needed to be "crucified," while urged them to "turn from their punk ways."

"They had one of their banners up quoting some verse about when the world turns to rottenness or whatever," Lydon gleefully reflected. That thrilled me. 'Ahh, they care. They've noticed, at last.'"[14]

"Protestors are part of rock 'n' roll," says Widner, who these days works as an editor at the *Arkansas Democrat-Gazette*. "People got outraged because of the way Elvis Presley moved his hips, the way Little Richard looked and acted. Johnny Rotten sang 'I am the antichrist,' so of course there was going to be a church-led protest. In retrospect, the religious protesters were more intense than the Sex Pistols' performance that night. Like I said, I was there to focus on the show. I don't recall the minister's name, but I'm sure he was interviewed by our news reporter."

Tom Dutton and his friends arrived at Cain's to find a bizarre dichotomy unfolding. "When we got to the ballroom there was a mob of kids waiting outside the door that seemed to be very excited to see the show. Directly across the street, however, there was a bunch of Christian protesters urging us not to go into the show, and quoting scriptures out of the Bible stating we would all be condemned to hell for going to this concert. They don't call Tulsa the 'Buckle of the Bible Belt' for nothing. We just laughed it off and went inside."

"I thought the Christian protest outside Cain's was rather silly," says Gowdy. "It was the first time I was ever aware of a group protesting a band. It was a quiet protest though, with no violence that I was aware of. I took a photograph of their 'Life is Rotten' banner, which was published in the college paper alongside a photograph of Rotten that I took later in the evening."

Annette Weatherman and her friends had estimated a three hour drive from Springfield to Tulsa. The rapidly deteriorating weather meant an extended journey time, and today she questions the sanity of their setting out in a "near-lethal," zero degree Midwestern mix of snow, hail, and freezing rain. "It was almost beyond conception that anyone could drive in such conditions, but we ate up that frozen stretch of Route 66 like a roadrunner on a bender.

"We were able to park right out front of Cain's, but had to force our way through a swarm of protesters who descended upon us like erstwhile angels out of the swirling snow.

According to Cain's Ballroom owner Larry Schaeffer, the Pistols showed only "mild curiosity" towards the protesters (© Robert Galbraith).

They were Christian evangelist types that had come from far and wide to dissuade us from attending this devilish show, handing out leaflets that swore Satan himself would be in attendance. There were also several news crews, and of course the film crew that was shooting footage for what would become the *D.O.A* movie. We got caught up in this, and three of our group can be seen in the film, with Jim even speaking on camera."

Larry Schaeffer recalls the Pistols showing "only mild curiosity" towards what was going on outside. "I seem to remember Johnny and Sid going out into the doorway to watch the protesters. They weren't out there long as it was freezing outside. There was some positive dialog between some of the protesters and those people waiting for the doors to open. A few snowballs were thrown, but there was nothing physical. It seemed to me as though the protesters weren't really sure what they were protesting against."

John Holmstrom is still baffled by the protest. "No way I would have stood outside to see the Pistols in such cold weather, know what I mean? These were very serious Christians, but it was all very peaceful. They were just Jesus freaks expressing their point of view, not the Ku Klux Klan threatening violence. I don't remember any reaction from the Pistols or anyone involved with the tour about the demonstrations other than bemusement.

"I enjoyed the show because you could stand right in front of the stage and fully enjoy a Sex Pistols concert without interference. Not their best performance, but it was good. If anything, the protesters brought a bit of excitement to the show. I think if anyone told them, 'Hey, you are helping the Sex Pistols here. You are falling into their trap!' maybe they would have up and quit.

"The Cain's audience was the most indifferent bunch I ever saw at any event, anytime, anywhere! I don't think there was a single punk rocker in that crowd. They were without doubt the most boring crowd of the entire tour. They didn't react to the show—negatively or positively! They just sat in their chairs, never even stood up! Many in the crowd left before the show ended. Of course, this was great for the photographers. There was no crowd to compete with, so Roberta and other photographers were able to take photos from up front and at all angles....

"The weirdest thing to me was that the best-looking woman in the audience was the transsexual groupie that Sid took back to the hotel after the show. There wasn't one sexy female in the crowd, which was 98 percent male (like many concerts back then). Those Oklahoma women were so unattractive: No make-

."NO FUTURE FOR YOU!!!"

So says Johnny Rotten and it's not all lies--. Punk Rock exposes the joke of man trying to save himself from the curse:

"The soul that sins will surely die."
So says God and he can't lie

no future for you...
not in music, in social friends, in plans and good deeds, and not in the rebellion that Punk Rock peddles...

BUT

There is a Life and a Future Forever: Jesus came to make a way back to

A FUTURE FOR YOU:

There is a Johnny Rotten inside each of us and he doesn't need to be liberated--
he needs to be crucified..
Our sin nature must die at the cross of Jesus Christ that we can be born again in the resurected Christ

TURN FROM YOUR PUNK WAYS
AND BE BAPTIZED INTO THE DEATH AND LIFE OF
JESUS

The Christian protesters handed out leaflets urging concertgoers entering Cain's to "turn from your punk ways" (© Robert Galbraith).

up, or maxi-dresses, nothing. The transsexual was hands-down the most attractive person there; the only woman wearing make-up and dressed in a sexy outfit. Well, except for Roberta, of course, she always looked amazing. You can see Sid's 'lady friend' in the *D.O.A* movie. Just don't blink!"

Roberta Bayley says she was "amused yet amazed" by the protest. "I don't know where they got the energy to do those things, make their banners, print out flyers, and what have you. It was snowing really bad! I mean, if someone is telling you that if you like this band, you're going to hell, it's like a wonderful endorsement that you're exactly where you should be. I loved the Tulsa show as I took some of my best photos there."

♪ ♪ ♪

The support act at Cain's Ballroom was Bliss, a typical late-Seventies rock act that was given the opening slot simply because they were managed by Shaeffer at the time. "Bliss was the band that I really liked," Schaeffer explained. "Somehow in the back of my head I thought they could make it. For that reason I put them on the show. They were straight ahead rock 'n' roll, absolutely not even close to punk rock. The problem we faced was that there weren't any punk bands in the Oklahoma area. Of course, that all changed after the Sex Pistols' visit."

"We weren't even remotely punk rock," drummer David Blue readily acknowledges. "We all grew up together in a small town called Bartlesville, the 'Home of Phillips 66 Petroleum.' We'd been together with the same personnel since 1970. We moved to LA sometime in '75, and played a number of showcases. Disco was hitting LA big time, and few record

Local act Bliss opened for the Pistols at Cain's. One reviewer would liken the five-piece as "an American, southern style Led Zeppelin." Members included lead guitarist Dana Martin (at left) and drummer David Blue. The others are unidentified (© Robert Galbraith).

companies were interested in hard rock. One showcase newsletter compared us to 'An American, southern style Led Zeppelin,' whatever the hell that means! But it provides a sense of our sound and style. We came back to Oklahoma, and Larry got involved after hearing us play at one of the big rock clubs in Tulsa. Yes, we were a cover band but only because Tulsa club owners frowned on original music. We were always writing and playing originals where and whenever we could, however. And yes, we also played a number of shows at Cain's Ballroom seeing as Larry owned it."[15]

"We were definitely doing exclusively original material by the time of the Sex Pistols' show," Bliss' lead guitarist and vocalist Dana Martin, added. "We'd quit playing bars, and contented ourselves working day jobs and opening for established groups such as REO Speedwagon, Blue Öyster Cult, Rainbow etc. We were essentially a southern rock band in the Kansas/Journey/Boston vein, though different as well.

"As to Larry's motivation for putting us on the show, I remember it somewhat differently. While he did find it convenient as our manager, he had a couple other motives too. One was to give us exposure on a newsworthy show as we sought a record deal. Second, since the Sex Pistols' whole trip was to piss people off and stir stuff up, he thought the contrast between the bands would make the Brits seem more outlandish and controversial. We discussed these things at the time and accepted the gig. It came as quite a surprise to end up on the bill, and frankly very humorous. The thought of sharing the stage with the Sex Pistols was a riot, and our friends were massively impressed. It was an honor to participate in such a major happening."[16]

Martin says that given the media explosion surrounding the tour, it was impossible for anyone with even a passing interest in music not to know of the Pistols. Blue, however, counters this. "No, we weren't aware of them at the time. Larry came into rehearsal one day—Cain's was also our rehearsal space—and told us of the Pistols. He was only putting us on the show because of the press corps traveling the tour with the Pistols. He said, 'This isn't your kind of show, but there is a lot media with them. It could be good for us.' We had played so many shows we really didn't have any opinion of the Pistols. It was just another show. But then the hype started coming out—how they had sex on stage with raw meat, cut themselves to bleed on stage, etc. That got our attention! We wondered how it would play out in the Bible Belt, which obviously was the tour plan. Shock Factor!

"It was a strange night to begin with as we arrived to find about 100 people carrying signs and banners gathered in a foot of snow next to the Pistols graffiti-laced bus, yelling 'Jesus Saves' and 'the Sex Pistols worship Satan' and some other shit. Numerous camera crews from around the country were filming the protests and asking people for their opinions on the Pistols."

"At the time, I was both surprised and somewhat irritated by the religious outcry," says Martin. "In retrospect, however, it makes sense. This was the Bible Belt after all, and those people felt genuinely concerned for the attendees and the band. We just tried to stay out of their way. Among my strongest memories of that night was the entrance the Pistols made into the ballroom. We had just finished our soundcheck and were sitting on the bench at the back of the room waiting for them to arrive. They blew in the door, strode past us, very much in 'badass Brit' mode, glaring at us and slowly swaggering by and showering us with stink-eye. We surreptitiously glanced at each other and tried not to smile."

Schaeffer's strategy in booking Bliss to open for the Pistols might have brought the band to the attention of the media, but they were nonetheless engaging on something of a fool's errand. "We didn't get punk rock, and the crowd didn't really enjoy us at all," Blue reflected. "After our first song someone shouted out, 'This isn't punk!' We always played the 'William Tell Overture' just before our closing song. That nearly created a riot, and was the first time we'd witnessed pogoing and slam dancing. Slam dancing to the 'William Tell'? Go figure! But for three minutes we had won over the quasi-punk crowd. For some reason, the Pistols' road manager wouldn't let us stack our Marshall cabinets, and there couldn't be any colored lighting on stage. So we played under glaring white light ... as did the Pistols."

Martin, however, says Bliss' performance was well received. "We had a pretty solid local fan base that didn't want to miss the show. There were some cries for 'Sex Pistols!' but altogether it was a fun set and the crowd was charged up for the main event. After our set, I noticed Sid standing by himself next to the stage and decided to talk to him. I was kinda expecting him to do something outrageous like pull out a knife or something, but he was quite congenial. Incongruously, he struck me as kind of a vulnerable, messed up kid trying to be big and bad. The actual conversation had a sort of 'How about all that snow outside' character, nothing deep. He didn't seem to be a bad guy."

Larry Schaeffer caught Vicious strolling about the ballroom in the company of a blonde. He says he didn't get close enough to verify the blonde's sex, and would subsequently assume that it had been Nancy.

Blue would jump to a similar conclusion. "Nancy was standing next to Sid when he gave an interview to a female reporter from one of the networks. I was standing a couple of feet away from them. The reporter asked Sid, 'So Mr. Vicious, how are you enjoying your trip to the U.S.?' Both he and Nancy were barely able to stand by this point. Sid murmured something, put a cigarette butt out on his bare chest, then proceeded to tell the reporter of a particular sexual encounter he'd had, which shocked the hell out of the reporter."

Blue had recognized the media circus surrounding the Pistols for what it was, and therefore wasn't shocked to find they didn't engage in meat sex or self-mutilation. "It was just hype, man! The Sex Pistols were just a guitarist and drummer who could actually play their instruments, a screaming John, and a muffled bass. The 'punks' in attendance were only weekend punks. There were as many cowboys in the crowd as punks, which is why half the crowd left within the first ten minutes of the Pistols' set. John was screaming at the 'halfwit cowboys' as they left. Sid was doing some crazy moves during one song and accidentally caught a security guard on the side of the head with his bass neck. He was very quick to apologize between songs, when the guard could hear him.

"My take on the Pistols is that they tore down some walls of the glam, big arena shows. They took music back to its rawest form, put their own brand of shock to it and became part of music history. So many bands that became successful in the Eighties can thank the Pistols for what they did. They were four guys who were generally nice, caught up in the time, and liked to drink a lot of beer."

Martin was forced to set off for home while the Pistols were still onstage for fear of being stranded at Cain's by the snowstorm. "I didn't see the whole set, but I saw enough to realize the Pistols weren't as outrageous as I had expected ... a sentiment I heard from several folks. Before I split, I did hear a few cries for us to go back on, which kind of cracked me up. Punk was not entirely uncommon in Tulsa, but the city didn't quite know what to do with the Pistols. I wouldn't say that the show really had a great deal of effect in Tulsa, although I believe it lent the city some cachet as a happening venue. And for us it afforded some pretty cool street cred."

Greg Sewell had seen Bliss playing various clubs in the Tulsa area. He readily acknowledges they were "good enough at what they did," but also couldn't wait for them to get off the stage. "It was all about the Sex Pistols that night. The ballroom, as I remember, was very full by the time the Pistols came out. But it was an older country crowd—curiosity seekers that had come along just because they'd read about the Pistols in the papers or seen them on TV. They had roped off the front of the stage area for the media, but that didn't last long. When the Pistols began playing their opening song I glanced over toward the side tables to check the reactions of the curiosity seekers. Most of them abruptly got up en masse and headed for the door in a hurry. But I remember sensing the tension amongst the people that stayed to watch the show. It was as though they did not know what to expect or what could possibly happen."

Vernon Gowdy had taken up a position to the left of the stage. "I was surrounded by the bigwig photographers from *Rolling Stone*, *Creem*, *Circus*, *Hit Parader* and *Billboard* Magazine. It was cool to be in such prestigious company, but it also prevented me from getting real close to the stage. I also remember seeing Annie Leibovitz at some point. One of the press members, I believe, was shooting with a larger video camera. The audience was rather rowdy, and I remember a beer bottle or two, maybe a pitcher of beer being thrown at the band but they kept playing. It seemed the Pistols were encouraging the crowd to get rowdy!

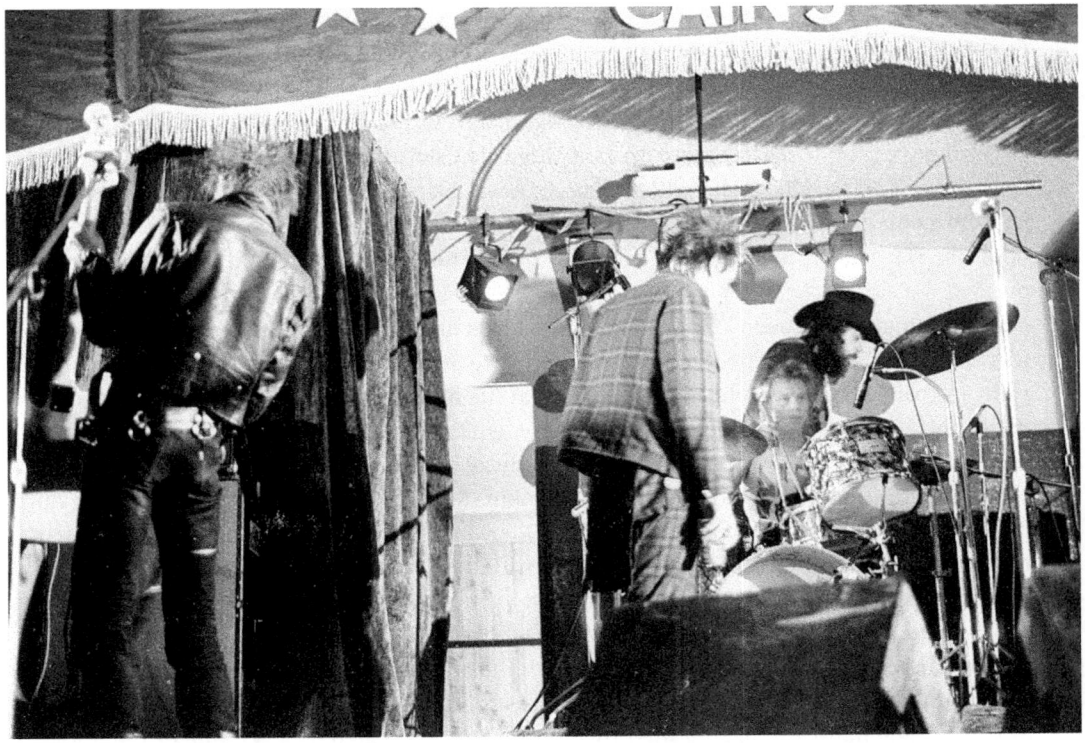

When the Pistols took to the stage at Cain's many of the curiosity seekers "abruptly got up en masse and headed for the door in a hurry" (© Robert Galbraith).

"I was using a 300 mm lens, and mainly concentrated on photographing Rotten. Rotten's energy was just incredible! I was particularly intrigued by his icy stare—the glaze in his eyes and his look was pretty intense and awesome. I snapped about three rolls almost entirely of him alone! The sad part about that evening is that the Pistols didn't play very long—it seemed like it was only 45 minutes at the most. They opened with 'God Save the Queen' and I know they definitely played 'Anarchy in the UK' as it was my favorite song. I don't remember much from the show now, I'm sad to say, but the bottom line is that when I saw the Sex Pistols that night I knew I was seeing a change in music. I knew a new style and expression was emerging…. It was exciting!"

"When the Pistols came onstage Johnny Rotten took one look at the hostile crowd and began verbally insulting them," Annette Weatherman reflected. "The audience returned the favor with a loud roar. Everybody appeared scared to death. No one had ever experienced anything like this. What happened next, however, caught everyone by surprise. We had been fed the bogus notion that the Pistols couldn't play their instruments, and right from the start this was rather obviously untrue. The rhythm was strong, the melodies apparent, and Rotten commandeered the ship like a pirate captain on the prowl. As one song fell into another the crowd became mesmerized. All eyes were on the fearsome foursome, and nobody missed a beat. Rotten kept the between-song jeering to a minimum, and the emphasis clearly was on playing a great set of music.

I've since heard tapes of all the other shows, and there is no question that the best set of all was played in Tulsa. How do I know? Because we taped the show! As tough as security was at Cain's, we were able to sneak in my Nikon camera and a nifty old fashioned analog tape recorder between our legs. We got a great roll of photos and a great recording. Still unreleased to the public, it's obvious to anyone who listens that the rousing set was inspired and with hardly a mistake; a near-perfect rendition of the album. It's top quality, and the performance it captures has more musical integrity than any other live tape I've heard. And it's nonsense to say that Sid couldn't play. Lou was also a recognized sound engineer, and he commented after the show that he couldn't understand why people said that. In his opinion, Sid 'was in there for almost every note,' and the tape we made totally bears this out.

"Sid might have been 'out of it' at other shows on that tour, but he wasn't at Cain's. He was sharp, and in fact quite the show-off, trying to steal the limelight from Rotten. I stood right in front of Sid and photographed him at his best. I made sure all of the Pistols saw me in the audience. Even Johnny gave me the 'wicked eye.'"

Ellis Widner had taken up a position midway between the stage and the exit. "There were kids massed close to the stage, dancing and doing their best to create a mosh pit out of what had been a reserved section for press. The kids moved in; some had the torn shirts, the spiky hair, the razor blades, all the accessories. It was a sight; cool, charming and funny, so very teenager. In hindsight, I suspect most were playing dress-up, but there were likely some genuine fans. The rest of the crowd was in their 20s or 30s, maybe a little older. One guy in particular caught my eye as he looked like a young college teacher: corduroy sport coat with elbow patches, flared jeans. He was standing on top of a table, holding a bottle of beer in one hand and gazing intently at the scene. He may have been one of the undercover cops Schaeffer hired for that night.

"The evening started with about 800 in attendance, they gradually began leaving. The band was pretty lackluster after the first three or so songs. By show's end, the audience had dropped to around 400 or so. Shaeffer said about 30 to 40 percent were people from Tulsa, most of whom didn't know who the Sex Pistols were.

"There were no computers back then of course, so I didn't keep a copy of my review. But I remember writing how the energy during the first few songs was bracing and invigorating, how the Pistols shook both the place and the audience, and that the energy, sloppiness of the playing, and the Pistols' drive, reminded me of a lot of early garage band rockers who could barely play their instruments. They were very loud, and the performance became dull when there was no shift in energy ... or shift in melody. They got sloppy, and at times, lost that early momentum and didn't seem to care. A couple of times, it seemed one or two players were on a different song from the others. It felt like the same two or three songs were being either recycled or repeated so after a while it did get kinda dull for me ... and for others. As I mentioned earlier, nearly half were gone by the end of the show. But it was definitely an event!"

Larry Schaeffer says he was as interested in observing the crowd as he was the Pistols. "I'd heard a rumor that undercover agents with the Oklahoma State Bureau of Investigation were in the crowd. Obviously, there was no way of knowing if that were true as they were operating undercover. However, I had no trouble picking out the undercover boys from Tulsa Vice. They were trying their darnedest not to look like cops, but you could still spot them a mile away."

Uniformed officers from Tulsa police department were also in attendance, but Schaeffer says that to his knowledge no arrests were made that night. "The fear was that the Sex Pistols would cause an insurrection—or would perform live sex acts on stage. That was soon receded much to the disappointment of both the cops and the crowd. In fact, there were no security problems that I can remember. People still say there was a bomb threat that night ... it simply didn't happen! There was no pogoing either, as no one apparently knew how. There were some rants from Johnny aimed at the more vocal non-fans who perhaps stumbled into the ballroom only because the lights were on, with no knowledge of even who was playing. Tickets were only $3.50 that evening, so it was not unusual to have some strays in the crowd."

"When the Pistols came onstage, Johnny Rotten took one look at the hostile crowd and began verbally insulting them," recalled Annette Weatherman (© Robert Galbraith).

Greg Sewell says he would have been happy to pay ten times the ticket price. "The Sex Pistols were blazing hot that night! The fury and fast-paced music was explosive. It was chaos, the way rock 'n' roll ought to be. The band looked great with their unusual style of torn clothing. I will never forget how manic Johnny Rotten was. He was so animated. I can still picture that blank stare, his jumping up and squirming around very aggressively while screaming his lyrics. He was just so captivating. When Sid took off his leather jacket his torso was covered in scratches. I don't know if he was junked up that night. He was coherent, but still didn't know how to play. Every other song Steve would have to go over to tell him what key to play, and then he would proceed to bang away.

"The Pistols seemed to be not quite sure what to expect from the crowd after what had happened in Texas, but there was no fights or real danger after they began their concert. I know now that they played their standard set. It all went by so quickly. Before I knew it they were on the last song. The crowd wanted to

Jones had come down with the flu and wore a scarf around his throat throughout the show at Cain's (© Robert Galbraith).

hear more, of course, and they came back out and played a cover of the Stooges' 'No Fun.'

"Over the years, the show has come to be seen as a historical event in the history of Cain's Ballroom. I often get asked about this show, and what it was like to have been there by the young concert fans of today. I tell them it was so exciting, and doesn't really compare to anything else. After it was over I kept saying to myself, 'Well, what's next? What more can the Sex Pistols do?' I wasn't surprised when they broke up after the last show. They came over and shot their wad on American soil. What was left?"

Annette Weatherman and her friends had hung around after the show in the hope that she might reacquaint herself with the Pistols. "We tried to get backstage, but we could see that it wasn't going to be possible. We could see Sid in the corridor. He was brewing up a storm with a tallish blonde woman who resembled Nancy, but obviously wasn't. One could only assume they would be getting it together after the show.

"We were turning to leave when suddenly, from behind the curtains, a figure broke loose and came bounding towards us. My friends couldn't believe their eyes. It was Paul [Cook]. When he reached me, he threw his arms around me in a big bear hug. 'What are *you* doing here?' he demanded with a huge smile. He'd last seen me on a dark street corner in London. 'I live here!' I told him. We were able to talk a bit more before he said he had to go. Mostly, it was about Steve. I'd noticed how rough he looked onstage, and Paul said it was because he'd come down with the flu—probably caught it from Johnny.

"My friends stood staring at this display like they'd seen an apparition. You mean the incendiary Pistols, the pirates of puke, gave hugs? They knew I'd met the Pistols, of course, but had no idea that I knew them to such an extent. Meanwhile, I was in a heaven that the diehard protesters out in the snow would probably never experience. On the highway home, in the middle of the night, Lou, an expert if there ever was one, pronounced, with all sincerity, 'That was the greatest thing I've seen or heard since Elvis Presley.' What else needs to be said?"

♪ ♪ ♪

January 11 also happened to be John Holmstrom's birthday (his 25th), and upon returning to the Holiday Inn a party was soon in full swing in Bob Gruen's room. Oklahoma was a "dry state," which meant that while alcohol was legal, it was only available in certain areas between certain times in the day "Thankfully, Roberta knew about the Oklahoma liquor laws," says Holmstrom. "She knew that it would be impossible to buy booze anywhere after

Local resident Greg Sewell says the Pistols were "blazing hot" that night at Cain's. "The fury and fast-paced music was explosive. It was chaos, the way rock 'n' roll ought to be" (© Robert Galbraith).

Roberta Bayley says Cain's was her particular favorite of the five shows she covered during the tour. "I loved the Tulsa show as I took some of my best photos there," including this one of Rotten (© Roberta Bayley).

8 p.m. Eight p.m.! We stocked up on a bunch of booze before the show and, not surprisingly, we attracted pretty much everyone to the party."

There was one person Holmstrom wasn't so keen to see at his party, however. "Sid was there with the 'he/she' blonde. The blonde took some marijuana out of her sock, but as soon as she started to roll a joint, Noel Monk freaked out and threw the marijuana into the crapper and flushed the chain. Yes, Oklahoma drug laws were so severe the entire tour party could have spent twenty years in jail if we were caught smoking a joint....

"I saw some very violent and ugly incidents on that tour, and I am surprised there weren't lawsuits. It was similar to the *Gimme Shelter* movie, where the Hell's Angels went to war against the Stones' audience—it really was that bad! Like the Stones, the Sex Pistols did nothing to stop it. I lost some respect for Johnny Rotten, because he lost control over the security situation like Jagger did at Altamont. But while I think Jagger would have curbed the biker violence if he could have, Rotten seemed to enjoy the control in a weird way....

"Anyways, getting back to my birthday celebrations I got drunk early on after switching to Courvoisier brandy once the beer had ran out. Joe Stevens and Bob Gruen warned me that it was powerful stuff! I ended up passing out in my room, so I missed all the hook-up action. I heard Sid got lucky that night. From everything I heard about the blonde—from Gruen and Stevens, mostly—she had recently undergone reassignment surgery. When Sid asked her whether he'd be sucking on her cock or her cunt, she replied, 'Cunt.' Joe said her voice was as deep as his. "Sid's escapades aside, I didn't see any crazy sex stuff going on. I honestly wish there had been some! Especially for me, as I did not get laid at all during the tour. I truly believe there just weren't many opportunities for anyone while the band was touring the Deep South. If the Pistols had played shows in New York or LA there would have been countless tales of sexual debauchery for sure. But Tulsa? There was just no action there whatsoever."

The following morning Holmstrom was nursing a hangover in a local coffee shop when Rotten and Cook wandered in and sat down at a nearby table. Holmstrom went over and showed them the back issue of *Punk* he'd been reading. Cook had seemed genuinely interested in the magazine, whereas Rotten had churlishly dismissed *Punk* as being "disgusting" and "hideous." Despite this, Holmstrom later presented Rotten with six-foot pair of steer horns that he'd purchased in the hotel gift shop as a "little gift from *Punk*."

Whether Rotten would have taken the steer horns back to London and mounted them on his living room wall at Gunter Grove was rendered a moot point while en route to San Francisco. Upon learning how he'd had come by the horns, Monk, fearing Forçade might have secreted some illicit substance inside the horns as payback for his film crew being denied access to the Pistols, snatched up the horns and set about them with a pocket knife. His suspicions were quickly proved groundless, but the once precious horns now lay strewn about the bus in bite-size pieces.

EIGHT

San Francisco

> A girl, blonde, about seventeen, wholesome, stands motionless and white-faced. The band up on stage before her bangs out sloppy rock 'n' roll, while its singer burns dark thoughts into the stunned audience.
> The girl looks deep into the singer's eyes and she is frozen and he is wicked. For a fragment of a second, the singer returns the girl's stare. At that precise moment, the battle within her between disgust and exhilaration is over.
> The next night, over 300 miles away, the same band and the same singer crash out more rock 'n' roll for an equally unprepared audience. The same girl is there, too. She is smiling and jumping, her blonde hair cut butcher style and her discretely torn T-shirt hand-painted with the words GOD SAVE THE SEX PISTOLS. The band and singer remain unchanged but the girl is somehow less wholesome now. She may never be the same again.
> —*Stagelife,* February 1978[1]

The blonde featured in the *Stagelife* article wasn't a total figment of Jim Parrett's fertile imagination. "She was based on a young girl I encountered outside the Longhorn Ballroom waiting to get in. She seemed so sweet and pure. She also seemed to be alone, so I identified with her. I thought we were both strangers in a strange land. Later the night after the show, I saw her again and she had this glow of excitement about her. She looked much more animated." Whether the mystery blonde that had captivated Parrett's imagination took a pair of scissors to her hair and clothes before venturing to Cain's Ballroom or Winterland is, of course, pure conjecture on his part as he didn't attend either show. If nothing else, however, the blonde serves as a metaphorical standard-bearer for those that attended a Sex Pistols show out of curiosity, and came away again with their mindset irrevocably altered.

Parrett's choice of wording for the slogan the blonde has daubed onto her strategically ripped shirt is particularly interesting as "God Save Sex Pistols" was originally intended as the title for the Pistols' debut album. "Never mind the bollocks!" was apparently Steve Jones' preferred putdown when he thought someone was talking crap. The guitarist had in turn picked up the phrase from two hot dog-vending twin brothers who had attended early Pistols shows

♪ ♪ ♪

The cavernous, 5,400-capacity Winterland Ballroom was by far the biggest venue the Pistols had played to date. Bob Regehr and his team—as indeed, many pundits throughout America—viewed this show as being the acid test that would prove whether the Pistols were capable of making the necessary leap from clubs to arenas. Such concerns were salved when all 5,400 tickets sold out within 24 hours of going on sale, but Regehr knew there was a world of difference between pulling a crowd and keeping it entertained. The Pistols might have been the most happening band on the planet, but the number of times they'd played to a crowd in excess of 1,000 could be counted on one hand. Indeed, the total number of people who had seen the band on the previous six U.S. tour dates could have fit inside Winterland with room to spare.

Located on the corner of Post and Steiner in San Francisco's Marina District, the New Dreamland Auditorium, as it was then known, had first opened its doors in June 1928. Over the ensuing decade San Francisco's discerning theatre-going public had flocked there in their droves, and the theatre continued to turn a profit throughout the Great Depression. The venue underwent its more famous name-change sometime during the late Thirties following redevelopment to feature a state-of-the-art ice-rink that could be converted to stage tennis and boxing matches, labor rallies, and the occasional opera.[2]

Tower Records' marquee at the intersection of Columbus and Bay streets heralding the arrival of the band (© Roberta Bayley).

Winterland had staged its first live rock concert in September 1966. Legendary Bay Area promoter Bill Graham (born Wulf Wolodia Grajonca) hired the ballroom to stage a performance by San Francisco's psychedelic pioneers, Jefferson Airplane, as his own venue, the Fillmore Auditorium on nearby Geary Boulevard, held only 1,150. Graham would subsequently open the Fillmore West (located on South Van Ness Avenue), but following its closure in July 1971, he began booking the Winterland on a regular basis.

The year 1978 would see Winterland celebrate its half-centennial, but the year would surprisingly prove to be its last; the curtain coming down for the final time on New Year's Eve following a show by the Grateful Dead. (Winterland was torn down in 1985 and is now the site of a luxury apartment block.)

The Pistols were set to go onstage at midnight, with the performance being broadcast live via a local radio station KSAN-FM. According to John Holmstrom, McLaren had wanted an open stage from 5 p.m. onwards so that "any kid with a guitar could come along and plug in and play." He even went so far as to secure radio time to announce his "come one, come all" intentions. "Malcolm thought by inviting any kid with a guitar to come to the show he'd find a band that might blow the Pistols off the stage. He thought it would be fantastic!"

Graham, however, thought otherwise. Winterland was the cornerstone of his personal Bay Area fiefdom, and McLaren was expected to fall in line like everyone else. The doors would open at 5 and the Pistols would go on at midnight, but McLaren's "come one, come all" open invite was restricted to two Bay Area acts: The Nuns and The Avengers. Between sets the *Sex Pistols Number 1* movie was to be screened. The 25-minute compilation of interviews, live clips and promo videos had first been shown at the Pistols' Screen on the Green cinema show the previous April.

McLaren's entourage, which again included Jones and Cook, had arrived in San Francisco Thursday afternoon. They were booked into the sumptuous Miyako Hotel, located a couple of blocks farther along Post Street. "When we arrived in San Francisco I picked up the rental car and we drove to the hotel," Johnston explained. "The Miyako was regarded as *the* up-market rock 'n' roll hotel of choice at the time. Bob Regehr, Carl Scott, and the rest of the Warners team were already at the hotel. When we got to the Miyako, I had a message from Bob saying that we—i.e., the—wouldn't be allowed to check in. The rooms had been booked under my name by Warners well in advance, but the news from the road had obviously percolated through and the Pistols were no longer welcome. The staff on reception had been warned to look out for the band, but I managed to get Steve and Paul checked in because they could still operate under the radar."

Lydon says he elected to remain on the bus to keep Vicious away from drugs, but had nonetheless arrived in San Francisco expecting to share the luxuries being afforded everyone

McLaren, center, meets with legendary Bay Area promoter Bill Graham, left, at Winterland the day before the Pistols' final U.S. date. The person at right is unidentified (© Roberta Bayley).

else. He was therefore none-too-pleased on discovering he and Vicious were expected to bunk down with Monk and his crew at the rather less salubrious Cavalier Motel in neighboring San Jose. "You have to understand they stayed in a very nice hotel. Me and Sid were not allowed in that very nice hotel. We had to stay with the road crew in a *motel*. The sheer lack of respect. All from Malcolm … and his not returning a phone call. That was it for me"[3]

Cook, however, says there was no connivance on McLaren's or anyone else's part. "We got to our hotel, and booked in there. I wasn't aware that he [Rotten] didn't get a room there, so ended up staying somewhere else."[4]

Cook's version of events is backed up by Johnston. "Contrary to what John has said, he and Sid did have rooms at the Miyako booked in their names. But getting them inside was going to prove more problematic as they were more recognizable. This has to be the reason why Monk had to book them in with himself and the crew."

The Holiday Inn chain had already let it be known that the Sex Pistols' dollar was no longer acceptable, and Jones and Cook's behavior on the flight from Tulsa had brought a similar pronouncement from American Airlines. "That was an interesting flight," Johnston revealed. "It was just Steve, Paul, Malcolm, and I from the band side that flew. Sophie probably was with us, but she kept to herself and we were all separated. Boogie wasn't traveling with us as Malcolm had wanted him to stay on the bus. I was sitting towards the front with Paul, while Steve and Malcolm were towards the back. I was eating my dinner when a chicken bone came flying over my head and hit the guy sitting in front of me. When a second bone struck home, the guy jumped out of his seat and started yelling. I was explaining that I had nothing to do with the chicken bones, when the captain came bursting out from the cockpit and warned me that any further disruption would have severe consequences for everybody."

Tiberi, however, was on the flight, but says he now wishes that he had been on the tour bus. "By that time the Pistols had split into two camps. Rory was looking after Steve and Paul, while I had John and Sid. John was making things difficult for Malcolm—acting independently. His sole agenda was looking after Sid while he was going through his 'cold-turkeying.' And I'm not surprised Rory doesn't remember me being in the car. You're not likely to remember the guy you met for the first time ten days earlier when you've got Malcolm sitting in the passenger seat."

On the Friday, McLaren met with Bill Graham to sort out any last-minute arrangements for the show, as well as discuss promotional ideas such as having the Pistols pay a visit to Alcatraz and pose for publicity photos. Yet with all 5,400 tickets supposedly selling out the first day of going on sale, why bother with further promotion or publicity? McLaren and Johnston also accompanied Jones and Cook on a sight-seeing jaunt, but, as events would ultimately prove, the three-day gap betwixt shows left him with too much time on his hands when the news came through that the next show at the Helsinki Worker's Hall in Finland on January 18 had fallen through owing to the Finnish authorities having revoked the Pistols' work permits.

The revocation of the permits was due to mounting pressure in the Finnish press, which had begun in earnest the same day the Pistols had arrived in America. The country's leading newspaper, the *Helsingin Sanomat*, had published a hostile editorial in which it fancifully cited the Pistols' most important instrument was "a mechanical distorter which produced a sound like spitting." The paper also indignantly pondered as to why "Finnish children's money was being demanded for the sound of crows cawing."[5]

The latest revocation of permits had been called through from Glitterbest's offices on Shaftsbury Avenue. Roadent, a roadie, had taken a call from a tabloid journalist in search of a quote in relation to the news that the Pistols had now been banned from Finland. He thought it prudent to verify the reporter's tale before alerting McLaren and called the Finnish Embassy. He'd assumed he'd be put through to some minor official, and was therefore amused to discover the voice on the other end of the line was that of the Finnish ambassador.

The *Sun* made no mention of the fabled "mechanical distorter" when reporting the latest ban and instead cited the Pistols' collective criminal misdemeanors as the primary reason for the Finnish government's refusal to issue the band with work permits. According to the tabloid, the ban had come the day after McLaren had announced plans to "take Eastern Europe by storm [as] Communist youngsters [was] a huge, untapped market for pop music."[6]

The Helsinki cancellation provided more headlines, but it also presented an unanticipated five-day lay-off before a show in Stockholm on January 20. The sensible option would have been to return to London, if only to allow the leg-weary Pistols a couple of days' rest before then flying out to the Swedish capital. In *England's Dreaming* Jon Savage says the idea for a jaunt to Rio came about because Tiberi had mentioned his having a friend who worked at the *Daily Express* having a contact number for the fugitive Great Train Robber, Ronnie Biggs.

"It was Malcolm that had the contact number for Biggs," says Tiberi. "I think he had a hotline to the *Daily Express*. It was me that came up with the idea to go to Rio, though. But it was when it looked like we wouldn't be going to America, and not in San Francisco. Malcolm would often come over to my place on Davidge Street. During the recording of the album we'd stay up long into the night listening to rough mixes of the songs as he didn't want to go home to Vivienne for another berating. It can't be stressed enough the influence Vivienne had on Malcolm. It was very significant—especially throughout 1977. She would lecture him on a near-daily basis. And you could always tell when he'd undergone one of her lectures as he'd turn up all red in the face. The Rio thing came about while the visa thing was still up in the air. I got out my atlas and said to Malcolm, 'Well, if we can't go to America, let's go to Brazil.' I'm not sure if it's true about Warners agreeing to cover the cost of flights to any destination, but there was money available. And Virgin would have taken care of things in any case."

Biggs was one of the 15-strong gang that had held up a Royal Mail train at Bridego Bridge in Buckinghamshire during the early hours of August 8, 1963. The train was ferrying an estimated £2,500,000 that was either surplus cash being returned to various banks within the City of London, or old and damaged notes that were to be withdrawn from circulation. Biggs had received a 30-year sentence, and the world would have surely forgotten about him had it not been for his daring escape from Wandsworth Prison in July 1965. Biggs' subsequent flight from justice would take him around the world, firstly to Melbourne, Australia (where he narrowly avoided recapture), and then onto Rio de Janeiro as at the time Britain didn't have an extradition treaty with Brazil.

By January 1978, Biggs had come to be regarded as the public face of the Great Train Robbery. What the average man on the street didn't know, however, was that Biggs had only played a minor role in the so-called "Crime of the Century." Indeed, it was only his happening to know a retired train driver who was thought to be capable of operating an English Electric Class 40 locomotive engine that he was even brought into the gang. Biggs' share of the spoils was £140,000 (£793,000 at its 1978 value), and it's also alleged that he pocketed the £20,000 set aside for the retired driver.[7] The happy-go-lucky "Jack-the-lad" was still at liberty, but his ill-gotten gains had long-since been frittered away. Aside from the occasional odd job, he was reduced to wiling away his days rehashing the robbery for goggle-eyed tourists in return for a glass or two of his favorite tipple.

McLaren hit upon the notion for the Pistols to play a show in Rio and invite Biggs onstage to recite some of the poetry he was supposed to have penned while in exile. "When McLaren has this brainwave: 'Why don't we go to Rio?' Warners had to cover them," Joe Stevens told Jon Savage. "McLaren had a really bad head cold. So I spoke to Biggs in Rio, and we arranged a hotel where the band could play in the lobby."[8]

♪ ♪ ♪

With the exception of Vicious and Cook's encounter with *Today*'s Jack Perkins in Atlanta, the Pistols had avoided the media, but on the eve of the Winterland show Cook and Jones engaged with the locals during a phone-in on "The Outcastes" at KSAN-FM's studios. KSAN had been the sole major-market U.S. commercial radio station to embrace punk. "The Outcastes" was co-hosted by Howie Klein, and Rory Johnston's pal Chris Knab (a.k.a Cosmo Topper), and went out live every Friday night between 2 and 4 a.m.

McLaren out and about in San Francisco (© Roberta Bayley).

Despite the lateness of the hour before going on air, Klein—possibly remembering Jones' part in Bill Grundy's fall from grace—took the two Sex Pistols through a list of dos and don'ts; the primary prerequisite being to keep the language clean. He might as well have saved his breath.

It is obvious from the off that Cook and Jones had been drinking before heading for the station. They were far from intoxicated, however, and might well have provided measured answers if they'd have been asked any straightforward questions. The closest things came to a clear-cut Q&A was when a caller asked if there was any truth in Glen Matlock's claim that he'd quit the Pistols because they were "getting too much like The Monkees."

The tone was set early into the session when a caller asked how the Pistols had come up with their name. Without skipping a beat, Jones quipped that they'd "bought it out of Woolworth's for five pence." When another caller asked how it was possible that the Pistols had sold out Winterland, Cook silenced him in a heartbeat yelling, "Because fools like you bought tickets!"

The tongue-in-cheek humor was lost on the majority of the callers; the badinage inevitably becoming ever bawdier. When a female caller said she'd do anything for two tickets for the Winterland show, Cook playfully gives her his room number at the Miyako. The most amusing moment, however, comes with Roberta Bayley calling in to ask them to have Johnston stop off for "food and liquor" en route back to the Miyako as room service had seemingly been curtailed.

"I can't remember if we stopped off for booze or not," says Johnston, "but there was no way Steve and Paul were staying put in the Miyako for the night. They'd had a great time making new friends at the Mabuhay Gardens the previous evening, and were badgering me to take them again."

Johnston says he can't remember whether he acquiesced to Cook and Jones' demands, but there was one Sex Pistol at the Fab Mab that night. "That's where I met up with Sid," says Killer. "Trudie and I had got a ride up to San Francisco with Chase Holiday, Micol Sinatra, and a couple of others in Chase's station wagon. Chase and Micol were friends from the LA scene. Chase was a keyboard player in several bands, and I knew Micol from hanging out at glam glitter discos before we got into punk. There were a lot of gay and bi kids back then on the scene. It was all very acceptable.

"The thing I remember is we were speeding up the I-5, and we were drinking vodka and Hawaiian punch out of plastic cups. We got stopped for speeding, just like we did in Texas. I'm not sure if whoever was driving got a ticket. What I couldn't believe is that the cops didn't mention the cups of vodka! Not a word. Once again, we just got away with it."

Had she but known, Killer could have met up with Vicious the previous evening as rather than head straight for San Francisco he and Rotten had decided upon a stopover in LA. Monk had booked a set of rooms at a Holiday Inn in Woodland Hills, and following a quick change of clothes and brush-up—which included Vicious being forcibly manhandled into the bathtub by a despairing Glenn Allison—everyone headed out for a VIP trawl of the bars along Sunset Strip. Rotten even took in a live show.

"At the time we were being managed by Joseph Fleury and John Hewlett, who was in John's Children with Marc Bolan," Mumps' keyboardist Kristian Hoffman explained. "They had seen us play Club 82, the lesbian bar in NYC that had opened its doors to 'punk rock' during the late reign of the Dolls and the early days of CBGBs. When John and Joseph saw us there, they decided they wanted to manage us. Since they already managed Sparks, we were soon seduced. It was their idea to get us out to California before any other perceived 'New York band' got there. And any other CBGBs-era New York band who claims that distinction is lying. Joseph and John got us to open for Van Halen at their record contract party at the Whisky. I'm fairly certain it was the first time we ever played there mid–1977. Van Halen had signed with Warners, who of course signed the Sex Pistols later that year.

"So, to the night of Johnny Rotten and the Whisky. We could have also been playing with Van Halen that night? I'm old now, and so my memory isn't what it once was. We had a somewhat interesting long distance relationship with the Sex Pistols. Malcolm McLaren famously came backstage after a Mumps show at CBGBs. He was wearing one of his trademark drippy, loose-knitted day-glo Vivienne Westwood sweaters. He told us, 'Other than Richard Hell, you are the only interesting musical act for the Sex Pistols!' We had no idea who the Sex Pistols were at the time, of course. That didn't lead to anything for us, but it led to a lot of ripped clothing for the Sex Pistols, who before then I later heard, had been doing some unremarkable rockabilly haberdashery slumming.

"Then, of course, our singer, Lance [Loud], lived one floor up from Nancy Spungen's apartment on 9th Avenue; they would regularly help each other out by hiding their drug stashes in each other's refrigerators. When Sid and Nancy were in New York after the Sex Pistols had split, he once bumbled up onto stage during a Mumps performance at Max's [Max's Kansas City] and insisted we do 'Stepping Stone,' which the band valiantly attempted while Nancy squealed, did some ill advised retard-adjacent calisthenics, and burbled indecipherably from the side of the stage.

"But the Whisky instance was before all that. We were all apprehensive of the 'neu British Invasion.' As Patti Smith memorably intoned: 'We started it—let's take it over.' Who were these upstart, Limey interlopers, pretending they invented the very thing we had arduously worked to incite, with an entire community of similarly disenfranchised wannabes, every since the first New York Dolls sighting? But none could deny the power of the Sex Pistols' first fabulous recordings—even if they were overseen by old school, high end producers!

"So when we heard that Johnny Rotten had not only invested the time to inhabit one of the Whisky's wonderfully Sixties curved red-leather banquettes, and was likely imbibing one of their famous Long Island Ice Teas which were served in giant wax paper Dixie milk shake cups ... we were thrilled and a little flummoxed. There was already a 'royalty' caste system in punk, and Johnny Rotten was the Queen!

"After our set we were nervously shepherded over to his table to meet the 'great man.' He was very civil, which again, was odd! He didn't say anything mean to us, and I shook his hand. I've since heard that Sid was also in town that night, but he obviously found something better to do with his time. Later Joseph said to us, 'Well, here's what Johnny said. I think it's a compliment. He said, 'Look, they're a good band. Okay? But I wouldn't buy their record.' It's most likely the best review we ever got."[9]

Theresa Kereakes' blog site (punkturns30.blogspot.com/2008/05/punk-rock-parking-lot-socials.html) features a neon-tinged photo purported to be Rotten and McLaren walking past the Whisky on the night of the Mumps' show. According to Kereakes, it was Belinda Carlisle who had identified the two as the future Go-Go had been outside the Whisky awaiting the Mumps to take the stage. Rotten is instantly identifiable, but whoever it is with him it most certainly isn't McLaren. "Yeah, my friend Theresa, who was the in-house photographer for the LA-based punk fanzine *Lobotomy*, sent me the photo a few months ago," says Rory Johnston. "It's impossible to say who it might be, but I can categorically state that it isn't Malcolm. Aside from the fact that he was in San Francisco at the time, the guy in the photo is wearing bell-bottom trousers! Malcolm had a mini-clothing empire and wouldn't have been seen dead in bell-bottoms. And the other factor ruling against it being Malcolm is that by that stage of the tour Malcolm and John weren't speaking to each other, so there was no chance of their going out for a stroll together."

When Killer and her friends arrived in San Francisco they headed straight over to the Mabuhay Gardens to meet up with Lamar St. John. "The Bags were playing that night. I recall that some of the band was doing a radio interview at KSAN. I was happy to see Sid. And he was happy to see me! The girls had slipped over the border while they were in Texas and gotten Sid a bottle of mezcal, and that's where they presented it to him. I think Sid actually got up on stage for a bit, and then he and I went backstage for a rest. That's where Ruby Ray took the classic photo of me and Sid. Sid's lying on the floor with a cigarette and holding my hand. It's funny how everyone thinks that photo's from when he OD'd at Lamar's!

Jones poses outside the WEA record store in San Francisco. In the lead-up to the tour, Warner Bros.' national director for special projects, Ted Cohen, sent out letters to the heads of the WEA record stores in each of the seven cities the Pistols were set to visit on the tour. In the letter, Cohen stated Warners was in the process of attempting to "firmly establish Punk/New wave music as a viable and saleable commodity" in the United States and it was therefore imperative that each appearance was "supported to the fullest extent possible" (© Roberta Bayley).

"After the [Bags] show we went to a party somewhere and ran around town for a bit as Sid was constantly trying to find dope. But Trudie and I had taken it upon ourselves to try and convince Sid that he shouldn't do dope. And also to protect him from everyone that wanted to get it for him.

"The next day Trudie and I went to Lamar's place in Haight-Ashbury to get ready for the show. When we got to Winterland there was already a huge line of people waiting to get in. We just walked past the line and went up to the window and said we were on the guest list. We were the only ones on the guest list. Sid made a promise to put his 'friends from Dallas' on the list, and damn it, he kept his word."

Killer doesn't know anything about the hotel's attitude towards the Pistols, but says she spent the night there with Vicious. "It was definitely the Miyako, and it was definitely the night before the show. Sid OD'd at Lamar's on the Saturday night so it couldn't have then. I didn't see Sid again until I went to London, so how else that could that have happened?"

♪ ♪ ♪

Sylvie Simmons has come to be regarded as one of the principal players in music journalism, but by her own definition, she was a "rookie rock journalist" at the time of the Pistols' U.S. tour. Born and raised in north London, Simmons had decamped to LA the previous August. Among other assignments, she was serving as *Sounds*' U.S. correspondent, and come the day of the Pistols' Winterland finale there was only one place to be. "Most of the flights from Los Angeles to San Francisco are fully booked. Undaunted by the Pistols choosing northern California over the South for their first U.S. tour, punks, poseurs and the press were making the 400-mile trip to check out the action and check out each other—the principle being, if the Sex Pistols won't come to LA, then LA must come to the Sex Pistols."[10]

Legs McNeil claims he was hanging out with The Ramones and Alice Cooper at the Tropicana in LA when the Sex Pistols had landed in Atlanta. And that he'd begrudgingly driven up to San Francisco after John Holmstrom had reminded him that as *Punk* magazine's "resident punk" it was his duty to be at Winterland for the final show of the tour.[11] Holmstrom, however, disputes his erstwhile business partner's claim. "The Sex Pistols ruled, and I am so glad we [*Punk* magazine] were the first U.S. magazine to introduce them to America. I always had great respect for the Pistols. And Roberta and I both feel that going on that tour—thanks to Tom Forçade, the world's most misunderstood genius—was the experience of a lifetime."

(In November 1978, the "world's most misunderstood genius" put a gun to his head at his Greenwich Village apartment. He was 33.)

♪ ♪ ♪

On the Saturday afternoon Rotten and Vicious headed over to KSAN's offices, where they were interviewed by another of the station's resident DJs, Bonnie Simmons. (Simmons would be at Winterland as part KSAN's broadcast team.) KSAN's chiefs were understandably on tenterhooks given Jones and Cook's laddish antics of the previous evening. Despite Rotten and Vicious' reputations preceding them wherever they went, however, there was little likelihood of their giving a repeat performance. Vicious would prove the more playful of the two by occasionally dropping into mock-Jamaican patois to confuse their host. Midway through the interview, Rotten confessed that he was only there as the station had offered the four Sex Pistols brand-new motorcycle jackets as a bribe in return for the interview/phone-in. This proves a surprising revelation given the biker jacket had become the quintessential centerpiece of the "clichéd punk uniform" he supposedly despised.

Simmons' line of questioning would prove equally hackneyed. Rotten and Vicious must have been sick to death of talking about the A&M sacking, and the reasoning behind the decision to omit LA and New York from the tour itinerary, but politely provided formulaic responses. Simmons pondered whether the Pistols having a song called "New York" had played any part in the decision, and asked Rotten to explain the lyric. "It's about imposters from New York—cheap arseholes who call themselves poets and take themselves seriously," he retorted. "And all they're doing is destroying music in a ridiculous way … at least we're destroying it practically."

Vicious then sells Simmons a line saying the band had written a new song against the apartheid in South Africa, before telling her about "Sod in Heaven." "We've got one about God. And it's an attack, a real attack. And it will be played to the Death March."

When reflecting on the Winterland show in *The Filth and the Fury*, Lydon bemoans the Pistols being denied the opportunity of conducting a soundcheck and of McLaren's willfully setting things up to make the band "look ridiculous." While it's true that the soundchecks in Atlanta and the other venues were slipshod affairs, the soundcheck at Winterland lasted some 20 minutes with run-throughs of "Belsen Was a Gas," "Pretty Vacant," "Problems," and "No Feelings."

KSAN's outside broadcast team were busy setting up additional audience and instrument microphones and running cables from the remote truck when the Pistols arrived for the soundcheck. "Their bus pulled in not long after our recording truck arrived," says Jim Draper, one of the assistant engineers that day. "It wasn't considered 'kosher' to bring a camera as a crew member, [but] I was a huge fan of the [album] and very excited about the band coming to town. As I grabbed my camera Sid came out of the bus. He walked right up to me with this big grin on his face, and a cigarette hanging out of his mouth. I tried to focus, but he got too close and stuck the cigarette right into my lens. There was no malice, he was just being Sid."[12]

KSAN had broadcast dozens of live shows, and while it was customary to record the soundchecks as it allowed the engineers to test the reel-to-reel recorders, Draper's forethought in bringing a camera saw him inadvertently capture the penultimate act in the Pistols' endgame.

During a break in "Belsen," Rotten grumbles about the monitors, while Vicious tells Tiberi to turn up the bass on the mixing desk. Rotten was obviously too preoccupied with his own grumblings to have heeded Vicious' request, but they're barely into "Pretty Vacant" when he demands that Tiberi restore the bass to its original setting as he can no longer hear himself. He also vents his spleen at the others for playing "Problems" so fast to render it "a fucking joke!"

Rotten's mood doesn't improve when Jones suddenly bursts into the opening bars of what sounds like Sham 69's "Borstal Breakout," but he stays long enough for a half-hearted run through of "No Feelings." What is particularly interesting about the soundcheck is how Jones remains silent throughout; a shadow of the prankster behind the phone-in frolics of the previous evening. It's as though Rotten and Vicious have killed the mood with their mere presence.

"The atmosphere was heavy once John and Sid arrived," Tiberi acknowledged. "It could have been because John wasn't happy about the hotel situation. I didn't find out about him and Sid having to be booked in with Monk's crew until later that day when I went back to the Miyako with Steve and Paul and found Malcolm with Bob Regehr. But if you listen to that recording of the soundcheck John is still being very professional. There was a lot at stake, because Winterland was the Pistols' biggest show to date. He might have had issues with Malcolm by that point, but he wanted to end the tour on a high."

Another telling instance where Vicious was "just being Sid" came when the bassist went outside to speak with some teenage kids who were already standing in line. One of these was 17-year-old aspiring drummer Jane Weems, who was set to make a name for herself on the Bay Area punk scene with her band, The Maggots. Prior to being introduced to the Pistols through a friend in high school, Weems had lived and breathed The Beatles, going so far as to cover the front of the family home on Precita Avenue with a huge mural in homage of the Fab Four. (The "Beatles House" as it soon came to be known, would become something of a San Francisco landmark and tourist attraction.)

"I still loved the Beatles, but as soon as I heard the Sex Pistols' music I wanted to know everything about them," Weems explains. "I began to see things on TV about the Pistols, including footage on our local news about their infamous interruption of the queen's jubilee on their punk rock barge in the river. It was fascinating and exciting for me and my ten-year-old foster brother, Michael. We began designing our own Sex Pistols T-shirts using acrylic paints. We didn't dare wear them to school lest we got the crud beat out of us for being 'weirdos,' but at home we were punks. I'd already bought the album, and when we heard the Pistols were coming to the States on tour, we were probably one of the first in line at our local record store when the tickets for Winterland went on sale.

"Dad was an old country and western musician who was very open to the idea about punk, while my mom just thought it was funny. Dad's reaction when he first heard 'God Save the Queen' was, 'Well, they got a good beat going, but the singer needs some lessons.' As the day of the show got nearer, however, my parents became extremely worried because of the news stories about the chaos surrounding the tour. Dad offered to buy our tickets from us for $20 each, but of course we said 'no.' They reluctantly let us go, but warned us to be careful and told us to come directly home if things got out of hand. We got ready in my room, putting on our homemade Pistols shirts, greasing up our hair, and putting safety pins on our clothes.

"There were only two other girls waiting in line when we got to Winterland, and one of them, Betty Fremont (a.k.a Devorah Ostrov), is still one of my best friends. People in cars passing by were pointing at us and laughing. Some even stopped to take pictures of us, but nothing could shake our excitement—especially when one of the other kids screamed out, and we looked up and saw Sid ambling towards us. He'd come outside to have a look around, and was surprised to see people already waiting in line like nine hours early. He had this huge smile on his face. 'So, you guys are gonna be first in line, eh?' Betty and her friend had brought along the *Bollocks* album sleeve in the hope of getting it signed by the Pistols. Sid gouged the pen into cover, as though trying to scratch the record inside, with a big 'SID.'[13]

"I knew it was a geeky thing to do but I liked meeting bands and it gave me something to say," says Fremont. "I'd brought the cover to Winterland—just in case. I only had a ballpoint pen with me; I hadn't discovered Sharpies yet. So, I asked Sid for his autograph. He gouged his name [with some difficulty, it seemed] into the cover with the pen. He was probably trying to wreck the vinyl, but I wasn't that stupid—the record itself was safe at home. Afterwards we thought it was funny that he only wrote his first name, and we wondered if maybe he couldn't spell 'Vicious.' Then Sid took a liking to my sunglasses. He put them on and walked off. I tried to get them back, but he was quite tall! And he was Sid Vicious ... so, I let him keep them. I also remember he reeked! But mostly I thought he was cute!

"My friend Collette and I got to Winterland really early—we were first in line. We lived out in Fremont, which is how I got my nickname. Jane arrived around 11 a.m. with her little brother thinking they'd be first, but we were already there. I'd been to the Mabuhay quite a few times by then. In fact, Collette was wearing a yellow plastic Devo boiler suit which she'd stolen off the stage when they played there. Neither of us looked like punks, though. We both had long hair, and I was probably wearing flared jeans! I absolutely loved the Nuns from seeing them at the Mabuhay and was just as excited about seeing them on a big stage as I was the Sex Pistols."[14]

"Michael and I didn't want Sid's autograph; we just wanted to talk to him," Weems continues. "Sid was really stoked that my little brother was there. When Michael said we'd turned down $20 each for our tickets, he said, 'You can buy a lot of sweets for $20, but I'm really glad you're here.' As we were talking, a guy came up wearing these wraparound sunglasses. He obviously didn't know anything about the Sex Pistols, as he didn't even recognize Sid. He asked us if we had a spare ticket for sale. Sid turned and looked at him, took the guy's glasses off and said mockingly, 'Hey man, you got a spare ticket for sale? No, I don't ... so Fuck Off!' Then he threw the glasses out into the street, where they were promptly run over by a passing car, which made us all laugh. He then said, 'Well, I'll see you all later inside.' As he turned to go, he reached down and wooled Michael's hair and said, 'You're so fucking cool.'

"After hours of waiting the crowd was getting bigger and bigger, and they were pushing at the doors. A security guard came out to try to quell everyone. He pointed at my little brother and said, 'Hey, how old is this kid?' When I said ten, he said, 'He can't come in here, it's for grown-ups only.' When he saw the crushed look on Michael's face he said, 'Nah, I'm just fucking with you, man.'"

KSAN's outside broadcast team wasn't the only camera crew in operation that night as Bill Graham employed his own in-house crew. One of these was 27-year-old self-confessed adrenaline junkie, Susan Campbell. "Through friends I got a job working part-time receptionist at Winterland for BGP. There was an all-female video crew—a director and two camera operators—that shot all the concerts for Bill, and projected the images above the stage on a huge screen, and in the bar on an old Madman Muntz projector TV. When one of the ops left to go live with Jackson Browne in LA, I was asked if I wanted to take her job. I mentioned that I was a television major at college [Sonora State] so they were sold."[15]

Campbell never did get to finish college, however. While attending the Rolling Stones' show at the Olympiahalle in Innsbruck, Austria, on September 23, 1973 (the '73 European tour to promote the recently released *Goats Head Soup*), she was hired by the production crew to decorate the Stones' dressing rooms, as well as paint the weather balloons Jagger would toss out into the audience each night. This in turn led to her relocating to London and working as Keith Richards' live-in assistant. It was nice to see how rock royalty lived, but after a near-death incident when she was attacked by a burglar she packed her bags and returned to San Francisco.

"My first encounter with the Sex Pistols came on the afternoon of the show during the load-in. I went onstage to run a cable to the mix for video. Someone was blocking my path. I looked up and saw Sid Vicious at the top of the ramp. He very menacingly said, 'Who are you?' I managed to stammer, 'I, I'm, I'm Susan.' Sid put out his hand and said, 'Hi Susan!' He wasn't wearing a shirt, and I remember being struck by all the little razor cuts over his torso.

"My abiding memory of Johnny is equally vivid. He had just taken a swig of beer, and as I was zooming in on an extreme close-up, he blew the beer out of his nose back at the crowd … ewww.

"KSAN were broadcasting the show. There's a misconception that KSAN were also filming the performance, but it was audio only. They may have taken a video feed from us, but then the sync would have been a serious issue if we'd have tried marrying our video to their audio. There was certainly no need for us to take an audio feed of their commentary, as we ran our audio feed from the FOH [front of house] mix position. It was such a cheaply thrown together shoot that it would have surprised me if someone had tried to do that. It still amazes me that the video is as good as it is, only two cameras, no editing, or post-production. We were good at what we did, but it's only because of Todd [Junkin]'s generosity that we succeeded in capturing that footage somewhat cleanly

"Cindy Sterne was the director, while Maxine Nunes and I operated the cameras. Jerry Pompili, he was the manager at Winterland, was also a fan of the Pistols, and he asked Cindy if he could direct the opening number, which, correct me if I'm wrong, was 'God Save the Queen.' Incidentally, Jerry and the tour manager, Noel Monk, used to work together at the Fillmore West.

"Anyways, everything was set for when the Sex Pistols came onstage, but KSAN somehow forgot about the guitar. If you've seen the video footage from the show, you'll notice that the guitar doesn't come in till midway through the song. But ironically, that made the song as it came in at the perfect moment. Jerry later told me how he thought it one of *the* 'greatest moments in rock 'n' roll.'

"We kept rolling tape even after the Pistols had stopped playing and the concert was over and the crowd was exiting. It was all very odd. Johnny was walking around the stage picking up various things the audience had thrown at them. During the concert I remember him getting hit by pennies and whatnot, and he said, 'Why don't you throw something good at me! Throw your cameras!' or words to that effect. For the longest time after the show, he and the rest of the band were just wandering around on stage, scavenging, picking up coins, lighters, etc., tossing some stuff back into the pit. In all of my years of shooting concerts, and I've shot upwards of two thousand, I have never seen another band do that.

"We normally shot the concerts in black and white, but our good friend Todd Junkin from Hitachi got us a free demo of their color cameras to use to try and convince Bill Graham to invest in a new system. Bill once said to me, 'What do I know about cameras …

San Francisco's leading punk band, the Avengers (Jimmy Wilsey and Penelope Houston), were invited onto the Winterland bill at the behest of Pistols' U.S representative Rory Johnston (© Richard McCaffrey).

and why would I want to invest?' I answered, 'What do you know about planes, yet you own one…' We never got our color cameras, but the Sex Pistols concert is in color thanks to Todd."

♪ ♪ ♪

San Francisco will forever be indelibly linked with the flower power hippy movement and the fabled Summer of Love of 1967. Yet while the air over Haight-Ashbury remained incense-tinged two decades on, the city now boasted a thriving punk scene. The epicenter of said scene was the aforementioned Mabuhay Gardens in North Beach as the one-time Filipino restaurant was now serving up raucous rock 'n' roll seven nights a week from the likes of Crime, Negative Trend, The Offs, and The Mutants. Two other "Mab Fab" favorites, The Avengers and The Nuns, would both be appearing on the bill at Winterland.

Alejandro Escovedo and Jeff Olener had been enrolled on a film course at the College of Marin when they'd formed The Nuns in the fall of 1975. Their sylphlike, blonde keyboardist/vocalist, Jennifer "Miro" Anderson (who would sadly lose her battle against cancer in January 2012), had been wasting her considerable talents in a covers band at the time and she'd jumped at the chance to join a band intent on penning original material. A third vocalist was found in gravely voiced New Yorker Ritchie Detrick, while Jeff Raphael and Pat Ryan were brought in on drums and bass respectively.

Miro's striking looks and blonde tresses inevitably saw The Nuns being viewed as a West Coast version of Blondie. However, as with Debbie Harry, Miro was way more than just a pretty face. "Jennifer was an exceptional talent," the band's first manager, Edwin

Heaven, told www.sfgate.com at the time of her death. "She had this tremendous stature. She sat there like Marlene Dietrich. Her skin was whiter than white. And she could write these pop songs that went well with these two-chord punk anthems."

Miro swanned Dietrich-esque onto the Winterland stage. Seating herself at her keyboards, she performed a seductive ballad, "Lazy," before the rest of the Nuns joined her onstage and launched into the infinitely punchier "Decadent Jew." Legend has it that Bill Graham, who was himself of Jewish descent, would offer the Nuns a management deal on the proviso they dropped "Decadent Jew" from their set. The band would refuse Graham's offer, if only as a show of artistic integrity.

Olener and Detrick, who was wearing another of McLaren's salacious SEX T-shirts, provided a twin vocal attack on Stooges-esque "two-chord punk anthem"s with inflammatory titles such as "World War Three," "Heroin," "Child Molester," "Turning Straight," and a version of the Stooges' own "Search & Destroy," while Miro took the spotlight on numbers such as "Savage" and "You Like to Bleed." Such was the Nuns' popularity in the Bay Area that they were invited back for an encore.

Their playing two sell-out shows a week at the Mabuhay Gardens, coupled with Heaven's promotional talents, led to The Nuns being courted by both Sire and CBS Records. They would release an eponymous-titled EP featuring "Decadent Jew" on Howie Klein and Chris Knab's independent label, 415 Records, but a major record deal would sadly elude them prior to their initial break-up that same year. "They were like a shooting star," Heaven lamented. "I always felt like their moment came when they were very young and didn't quite know what they were doing."[16]

The Nuns would reunite without Escovedo in 1980 to record an album. Escovedo's decision to chance the New York scene would ultimately pay dividends as he has carved out a successful solo career. At the time of writing he has just released his thirteenth solo album, *Burn Something Beautiful.*

Renowned rock critic Richard Meltzer was emceeing between acts as Rory Johnston was worried the Winterland crowd would prove too placid. "I thought that having Meltzer introduce the bands would provide the necessary spice. I'm not sure who pitched the idea to me, but it most certainly wasn't anyone from Bill Graham Productions. It might even have been Richard himself. He was a character on the scene and had good punk credentials."

Whoever was responsible for the pitch, Meltzer didn't disappoint on the night as he himself explained. "I went out and provoked the audience and they threw things at me. Bill Graham chucked me out of the building. What a rush!"[17]

"Meltzer totally insulted the crowd," Avengers' guitarist Greg Ingraham reflected. "He was saying things like, 'Your mothers suck cock in hell!' while pacing the stage from one side to another. Bill [Graham] was furious! He was in such a rage you could fry an egg on his head. He had security kick Richard out of the show while he walked alongside yelling at him. Bill hated every second of that night and every one of us. He kept stomping around cursing, and I heard him say he would never promote another punk show. We were all laughing our heads off. Bill's mood wasn't improved much by the apple fight we had backstage, either. He had these big baskets of apples and we were throwing them about."[18]

Johnston was also responsible for getting The Avengers onto the Winterland bill, as he'd caught them live a couple of times in LA and thought they'd "be a good fit" for the Pistols. Indeed, he'd been so impressed with what he saw that he'd offered to manage them.

"The Avengers basically came about from me and Danny [O'Brien] deciding to put a band together," says Ingraham. "We both grew up in Fullerton [Orange County]. We met when we were around 12 or 13, and became close friends. We shared a lot of the same ideas, and had similar tastes in both music and art. Dan was a drummer and I played guitar. We were in a band together called Head over Heels when we were about 18–19. Dan came up to San Francisco to go to the Art Institute and after about a year or two later, April 1977 to be exact, I moved up to start a band with him. We were living in a big warehouse with a few other artists from the Art Institute. We used to have these big parties all the time. Penelope [Houston], who was also from the art institute, happened to come to one of the parties. That was around May 1977, and it was the beginning of the Avengers."

Though born in Los Angeles, Houston had spent her formative years in Seattle before recently relocating to San Francisco and enrolling at the city's Art Institute. "I was 19 years old and thought that sooner or later I'd be famous. So after a day of falling in love with a microphone, I told Danny and Greg that I was going to be their singer."[19]

The Avengers had only been together since the previous summer, yet were already regarded as one of the leading lights on the Bay Area scene. They'd even released their own three-track "We Are the One" EP via the LA-based indie label Dangerhouse Records. (The other two tracks on the EP were "I Believe in Me" and "Car Crash.")

Houston says she was "thrilled" on learning the Avengers would be playing the Pistols' Winterland date. "We were really into the Pistols. They had such great songs. Rory was working with Malcolm at the time, and it was through his wanting to manage us that we were invited onto the bill."

The Avengers had released an EP, but the Nuns were nonetheless viewed as being the more established of the two acts and many of their fans were therefore confused at their being placed bottom of the bill. Some went so far as to accuse Graham of foul play because of the song "Decadent Jew." Houston, however, says the decision had nothing to do with Graham. "Jeff Olener called me on the phone. He was concerned that we might not be able to handle being the support act and offered to change places with us. If there was any rivalry between us, then it started from the Winterland show. They had a manager who was holding out for a big record deal, and subsequently never had any real releases."

"The Nuns were good friends of ours," Ingraham adds. "I always liked them as they were one of the bands that gave us our start. I wouldn't say there was any rivalry, but I do remember them not being very happy about their having to open the show."

As was their wont, Jones and Cook once again proved the most amiable of the Sex Pistols towards the support acts. "The Pistols' dressing rooms were far away from the stage," says Houston. "John pretty much stayed up there, but Steve and Paul came down and mingled with everyone. I've no idea where Sid was—probably off getting high as he'd managed to connect with people in the scene who had drugs."

Ingraham remembers talking to Jones about guitars and amps. "I guess you might say we were 'geeking out.' We also talked about the tour, though. Steve and Paul really weren't happy about the tour. They thought it had been 'dreadful.' They told us stories of almost getting the shit kicked out of them in some of the venues they played. You could sense there tour had really taken a heavy toll on them."

While in Dallas, Jones had purchased the vintage Gibson Firebird III (either a 1964 or '65 model with a tobacco sunburst finish) he would use both at Cain's Ballroom and

Winterland. Rory Johnston was present when the deal was struck. "It was the first opportunity Steve had to buy a guitar on the tour—probably the first occasion he'd ever paid for one! A guy came to the hotel with the Firebird, and he asked me what I thought. It seemed authentic, not that I was an expert, and I suppose Steve liked it. I can't remember how much the guy was asking, but it seemed reasonable for what it was. Of course, Malcolm was the one who handed over the money as Steve and the rest of the band were only on $25 a day. That wasn't bad at the time, though. I know plenty of bands that are expected to survive on that today."

Houston says she doesn't remember anything from her conversations with Jones and Cook as everything was "all a bit of a blur" until the Avengers had come off stage. "I was so nervous because the show was about ten times bigger than our biggest audience to date. As I walked out on stage there was spit everywhere from the tough reception the Nuns got. People were throwing all kinds of things at them. There's a story that Jennifer got hit with a loogie and kept playing with it hanging there—like one of the guards at Buckingham Palace or something. As I crossed into the lights of the stage I slipped and caught myself from falling. That didn't help my nerves any!"

Houston wasn't the only Avenger on edge, as Ingraham revealed. "I remember not moving much on stage like I'd normally do because I had a bit of stage fright. After a couple of songs I loosened up, but stayed somewhat composed because I wanted to play really well and not make any mistakes. I still feel it was one of the best performances we ever did."

The Avengers opened their 13-song set with "The American in Me," a relatively new song that centered around the "Ask not what your country can do for you" couplet John F. Kennedy had used in his inauguration address in January 1961. This, along with other songs such as "Desperation," "Open Your Eyes," "No Martyr," and a cover of the Rolling Stones' classic 1966 single "Paint It Black" would subsequently appear on the band's eponymous 1983 compilation album (also known as the "pink album" owing to its magenta-hued cover design). The full set features on the 2010 *Live at Winterland 1978* CD.

With the Winterland crowd again proving receptive to homegrown talent, the Avengers began to relax into their stride. Houston says that anyone listening to the live album or watching the video footage of the set on YouTube will detect her voice shaking between songs. "But as the set progressed we girded ourselves and blasted through our best material. By the end we felt triumphant." Such was her confidence that during "I Believe in Me" she playfully launched into an ad-lib about how the Avengers weren't playing for the money as they were being "paid shit anyway." And how much did they receive? "We made $250. Not a terrible insult, but considering the crowd it was kind of small. Two weeks earlier we'd played the Mab and got $420 on a $3.50 ticket price. The tickets that night at Winterland were $5.00."

(Little did she know the Avengers were getting almost four times what the headliners would receive? Out of the $2,800 door receipts, the Pistols earned a pitiful $66.)

As with The Nuns, the Avengers would fail to realize their potential. Following Ingraham's departure in 1979, the band stumbled on for several months before breaking up. Prior to Ingraham's leaving, however, the Avengers were reunited with Steve Jones when the ex–Sex Pistol was brought at the behest of Rory Johnston to produce the recording session that resulted in the four-track "Avengers" EP. "Steve came and worked with us in mid October of '78," Houston explained. "I felt that he was just feeling around for his next gig, and that Rory had suggested his producing us. I could be wrong, though. He ended up leaving before the tapes were completely mixed or maybe completely paid for, however. The studio held on to the tapes as security and I ended up buying them from the studio."

Houston hadn't spoken with Jones since the Winterland show, yet surprisingly says she didn't engage him in conversation about the show, or the Pistols' breaking up during the sessions. "The topic simply never surfaced. The last time I'd seen Steve was at the Winterland after-show party. It was at a house somewhere in the Cole Valley neighborhood. Paul and, I think Sid, were also there. I don't remember seeing John, but the place was insanely packed with people. The next day we heard Sid had OD'd, and had been taken to the Haight-Ashbury Free Clinic.

"Punk is supposed to have ended with the Pistols' breaking up. It didn't, of course, but it was never the same. Our scene had been small and fairly friendly up until that point, but then more dudes from the suburbs started coming to the Mab and fistfights would break out during our shows. It wasn't so much a case of turning a corner, but more of a slipping down into cynicism, drugs, and the commodification of punk."

Following the Avengers' break-up, Houston relocated to London where she collaborated with Howard Devoto on the ex-Buzzcocks and Magazine front man's solo projects. (Devoto, of course, had been inspired to form the Buzzcocks along with guitarist Pete Shelley after their seeing two early Sex Pistols shows in February 1976.)

On her return to San Francisco in the mid-Eighties, Houston signed a deal with Subterranean Records and released her debut solo album, *Birdboys*, in 1988. She has gone on to enjoy a successful solo career, but the Avengers are still close to her heart. She and Ingra-

Vicious' battle-scarred torso tells its own story as Rotten gets close to the audience (© Richard McCaffrey).

ham first reconstituted the band in 1999 in support of a compilation Avengers album, and have been playing sporadic shows since 2004.

♪ ♪ ♪

Gabi Berlin can't remember why she and the rest of the LA gang headed home instead of trailing the tour bus to Tulsa. "I'm sure that Malcolm had put us on the guest-list for Cain's, so I can only suppose it was because we didn't have the gas money to get us to Tulsa and then back to LA. Maybe if we had have gone to Tulsa I would have something to gauge the contrast between the shows in Dallas and San Francisco, because comparing those shows is pretty much like trying to compare apples and oranges. At Winterland I was left wondering what had happened to the happy-go-lucky guys that I had met in Texas just five days earlier. Johnny was so remote and polished—he seemed like a different person."

Berlin was late getting to Winterland but since Vicious had given her a backstage pass before leaving Dallas she was able to bypass the queues and make her way through to the backstage area. She soon wished she hadn't. "There was the usual yucky atmosphere that you find in backstage areas—everyone trying to put one over everyone else. I felt so disillusioned. It was pretty obvious that Sid and John detested Paul and Steve—at least to me. They never spoke or even looked at each other before going out onstage. It was a totally different vibe than most bands where all the guys are glued together. But Malcolm couldn't do anything about the situation because the Pistols were so different psychologically. But I've always thought Malcolm looked on the Sex Pistols as his 'art project.'"

Berlin's "art project" assessment isn't all that far off the money, as there's no arguing that the Pistols' career had never been of primary concern to McLaren. In *The Great Rock 'n' Roll Swindle* he'd boasted that he'd nurtured the Pistols as a means of promoting the shop and "sell lots of bondage trousers." He also makes the grandiose claim that the Pistols had been part of some Machiavellian master plan to enable him to swindle his way to the "top of the rock 'n' roll industry," but in reality he'd never thought beyond the next outrage. In hindsight, he should have walked away after "God Save the Queen," because after putting a safety-pin through the sovereign's nose in her silver jubilee year where else was there to go?

In the *Swindle*, McLaren would also make the claim that the Pistols' "cover had been blown" during the U.S. tour owing to their publicity working against them and making them the "most important name behind the president of the United States." He also decried the Pistols as now being a "dying horse that needed putting out of its misery." But of course, it was his own naivete in thinking his own cover wouldn't be blown—that Warners would roll over as EMI, A&M, and Virgin had done—that ultimately brought matters to a head in San Francisco.

John Holmstrom has his own theory as to why the "craziest rock 'n' roll tour" he's ever experienced ended in a damp squib. "Compared to the shows in San Antonio and Dallas, Winterland was definitely a let-down. But you have to remember that this was the Pistols' first show in a big auditorium, so the sound was uneven. In my experience, it takes a while for any performer or band to adjust to working a big stage. And you have to take into account everything that was happening offstage by the time we got to San Francisco. Everyone was feeling the strain. I only spoke with Boogie and Rory Johnston a couple a times, but I sensed they were encountering a lot of frustration with the Warners thugs during the tour—as all of us did. It started off bad, and got worse and worse as the tour went on. I remember seeing Boogie getting physically manhandled out of Winterland. 'But I'm the fucking sound man!' he yelled."

Tiberi, however, is puzzled by Holmstrom's comment. "I don't know where he got that from. Maybe he was confusing me with someone else? I had no problems with either Graham, or getting in and out of Winterland. I had every piece of laminate you can imagine on that tour. I also had a pocket full of complimentary passes, which I still have incidentally."

Despite Monk's assurances back in Tulsa, there would be no complimentary passes awaiting Holmstrom and Bayley. "Yeah, we found ourselves barred when we arrived at Winterland," Holmstrom explained. "We snuck in though because Roberta bought tickets. We ran up to the balcony.... One moment we were sitting with Malcolm before the show, the next we were being forced out the door. Roberta objected, so they got physical—which I thought was gutless. But the roadies were mostly bullies, picking on anyone smaller than them, insulting and intimidating journalists, picking on women. This tour kind of marked the beginning of the 'us versus them' attitude between 'security' and the rock press and fandom."

"Tell us, what's it like to have bad taste?" Rotten addresses the Winterland crowd (© Richard McCaffrey).

Despite being ejected, "Steve and Paul would visit our room at the Miyako," he added.

♪ ♪ ♪

The Pistols may have been unraveling at the seams, but playing Winterland was at least serving as a distraction for Steve Jones—if only because it "seemed like a great venue for a proper rock 'n' roll show, [unlike] the shitty cow palaces we'd been booked into up till then"[20] Winterland was indeed a great venue for a "proper rock 'n' roll show," but only when the act onstage is of a mind to put on a show. The Pistols were best playing within intimate settings, creating a synergy with the audience. They had no experience of having to project themselves beyond the front twenty rows, so the performance at Winterland would have suffered even if they had been on top of their game.

The stage was certainly set for a climactic tour finale, as the auditorium was cloaked in complete darkness until the moment the Pistols launched into "God Save the Queen." All the harsh lighting did, however, was illuminate the Pistols' shortcomings. Indeed, the performance is so poor that at one point Rotten playfully enquires of the crowd, "Tell us; what's it like to have bad taste?"

As "New York" came to a close, Rotten—dressed in leather trousers and a striking leather waistcoat that he'd purchased while in America—decided the "presents" being hurled onto the stage were inadequate and challenged the crowd to improve the quality of their offerings. "Cameras, can we have a couple of cameras?" he deadpanned, pausing to check the denomination of a crumpled bill he'd grabbed up from the floor before stuffing it into his pocket.

Vicious might have been too strung out to care whether he was in sync with the "tuneless racket" emanating from the stage, but he made sure the latest recruits to his ever-burgeoning Californian fan club got their money's worth. "Sid spotted us in the crowd and waved at us," Weems explained. "During 'Problems' he came over to our side of the stage, and was pointing at us as we sang. ... He even tried to pull us up onto the stage, but everyone who got pulled up there got slammed by security and chucked back in, losing their front row place so we didn't take his hand. He understood, and kept smiling and nodding at us. It was wonderful, and I will always be grateful that we got to go to that show. I'd always been something of an outcast at school, but now I felt for the very first time in my life that I was actually a part of something new and exciting—something that we were making ourselves!"

Another who'd gotten in line early to ensure a spot close to the stage was 20-year-old Dan Young. He lived in Healdsburg, some fifty miles north of San Francisco, but was something of a regular visitor to the city. He'd come across an import copy of "Anarchy in the UK" during the fall of 1976 on one of his weekly forays to Ripped Records. "It was an exciting time to be alive. I felt like I was one of the few people alive who had been let in on this tremendous secret. I was definitely the only punk fan in Healdsburg. I was an avid fan of "The Outcastes," which is probably how I learned the Sex Pistols were going to tour the U.S. It was a bonus that they came to San Francisco, but I was ready to travel to wherever they were appearing."[21]

Young's determination to get up close and personal with his heroes almost ended up with his life, however. "We all jammed up as close to the stage as possible, but as more people crammed into the hall those of us at the front began to be squeezed together so tightly it was struggle just to breathe. During the Nuns' set, the people at the edge of the crowd began to push against the crowd, rocking us back and forth. We were being rocked from side to side, harder and harder. We were screaming at the people at the sides, begging them to stop, but they kept right on doing it. Things were really getting out of control. A girl I had been talking to in the queue earlier passed out. Her boyfriend managed to lift her over the crowd and she was passed from one to another, up on to the stage and away.

"The rocking stopped for a bit, but then started again during the Avengers' set. This time it escalated quickly—people were being knocked over and getting hurt. I was struggling to remain upright, like standing in the ocean during a tsunami. Suddenly I got slammed hard from the right and down I went. I tried to get back up, but the crowd actually climbed on top of me so they could see better—and most likely get some air. I started screaming, but my voice was drowned out by the music. People were standing on my face. My glasses were off and I blacked out. Somewhere off in the distance I heard Penelope on stage, asking the crowd to 'please quit shoving,' and to 'let that poor guy up off the floor.' She probably saved my life. I never did find my glasses, though, so when I say I saw the Sex Pistols that night I'm stretching the truth a bit."

Houston could have watched the Pistols' performance from the safety of the wings, but says that wasn't her style. Despite having seen the danger first-hand, she decided to go out into the audience. "I worked my way through the crowd up towards the stage. It was so packed that my feet barely touched the floor. There was perhaps more energy in the crowd than on stage—not all of it friendly! I'd say the audience was a mix of adoration and hate."

On her website, www.penelop@penelope.net, Houston playfully says the Avengers had "blown" the Pistols off the Winterland stage. "I still stand by that, because that night it seemed like the Pistols were each playing for a different reason. We know now, they were simply sick and tired of each other, but it still ruined the show."

Greg Ingraham is rather more pragmatic in his assessment of the Pistols' performance. "They were horrible! I remember Steve kept telling the stage guy, Terry Nails, to turn off Sid's amp. He was so wasted that he could hardly play. I was disappointed when I heard they'd broken up. Disappointed, but not surprised. I still hoped that they might somehow pull it back together though because they were such a great band."

Rory Johnston's photographer friend, Hugh Brown, was another left feeling underwhelmed by the Pistols' lackluster performance. He was already a familiar face on the Bay Area punk scene from his photographing bands at the Mabuhay Gardens on a near-nightly basis. Brown was also acquainted with McLaren. He'd lived in London circa 1974–1975 while

In *The Great Rock 'n' Roll Swindle*, McLaren would decry the Pistols as being "a dying horse that needed putting out of its misery" by the time of the Winterland show (© Roberta Bayley).

studying at the University of Sussex. He'd paid a visit to Let It Rock, as the shop was then known, and had chatted briefly with McLaren. Having subsequently come across McLaren's name mentioned in a *Melody Maker* article on the Sex Pistols, he'd purchased an import copy of "Anarchy in the UK."

Brown had first met Johnston a year or so earlier while the two were working independently out of then-Blondie manager Toby Mamis' LA offices. Upon his discovering Johnston was acting as McLaren's U.S. representative, the two had quickly struck up a friendship. "Rory was selling T-shirts from Malcolm's shop, and at one point he came up to Berkeley and slept on my couch. I took him around to the local record stores such as Rather Ripped Records, and Aquarius Records on Castro Street in San Francisco, which was owned by Chris Knab, as both stores had all the new punk 45s. They both took some shirts, as I remember.

"I'm a little hazy as to how it all came about, but one day in either February or March 1977 Rory, Chris, and I ended up driving around LA in Chris's Citroen listening to a demo tape of the songs that would make up the Pistols' album. Chris's car had a great sound system. I also distinctly remember reading a short article in a weekly LA music mag as we drove about. The article was about local band Van Halen signing that week to Warner Bros. I remember saying to Rory and Chris that Halen would be 'nothing compared to the Sex Pistols.' I was really excited about the album after hearing that tape."[22] (The demos Brown refers to are those recorded by Dave Goodman during the latter half of 1976 and early 1977.)

Brown had also tagged along when McLaren flew out to LA in early July '77 to meet with Russ Meyer to discuss the latter's directing the Sex Pistols film, which at the time had the working title *Who Killed Bambi*? "One evening we went out to dinner, and after that we drove over to the Pleasure Chest sex shop on Santa Monica Boulevard in what was known as 'Boy's Town.' Pleasure Chest had the naked cowboys T-shirt and Malcolm bought one along with a few others.... I do remember Malcolm being quite interested in the store's merchandise. For some time now I'd been selling screen-printed T-shirts of bands using my photos. I had Pistols' shirts on sale at both Rather Ripped and Aquarius, and I'd brought some to LA to sell at some punk shops there. Malcolm took a few of them, and stiffed me for $31.00. I still remember!

"If memory serves, Rory and Malcolm met with Russ at his place on July 4. I wanted to go, but had other plans seeing as it was Independence Day.... I had intended on joining up with the tour in Dallas but was short on funds. Rory put me on the guest list for Winterland. I also had backstage passes, but I got those off of Bill Graham. By that point, I used to get in free to most of Bill's shows as I'd done some posters for BGP. I saw many great shows there. Sadly, the Sex Pistols wasn't one of them."

The *San Francisco Chronicle*'s Joel Selwin would surprisingly laud the Pistols for "turning out a tight, tidy hour-long blitz of hard, driving rock." He would end his critique by "questioning the future relationship between the Pistols and audience when it is so clearly based in violence and outrage." This, of course, would prove a moot point as the Pistols' relationship with their audience was already over.

The proceedings were brought to a close with another rambunctious run-through of "Anarchy in the U.S.A," and the Pistols probably wouldn't have returned for an encore had KSAN not been staging a live broadcast. In hindsight, the lyric to "No Fun" was so prophetic.

Midway through the song Rotten paused to intone "Oh bollocks, why should I carry on?" The bemused crowd would have assumed he was referring to the song, but we know now that he was questioning the worth of his carrying on as a Sex Pistol.

Jones and Cook were pondering the same conundrum, but continue the song's dirge-like mantra; the latter pounding the tune into submission. The last cymbal crash is still resonating about the hall when Rotten faces the crowd and utters his immortal teaser: "Ah, hah-hah, ever get the feeling you've been cheated?"

There were undoubtedly more than a few San Franciscans ruminating over whether they'd been shortchanged as they headed for the exits. Dan Young, however, wasn't one of them. "The Sex Pistols show was about what we expected. It was so much more than a musical performance. It sounds like a cliché now, but it really was an event. In fact, I still think of that night as being the funeral of rock 'n' roll. After twenty some years of rock, it was the perfect way to end it. Everything that came after the Pistols was superfluous. I was damn glad to hear they broke up after the U.S. tour because they'd made their mark, and there was nowhere else really to go with it. Johnny was an amazing presence on stage, and PiL was better than anything the Sex Pistols would have done."

Nine

Endgame

> The Pistols' road manager, scarlet and fuming, is trying to push his way through the crowd. No one seems to believe he's who he says he is. "This is no way to treat the press!" says one unhappy woman in what might be the quote of the evening. Meanwhile Sid is back onstage selecting tonight's groupies from among the punkettes who remained behind when the lights went on and pulling them onto the stage and round the back.
> —Sylvie Simmons[1]

What Sylvie Simmons didn't know, of course, was that the "groupies" Vicious was seemingly plucking from the gaggle of punkettes at random were already known to him. Just as they had at the Longhorn Ballroom four days earlier, Hellin Killer, Trudie Arguelles, Gabi Berlin, and Lamar St. John had taken up position stage right so to be as close to their hero as possible. "The show was sold out, but the crowd was nowhere near as manic as Dallas," says St. John. "The Winterland stage was higher than at the Longhorn, but we got a good spot right in front of Sid. He knew we were there, and we knew we'd be meeting up with him after the show."

Legs McNeil was still upset at John Holmstrom for dragging him away from LA, and his mood didn't improve when the latter insisted he be the one to go backstage after the show to speak with Vicious. "The Pistols sucked at Winterland. The show was awful, but it didn't seem to matter. Everyone was just thrilled to be there in the presence of the Sex Pistols. Holmstrom handed me a pass and said, 'Go talk to Sid. You'll like him, he's just like you.' I thought, 'Fuck you! Sid's a fucking moron.'"[2]

While McNeil was watching Vicious with green-eyed envy, Annie Leibovitz came bursting backstage. She was there to get a photo to accompany Charles M. Young's tour feature and she and her assistant hurriedly began setting up the gear. Bill Graham had arranged for a local artist to paint a Sex Pistols mural on one of the walls in the dressing room. In the mural, the band is standing in line waiting to be knighted by Queen Elizabeth II; that all four are sporting the KSAN biker jackets suggests Graham was made aware of KSAN's benevolence beforehand. Bob Gruen had snapped a photo of the Pistols huddled together on sofas beneath the mural prior to their going onstage. The band appears relaxed in the photo, smiling for the camera even, but it was literally nothing more than a pose. Leibovitz's repeated pleas to get the Pistols to again pose beneath the mural fell on deaf ears, as did her attempts to get Rotten and Vicious in the same frame.

Hugh Brown watched Leibovitz's mounting frustrations with bemusement before heading back out into the empty auditorium in search of Johnston. In doing so, he found himself being privy to an explosive piece of news. "I remember sitting on the bleachers with Malcolm and Rory when a crestfallen Malcolm said that Johnny wouldn't be going to be joining them in Brazil as he was quitting the band. I was shocked, of course, but in hindsight it kinda explained Johnny's performance."

Ted Cohen claims it was he who broke the news to Rotten about the proposed Rio jaunt prior to the band going onstage. "John had finally gotten kind of unbearable by that time. I was laughing and joking with him trying to lift the mood before show time, and said something along the lines of, 'This is it, one last show and then onto Brazil.' John said, 'What are you talking about, going to Brazil?' One of the others, I think it was Steve, said, 'That's right; we're going to Brazil to meet up with Ronnie Biggs.' John said, 'And when was all this planned?' And Steve said, 'While you were on the bus with Sid.' He thought Steve was joking, and when he found out the Brazil trip was true he got angry … very angry."[3]

Instead of going in search of McLaren to vent his anger, Rotten headed back to the Cavalier with a female who had latched onto him backstage. Leaving Vicious holding court with his coterie of admirers, Jones and Cook returned to the Miyako with Ted Cohen, Bob Merlis and the rest of the Warners team.

"We headed back to the hotel because while the band were onstage someone poured the butter for the popcorn onto the floor to turn the area into a skating rink," says Merlis. "I thought we had a fun party backstage even if others didn't. We [Warners] were very happy with how the tour had panned out. It had been a relative success, and the Pistols had got a great reception at Winterland. I was surprised when I heard they'd broken up a couple of days later, but I wasn't aware of the internal dynamics in the band at that time."

Susan Campbell and the rest of the video crew arrived backstage to find the floor awash with goop. "The popcorn stand was lying on its side, and the oil had spilled all over the wood floor. I was gripping the handrail so I wouldn't fall, while calling for sawdust. Everyone was slipping and sliding all over the place!

"We later headed over to the Miyako for the after party. The room was really crowded, loud and smoky. You had to have a backstage sticker/pass or a Winterland ID to get in. Nothing much happened from what I recall, but we three gals saw it as a badge of honor just to get in!"

Rory Johnston says the popcorn butter wasn't spilled on purpose. "It was definitely an accident. What made it worse was the backstage area was already wet because it was pouring with rain that night. The rainwater got mingled with the butter and, yeah, a skating rink pretty much describes it. My friend Theresa Kereakes, the soon-to-be photographer for the LA-based punk fanzine *Lobotomy*, was backstage when the Pistols came offstage. She told me that Rotten came through, slid on the butter, and crashed right into her."

"Rotten just fell into me and he was so apologetic for doing that," Kereakes explained. "He apologized in a very public school, well-raised young man kind of way. It took me aback! There was an old time movie theatre popcorn popping machine backstage, and the butter was leaking all over the already slick and smooth cement floor. Everyone was slipping and sliding. I vividly remember Penelope [Houston] sliding around on the spilt butter as if she were skating."[4]

Kereakes was enrolled at the University California at Los Angeles with ambitions of becoming an English teacher before punk rock "got the best" of her. "I was already familiar with the Sex Pistols because I'd spent a semester in London in 1976. Prior to that, I always read the music papers from England. I also listened to Rodney Bingenheimer, who played

Nine. Endgame 167

the latest underground music. He was the first one to play the Pistols in Los Angeles. My friends and I were over the moon excited on hearing the Pistols were coming to the U.S. We also got very excited when we heard Hellin, Gabi, and Trudie had gone to Dallas and had become friends with the band.

"You'll get one number and one number only, 'cos I'm a lazy bastard…. This is 'No Fun'" (© Roberta Bayley).

Vicious (center, open jacket) joins in the backstage frolics while Cook, right, and fan Penelope Houston watch (© Roberta Bayley).

"We all knew each other. There were about fifty to a hundred of us who knew each other from going to punk shows. After the shows were over, we all hung out in the parking lot at the Rainbow Bar and Grill on Sunset Strip—you could bump into rock 'n' roll people there. We all also used to frequent the monthly Capitol Records Parking Lot Swap meet to buy records, memorabilia and such.

"I still don't remember how we got backstage at Winterland as we didn't have passes or anything. But I think if you act like you belong somewhere, no one questions you. Everyone just went about chatting with people, milling about—very casually, as if it were a school function and not the most-anticipated rock show ever! I remember that in addition to Pleasant [Gehman, a.k.a Princess Farhana, *Lobotomy* co-founder] and me, and our car full of people, there was Sal Maida from Roxy Music and Sparks. At the time, he was playing bass with Milk 'n' Cookies so we may have brazenly walked backstage with him."

"We definitely didn't have passes," says Gehman. "*Lobotomy* had only just started when the Pistols played Winterland. In fact, we were still working on the first issue. We had to buy tickets. And they were expensive—$5.00! It sounds ridiculous now, but my rent was like, $25.00 a month. To put in perspective, cigarettes were about thirty-five cents a pack, so yeah, that was a pricey ticket … but worth every penny!"[5]

Gehman says she first became aware of the Pistols in the spring of 1976 after spotting Neil Spencer's "Don't Look Over Your Shoulder, but the Sex Pistols Are Coming" review of their February '76 show at the Marquee—the band's first bona fide press event. "I was 17, smart, sarcastic and streetwise. I was 'bicoastal' between LA and New York, by way of Greyhound bus. I was in high school, but cut school constantly because it bored me. I was artistic and obsessed with rock 'n' roll, and would read the English rock papers: *NME, Sounds, Melody Maker*, and any other British music press I could get my hands on. We bought the magazines as 'imports' at record stores, so they were expensive. The papers were usually a bit outdated by the time they got to LA, that's why I'm not exactly sure when I first heard of the Pistols as there was always a couple of weeks' lag time before I saw the 'current' issues!

"I remember seeing postage stamp-sized images of Johnny Rotten and Sid Vicious, as well as Siouxsie Sioux, the Damned, the Clash, etc. I'd stare at those teeny-tiny photos on the grainy newsprint and try to absorb every shred of coolness that I could. Even in an inch-square pixelated photograph, the genius of the Sex Pistols was apparent … at least to me! I was totally following the tour in the media, as much as I could; to the extent that it was possible in the late–Seventies. The American news stations had short, but sensationalistic clips of the Pistols as they made their way across the South and Midwest.

"The Pistols went beyond my expectations! It's always amazing to see your favorite bands live, but back in those days, there was no YouTube and no social media, so if a favorite band of yours wasn't on tour, you'd pretty much just have to imagine what they'd be like live, supplementing your fantasy with live shots that would appear in rock magazines weeks or months after the fact. I was standing dead center, in the second and third rows of people against the stage at Winterland. There were long periods of time during that show when my feet literally did not touch the ground! There was such a surge of bodies pressed up to the mouth of the stage from the moment the Pistols started, that it was hard to move. Finally, some hippy guy just kind of pulled me upwards and I was suspended there, held up by the crowd. It wasn't violent; it was just that the entire crowd surged forward when the band started playing.

Nine. Endgame

"No matter what anyone in the press said, or what anyone nowadays might say looking at a tape of the show, if you were *actually there*, the experience was phenomenal. The energy in the room was extraordinary; it was electric. And at the time, right there, during the concert, there was a sense of history being made. We all knew this wasn't just a 'regular' concert, even if most of us had no idea it would be the Pistols' last!"

Kereakes was equally enthralled, and hadn't wanted the show to end. "I thought the Pistols didn't play nearly long enough. Although in hindsight, I suppose they probably only had thirty minutes worth of material plus a cover or two. But it was over too fast for me. I didn't know what to expect, but I was not disappointed. I was, however, disappointed that they broke up. At the time, the Pistols really did seem more like an art project than a band ... almost as if Malcolm planned it all, thinking cynically about it. But I really loved the album, and wanted more from them both on record and live. After Winterland some of the band decamped to LA and were staying at the Tropicana. We hung out with them and would tease Steve Jones for wearing that red hunting jacket."

In her 2010 autobiography, *Lips Unsealed: A Memoir*, Belinda Carlisle says she was determined to get to Winterland by any means possible. Her introduction to the Pistols came the previous summer while repeat-listening to "God Save the Queen" with Germs duo Darby Crash (born Jan Paul Beahm) and Pat Smear (born Georg Ruthenberg). Carlisle had intended on being the drummer for the fledgling Germs—rechristening herself Dottie Danger—but had to abandon her dream before ever playing a show after sidelined by a bout of mononucleosis. "They [Crash and Smear] played it over and over, as if they were tattooing it in their brains. It provided our revolution with an anarchist anthem."[6]

Hearing *Never Mind the Bollocks* following its U.S. release—coupled with what she'd read about the band in the music press—convinced Carlisle that the Pistols were a "fast-moving cyclone," and that she'd "better do everything she could to see them before they blew apart."[7]

Carlisle wasn't the only founding Go-Go at Winterland as both Jane Wiedlin and Margot Olivarria had also made the trip up to San Francisco. Olivarria recalled, "I had only recently returned to LA from traveling around Europe. I was just getting to know people in the punk scene in San Francisco and LA. I was going to school and working as a babysitter for rich people up in Laurel Canyon. I flew up by myself the day before the show. I remember going to a house in Haight-Ashbury where there was to be a party that night. I remember I met a girl named Delphina there. She later was a neighbor at the Canterbury in Hollywood where I was living at the time. She was an artist and drew shoes ... lots of shoes. The party was totally wild and I met Hellin Killer for the first time that night. She was hanging out with Sid, who of course, was the center of attention. Sid took a piss in the closet and kept bumping into walls."

Her name "plus two" was added to the guest list. "I ran into Rod Donahue and Rock Bottom outside Winterland. Rod was an LA scene punk, and a friend. He later joined the Mau Mau's. Rock was also an LA scene guy, but I don't remember him ever joining or forming a band. They didn't have tickets so they came in with me."[8]

The last thing Gabi Berlin remembers about being backstage at Winterland is hanging around waiting for Vicious and Hellin Killer to emerge from an adjoining room. "There wasn't anything sexual going on as Lamar and some of the guys from the Nuns were in there as well. When they came out we all went to a party at Mark Mothersbaugh's house.

He was one of the guys in Devo. This is when everything becomes a bit of a blur as when we got there I drank something with acid it, passed out, and missed all the fun. I didn't even find out about Sid OD'ing at Lamar's place until later.

"The Sex Pistols' breaking up was the beginning of the end for me. I had some bad experiences when the Orange County violence came in. After Darby Crash died [December 1980] I didn't want to have anything to do with the scene. I didn't even know about Hellin going over to London and moving in with Sid and Nancy. Then when Sid died I just up and left that scene and completely cut it off. I haven't read any books or seen very much from those days. In fact, this is the first time I've ever spoken about any of this."

According to Kereakes, Berlin would make one final gesture before bidding punk a final farewell. "When Sid died, Gabi and Nicole Panter climbed up on to a billboard advertising the Warren Beatty movie *Heaven Can Wait*. They spray-painted 'RIP SID' on it. Stiv Bators from the Dead Boys called me up after he saw it and we went and took some pictures. We never interviewed any of the Sex Pistols for *Lobotomy*, but I did get to know Sid through Stiv while he was in New York. Sid was one of Stiv's biggest fans and followed him around like a puppy. Stiv was very close with Sid and needed to have this last bit of memorabilia. One of the photos was featured in Sid's obituary in *Creem* magazine."

♪ ♪ ♪

Rory Johnston still maintains that the Sex Pistols could have been pulled back from the brink if McLaren had showed the slightest interest in saving the band. But in a reversal of the Little Dutch Boy legend, McLaren had willfully picked at the crack hoping the damn would burst. He was bored with the responsibilities that came with managing a successful rock band, and was only interested in the next salacious headline. Tours and albums were only of interest to the *NME* and *Rolling Stone*, whereas stunts such as meeting up with a Great Train Robber in Rio de Janeiro would be front page news. He could easily have salved Rotten's wounded pride by conferring with him about the trip. Instead, he blithely instructed Warners to sort out booking the tickets for Rio as per the label's agreement to fly the Pistols to the destination of their choice.

"Rotten was seething about the proposed Rio trip, but his hissy fit prior to going onstage at Winterland had pretty much gone ignored," says Johnston. "He was angry because he only found out about the Rio trip from Teddy Cohen, but he would probably have gone along with the Brazil idea—if only to poke fun at Ronnie Biggs!"

When Rotten called Joe Stevens the following day he'd given no indication that he wouldn't be at the airport at the designated hour. But at some point that Sunday he'd reached the decision that things couldn't carry on as they were. The only money he had to his name was the cash he'd grabbed up from the Winterland stage, but it was enough to cover the cab fare to the Miyako.

Johnston says John arrived at the hotel early Sunday evening. "I remember this because I'd fallen asleep—I was exhausted by this point—and I obviously hadn't heard him knocking. The next thing I knew, he was coming through the open window. He'd climbed over the balcony from Steve and Paul's room next door. He was looking for his bag and thought I might have it. All I can assume is that Noel Monk dumped everything at the Miyako before heading off home....

"Like I say, there was a room booked in John's name, but he wouldn't have been able to check in as the management was still on the lookout for the Pistols—even though they already had half of the band under their roof."

Johnston says he is unaware of any flights being booked for the following morning, but Joe Stevens' photo of a despondent-looking Cook and Jones sat beneath the departures board at San Francisco International is evidentiary proof. As the *NME* were happy to continue paying his expenses, Stevens had accompanied Cook and Jones to the airport for the 07:00 Pan Am flight 515 to Rio de Janeiro. Like McLaren, Stevens knew a snap of the Sex Pistols lounging about with Ronnie Biggs would be syndicated around the world.

With Rotten and Vicious failing to put in an appearance, Stevens—realizing he might have a far more important scoop for the *NME*—returned to the Miyako with Cook and Jones sensing "something deadly was going to happen."[9]

Later in the year during an interview with the *Record Mirror*'s Rosalind Russell, Vicious revealed the reason behind his no-show for the flight to Rio. His version of events that Monday morning has McLaren collecting him from Lamar St. John's place in Haight-Ashbury, and that while en route to the airport he'd expressed his disinterest in "flying down to Rio to play to a bunch of 'Pakis' that didn't understand the Sex Pistols, and had no idea what they were about."[10]

Vicious had then supposedly expressed his disillusionment with what the Pistols had become before informing McLaren that he wanted to leave the band. He'd then insisted on being taken back to Haight-Ashbury where a couple of hours later he'd called Rotten at the Cavalier to vent his spleen.

Lydon makes no mention of Vicious' call in either of his autobiographies, but this isn't all that surprising as Rory Johnston is convinced these events didn't play out anywhere other than Vicious' drug-addled mind. "It simply couldn't have happened that way, as there is no way Malcolm would have gone to collect Sid. And how could Malcolm have known where to collect him? No one had had any contact with Sid since the Saturday night."

♪ ♪ ♪

Hellin Killer can't remember what time they arrived at Mothersbaugh's house with Vicious, but the party was in full swing. "There was a whole entourage of people there, it was packed with people! There was plenty of drinking obviously, but I spent most of the time keeping an eye on Sid, constantly trying to keep him from scoring. At some point we left to go to Lamar's place as we were staying there. I think some of the people who were at Mark's came as well."

Like all addicts, Vicious had only one thing on his mind. "Sid wanted to cop some dope and I suppose I knew where we could get some," St. John explained. "I hadn't seen much of the Pistols before the show as I'd mostly hung out with the Nuns and the Avengers, but afterwards I used my pass to get backstage and hung out with Hellin and Sid. By this point the security guy charged with babysitting Sid had pretty much given up. Vickie and I had planned an after-show party at the apartment. I knew the party would be in full swing by now, so we took a cab to a house where I knew Sid could score some dope. I wasn't doing heroin then, and as I recall, Hellin didn't do it either. I don't think she even smoked weed! I'm pretty sure we got him some. When we got to the apartment Sid mingled for a bit. We had a kitchen table that everybody would carve their name into. Sid added his name, so it was too bad that Vickie later tore the table apart and threw it out the window in a drunken rage.

"Everybody who was anybody was at the party. Sid was the only one there from the Pistols, though. Hellin hung onto Sid and just pampered him. I gave him the bottle of mezcal I'd bought in Juarez and told him not to eat the worm. He was already high, and now he was drinking 'crazy water.' Hellin and Sid were sequestered in my bedroom—such as it was. People forgot Sid was there because he was so out of it. The party wound eventually down, people left, and I slept in the closet."

"Lamar's place was pretty packed when we got there," says Killer. "It was so packed we had to hang out on the stairs. Sid was just talking to everyone and having a great time. And yeah, Lamar's 'bedroom' was the closet. Trudie and I locked ourselves in there at one point with Sid just to lecture him about not doing heroin. We were *so* against it. We partied till late, but eventually the place thinned out and we were able to find a space on the floor. Trudie, me, and Sid curled up and went to sleep.

"A fond memory I have is from the morning after. When we woke up we went into the kitchen. Lamar was making an amazing breakfast for everyone that was there. Terry was still there and a few other people … maybe Trixie? It was nice and intimate. I remember Lamar making these amazing fried potatoes with onions and peppers and scrambled eggs, and maybe toast! It was a great breakfast! The next thing I remember is being in the front room and Sid tying to give everyone something. He took the shirt Terry had loaned me and gave it to someone else—to my great dismay! He also gave Trudie his wristband in exchange for a necklace she had. He just loved to give and receive gifts."

Pleasant Gehman was at the party and made a futile attempt to connect with Vicious. "I tried talking to Sid, but although he was trying to talk, he was so out of it, just slurring unrecognizable sounds. Hellin was holding his hand throughout. She was very protective of him. I knew Hellin from the scene. We were thinking of putting a band together. We were going to call ourselves the Girl Scouts."

St. John says she doesn't remember the gift exchange the following morning; only that Vicious wanted to get high again.

"There is one thing from that day I feel I have to clarify," says Killer. "Later that morning, when there was hardly anyone left, a friend of Lamar's showed up. Maybe he wasn't really a friend, but she definitely knew him. Anyways, he knocked at the door and asked for Sid. I remember his face like it was yesterday. He'd brought heroin with him. Damn it, I was so mad because Sid had been pretty much clean the whole tour! I told the guy not to do it, but hey, people wanna be your friend so they give you what you want right? Well, the guy gave Sid some dope thinking he was fuckin' cool. When he took Sid into the bathroom I went in there too. I wasn't going to leave his side because I wasn't dumb! I'd seen people OD before.

"Anyway, the guy gave it to him and I couldn't stop him from doing it. I was sitting on the side of the tub with Sid. When he shot up he fell over backwards right into the tub. I knew something was wrong right away, and turned the cold shower on him. The dope guy was already gone out the door, so I shouted for someone to call an ambulance. Sid had OD'd! I was just trying to keep him breathing. I didn't know about Lamar rushing down to the clinic, only that a doctor from the clinic showed up. The doctor shot him up with what I now know was Narcan."

St. John recalled, "Sid immediately became unresponsive. We lived a block away from the Haight-Ashbury Free Clinic so I ran over there. I remember it was early, but it couldn't have been too early or they wouldn't have been open. I went inside and told them that Sid Vicious was at my house and that he'd OD'd. I didn't stop to think whether they'd know who Sid was or not. Anyways, it was either a doctor or one of the other staff that came back with me to the apartment and gave Sid a shot of Narcan which soon brought him round. I then called the Miyako and spoke with Malcolm. Malcolm said he would come round straight away."

This is where things get interesting, as St. John is convinced that McLaren arrived at the apartment with Johnston. And Vicious had said as much in his April 1978 *Record Mirror* interview. Rory Johnston, however, is equally adamant that while McLaren could well have taken St. John's call at the Miyako, it was himself and Tiberi that drove over to Haight-Ashbury.

Killer says that while everything was happening in a blur, she remembers all too clearly what happened on Vicious' receiving the Narcan shot. "We'd carried Sid into the front room. Within seconds of getting the shot, Sid was sitting up like nothing had happened, fixing his hair! Did I mention Sid was obsessed with his hair? It was total nuts after that. I thought Malcolm was there, but maybe I talked to him on the phone? It's too bad Malcolm's not here anymore to clear it up. I vaguely remember Rory and Paul being there, but I was paying attention mostly to Sid and his ridiculous behavior. He was acting like nothing had happened! But then I was to learn over time and experience that most junkies who OD act that way when they suddenly come to; like, 'Why is everyone looking at me like that?' Jeez…. When they took Sid away, that was the end of the innocence. So, so sad."

Johnson says he doesn't know anything about a doctor or a Narcan shot. "We must have got there just after Sid had shot up, because he was laid out on a mattress in the corner. I'm no expert, but it was obvious he was OD'ing! We managed to bring him round by walking about the room. I remember thinking, 'Boy, what the fuck is going on here?' He nearly died! I called Bill Graham, and he put us in touch with a doctor in Marin County. The guy was on a retainer from Graham. He was one of those 'hippy rock 'n' roll' types that just also happened to be an acupuncturist. Malcolm wanted Sid back at the Miyako, but the doctor said he was keeping Sid in overnight for observation. He didn't get any argument from me."

"I definitely went over there with Paul," says Tiberi. "I can't remember now if it was Rory that drove us there or if we took a cab and he met us there…. The only thing worth mentioning is what a truly horrible and frightening moment it was. If whoever it was hadn't made the call to the Miyako, Sid could have died."

Having bunked down at the Miyako, Rotten awoke sometime Monday morning determined to have a showdown with McLaren. With Joe Stevens in tow, he first went to state his position to Jones and Cook. He told them that while he was prepared to continue the Sex Pistols—either with Vicious or a new bassist—he could no longer work with McLaren.

Jones, however, had come to a decision of his own. "I was getting more and more where I wanted out of the [Pistols]. And that's when I said, 'I don't want to do it no more.'"[11] Cook was equally disillusioned, but he and Jones—at Joe Stevens' behest—agreed to accompany Rotten back to McLaren's room. Stevens ordered beers from room service, but Rotten was in no mood to sup with the devil who was making his life a misery. According to Johnston's recollections, Rotten accused McLaren of constantly trying to manipulate for McLaren's benefit and that the Rio trip was just the latest in a long line of such at his expense. McLaren had then retaliated in kind by telling Rotten he was "turning into Rod Stewart." Realizing he was wasting his breath, Rotten stormed out of the room and out of the Sex Pistols.

Johnston had purposely kept out of the way during the showdown as he felt that it was a situation that should be sorted out between McLaren and the band without external interference. "I had so many other things to deal with so I left them to it. I've no idea how or why Joe Stevens got to sit in on the meeting—even if he was rooming with Malcolm. But Malcolm always did like to have people around him in awkward situations.

"I'm not going to say I sensed a split in the air, but by San Francisco I knew we'd reached the point where something had to give. It was nothing specific, but there was definitely something hanging in the air. There was a darkness surrounding the Pistols. Warners were really pissed off with us, so that kind of matched the mood. In hindsight I should have done more to help, but I simply didn't have the experience. It was a tragic waste as we'll never know what the Pistols might have gone on to achieve had they carried on. I still see Paul on a regular basis. He makes light of the Pistols' legacy saying 'But we only made one album.' 'Yes,' I tell him, 'but what an album!'"

Tiberi says he'd long since come to recognize that a parting of the ways was inevitable. "I know I'm viewing these events with hindsight here, but John and Malcolm's interpersonal relationship was nonexistent by the time we got to America. Malcolm had stopped speaking to John from May 1977 onwards and the denouement came in San Francisco. I would have regular discussions with John—at least one a week—where I'd explain what was happening in regard to certain situations, and he'd say, 'Yeah, but Malcolm's got to run it by me, hasn't he?' I'd go and tell Malcolm that he needed to speak with John, but Malcolm simply wouldn't do it.

"Malcolm had been in love with rock 'n' roll since the Fifties. He loved the whole Tin Pan Ally scene, and saw himself as a latter-day equivalent to Larry Parnes. When I joined Glitterbest it was a fluid operation, but by the time we went to America it had become fragmented. I ran with it as best I could to ensure that John at least got his guarantees from Malcolm. John had theatrical dexterity, but he also needed to be inspired. But from October '77 onwards Malcolm's sole interest was the film; his latest piece of putty if you like. Sets were being built and Malcolm was fully occupied with the script. It didn't matter that Russ Meyer had already written a script. Malcolm wasn't the sort of person to sign off on anything. He was constantly rejigging the dialogue, literally changing it from day to day.

"In the early days Malcolm was heavily involved with the band, but as the Pistols got bigger they began taking up more and more of his time. People say today that Malcolm viewed the Pistols as his personal art project, and to a certain extent that's perfectly true. He wasn't what you would call a 'cash-till manager.' He was exactly what you see in the *Swindle* ... a manipulator. He was always looking to move onto the next thing. Steve and Paul's breaking away from John was totally down to Malcolm, because he'd severed his interpersonal relationship with John."

Jones has since come to regret his decision in siding with McLaren. "I regret leaving, I really do. I apologized to John that I fucking bailed on him, because we might have continued if we had got rid of Malcolm. But that's the way I felt—that I couldn't get away from my feeling at the time."[12]

"I saw John in the lobby when I arrived back at the Miyako after dropping Sid off with the acupuncturist," says Tiberi. "I guess I kind of knew why he was there. Rory and I had driven over to San Jose to speak with John the previous evening, but Monk—even though it was him that had given me the name and address of the motel—wouldn't let us see John. It seemed to me there was a lot of mind games going on. I was getting mixed signals from both John and Malcolm. I knew John had gone up to see Malcolm with Steve and Paul, but it wasn't my place to get involved. The only other person that had the right to be in there was Sid, but that couldn't be helped because of what had happened.

"I was outside in the corridor when John, Steve, and Paul went into Malcolm's room. Steve and Paul came out first, but didn't really say much. It was when Malcolm and John were alone that Malcolm told John about going to Rio. When John left I went in to see Malcolm and that's when he told me it was all over.

"John has always said that 'Malcolm broke up a good band.' And he's said that to me on more than one occasion. And he's right. I believe John, Steve, and Paul could and should have carried on. The Pistols now have that tag of being a 'great one-album band.' And while the follow-up album might not have been as successful as *Bollocks*, it would still have been special. Steve's guitar on 'Bodies' and 'Holidays' show you the direction they were heading in. The style of those songs was totally different to the songs they did with Glen."

The following morning Rotten accompanied Joe Stevens to New York, while Johnston drove McLaren, Richmond, Jones, and Cook to LA. The task of collecting a still fragile Vicious from Bill Graham's "Dr. Feelgood" fell to the hapless Tiberi.

"I've since read that Sophie picked Sid up from Graham's doctor, but I'm pretty sure it was Boogie," says Johnston. "I can't imagine why Sophie would volunteer, and Malcolm certainly wouldn't have told her to do it. I remember Boogie turning up at the Tropicana saying he'd managed to get Sid enough methadone to get him through the flight back to London. I drove them to the airport and accompanied them onto the concourse—as you could back then. We made small talk the whole way to the plane and it was really good. For the first time since I'd met the band in Atlanta, I felt that I was talking with John Beverley rather than Sid Vicious."

What Vicious failed to mention to either Johnston or Tiberi was that he had a stash of Valium capsules. As soon as the plane was airborne he popped a couple of the Valium, promptly overdosed again, and slipped into a coma.

Vicious was still unconscious when the plane touched down at JFK, and such was his condition that a doctor ordered him to be rushed to the nearby Jamaica Hospital in Queens. That night a raging blizzard descended upon New York, and with Tiberi holed up in a nearby hotel when Vicious regained consciousness the following morning he had no idea where he was or how he'd got there.

Johnston says McLaren, Jones, and Cook hung out at the Tropicana for at least a week before flying down to Rio. "I stayed behind in LA dealing with Rene Daalder as he was still working on the *Swindle* script. Russ Meyer had walked away by this point, but Malcolm still wanted Rene involved in the project. I had a house in LA, of course, but I ended up staying at Rene's place up in the Hollywood Hills. While Malcolm was in LA, I had Warners leaning on me to rearrange the cancelled shows—they fully expected Malcolm and John would work things out. Bob Regehr was holding out for the shows, and was constantly on the phone to me. What could I do at that point? I tried the whole time we were in San Francisco to convince Malcolm to rebook the cancelled dates, but he wasn't interested. 'No, we're going to Brazil!' And there was nothing Warners could do as they had nothing in writing.

"I've never understood why Malcolm found going to Rio to meet Ronnie Biggs so appealing. I kept thinking, 'Why are they going to Brazil? What's the point?' One of the things I did while Malcolm was in LA was finding an actor that looked as if he might have worked in a Nazi concentration camp to play the part of 'Martin Bormann' in the film. His name, if I remember rightly, was Jim Jeter." (At the time, the Texas-born Jeter was best known for appearing in *The Sand Pebbles* opposite Steve McQueen.)

♪ ♪ ♪

Tom Forçade had sensed the Pistols' story was far from played out. John Holmstrom says he and Roberta Bayley were in their room at the Miyako when their sponsor arrived with an offer neither could refuse. "We were packing our stuff, and all we could talk about was how much we wanted to get home after being on the road. Then Tom showed up and asked us if we wanted to go to Rio. Suddenly, the idea of going home wasn't so important. He gave us the tickets for the red-eye back to New York, and I'm pretty sure they were first class. We hadn't been home long when we started hearing the stories: that Rotten was in NYC staying with Joe Stevens, of Sid passing out on the plane and ending up in a hospital bed at Jamaica Hospital.

"I bumped into Rotten at CBGBs when I went to watch Ulli Lommel filming, *The Blank Generation* starring Richard Hell. Rotten is in the tracking shot when Hell performs 'Blank Generation.' He's standing next to Cheetah Chrome of the Dead Boys, wearing the blue tartan suit from the tour. It was the perfect ending to the craziest tour in rock 'n' roll history."

It's doubtful that Rotten was aware of Vicious' hospitalization, but even if he had its unlikely to have made any difference. Legend has it that with the blizzard having brought New York to a standstill, Vicious' only contact with the outside world during his overnight stay in hospital came courtesy of a telephone conversation/interview with Roberta Bayley. Tiberi disputes this, however. "I spoke with Sid on the phone several times. And when the hospital called me the next day to say Sid was being released, I rebooked the flights to London before going over to pick him up. While Sid was in hospital he received a telegram from the 'HA crowd' 'HA' as in 'Haight-Ashbury.' I still have it. It says something like, 'Hi Sid, we've burnt our leather jackets.'"

During the thirty-or-so minute conversation—besides bemoaning his having been abandoned by Tiberi–Vicious cast a disparaging eye over his fellow ex-Sex Pistols: Jones and Cook would "probably try and get another band together—and fail," while Rotten was "finished" as a performer. "He's just not what he used to be. Nobody will even want to know him. They'll say, 'Oh, didn't you used to be Johnny Rotten?'"

When the bemused Bayley enquired after his own post–Pistols future, Vicious expressed a desire to hook up with Johnny Thunders. "Just think what [The Heartbreakers] would be like with me, Thunders, Nolan and Walter Lure? Particularly if I was healthy."[13]

When Bayley ponders how Thunders managed to stay "pretty healthy" in spite of his own drug problems, Vicious says it's because Thunders had never suffered hepatitis. He then goes on to explain how he'd contracted the disease the previous summer, and on being released from hospital he'd purposely fucked himself up as badly he could [because] it was his basic nature. Bayley warned him that his "basic nature" was going to land him in trouble, Vicious responded saying his basic nature was "going to kill me in six months."[14]

Holmstrom is of the opinion that Vicious could and should have been saved from his self-destructive nature. "Having worked at *High Times* years later and learning about 'harm reduction' drug policies that treat drug addicts as human beings instead of 'problems,' I sadly think that Sid could have been saved. The record industry treated all drug/alcohol problems in the same way—a Band-Aid approach that helped no one and led to so many deaths: Keith Moon, Brian Jones, Jimi Hendrix, Jim Morrison, Kurt Cobain, Amy Winehouse, Michael Jackson, and so many others. The music industry has taken no responsibility for any of these drug deaths, but they profit greatly after musicians die and leave large estates behind. In many cases the record companies provide drugs to addicted musicians, and are complicit in creating the problem. I doubt you'll publish those above comments, but they need to be raised somewhere."

When the news about the Pistols' split broke in Britain, Glitterbest issued the following press release: "The management is bored with managing a successful rock 'n' roll band. The group is bored with being a successful rock 'n' roll band. Burning venues and destroying record companies is more creative than making it." The release duly appeared in the following morning's edition of *The Guardian*, but it soon transpired that the statement had been penned by mischievous Glitterbest employees rather than McLaren and was promptly withdrawn.

The music papers had already gone to press when the news of the split broke, so it wasn't until the following week that the music weeklies were able to offer their respective takes on the split. Speaking with the *Record Mirror*, Virgin's press officer Al Clark said that there wasn't much anyone could say about the Pistols' immediate future—at least until the label could get everyone concerned in the same room—other than the band were all still under contract to Virgin.

Ten

Aftermath

Sex Pistols Sensation
Punk band splits up as Rotten walks out

New York—Britain's top punk rock band, the Sex Pistols, have split up, said their manager early today.

The pop sensation came in Los Angeles when manager Malcolm McLaren declared: "It's all over. We will never perform again."

—Leslie Hinton, The *Sun*, January 19, 1978

In the same interview with the *Sun*, McLaren said that Rotten had been kicked out of the Pistols by the rest of the band following the showdown at the Miyako. The article, however, also gave Rotten's version of events in which he said that he was "sick of working with the Sex Pistols," and that he never wanted to appear with them again.

Warners had honored their commitments in taking care of the travel arrangements for McLaren, the other Pistols and their small retinue, yet there'd been no open-ended ticket waiting for Rotten. Indeed, it was only through Joe Stevens' munificence that the singer was able to get out of San Francisco. Aside from paying for Rotten's flight to New York, Stevens would also have to provide the funds to enable him to purchase a one-way ticket back to London. Upon his arrival in New York, Rotten had apparently called Warners' local office requesting assistance to get back to London. Yet, somewhat bizarrely, whoever answered the call refused to believe it was the Pistols' front man on the other end of the line.

When Rotten finally arrived back in London in late January, he was besieged outside Heathrow by a coterie of reporters all anxious to hear his version of events leading to the Pistols' split. Despite providing The *Sun* with its scoop while in New York, Rotten mischievously declared the Pistols were in fact still together, and that the split was just another of McLaren's "publicity stunts." Those reporters still wet behind the ears went scurrying off back to their respective offices, but the majority of the newshounds were sufficiently long enough in the tooth to recognize they were being fed a line and continued to press him as to what his next move might be.

Rotten probably had no idea as to his immediate future plans, other than to hire a solicitor to look into the tangled morass of Glitterbest's accounting. (Glitterbest was the Sex Pistols management company set up by McLaren with himself and Steven Fisher as sole directors. McLaren had bought the name off the shelf for £100 and the company was incorporated on September 23, 1976.) So when Rotten's photographer friend Dennis Morris called out of the blue to invite him on an all-expenses-paid trip to Jamaica to sound out prospective reggae acts for Virgin Records' new subsidiary reggae label, Front Line, he'd readily accepted. (Morris had carried out several photographic assignments for Virgin—including snapping the Sex Pistols while filming the promo video for "God Save the Queen" at the legendary Marquee Club.)

Virgin owner Richard Branson had intended to fly out to Jamaica himself but had delegated the task to Morris, who in turn had invited Rotten.

While in Jamaica, Rotten visited Lee "Scratch" Perry's Black Ark Studios, where he supposedly provided the vocal on Jamaica-inspired versions of the Pistols' tracks "Submission" and "Problems." There is some skepticism over whether the ad hoc recording session took place as journalist Vivien Goldman, who was covering Rotten's Jamaican jaunt for *Sounds*, and had accompanied Rotten and Morris to the studio, has no recollection of Rotten and Perry recording any material, let alone reggae-tinged Pistols numbers.[1]

Branson later flew to the island. Rotten had assumed Branson had come to check on his and Morris' progress, but it seemed there was an ulterior motive behind the Virgin supremo's visit. Devo was signed to Virgin at the time and Branson flew Mark Mothersbaugh, who had entertained Vicious at his home after the Winterland show, and rhythm guitarist Bob Casale to Jamaica. Mothersbaugh recalled: "He [Branson] said, 'Johnny Rotten is down here at the hotel [The Kingston Sheraton]. He's in the next room, and there are reporters downstairs. I'd like to go down to the beach right now, if you're into this, because Johnny Rotten wants to join your band ... and I want to announce to them that Johnny Rotten is the new lead singer for Devo.' And I'm going, 'Oh my God, I'm really high right now.' Regrettably, I didn't just go, 'Yeah, sounds great. Send him to Akron. He can do it for a week or two, just for the hell of it.'"[2]

Speaking in 2007, however, Lydon said he hadn't thought there was any serious intention to Branson's thinking. "He may or may not have been trying to get me to be their singer. I certainly don't think he ever asked me."[3]

Branson wasn't the only one harboring ulterior motives where Rotten was concerned, however. Warners had suspended the £200,000 they had invested into the ongoing *Swindle* project, and his only hope in getting his hands on the cash was in resolving his differences with Rotten. Upon hearing about Rotten's Jamaican jaunt, McLaren had handed Tiberi a cache of blank sheets of paper bearing his signature and packed him off to Heathrow. The signed sheets of paper were to be used to make various promises to Rotten if he would agree to a truce and cooperate on the movie. Rotten, of course, was savvy enough to know that whatever promises Tiberi was making on McLaren's behalf literally wouldn't be worth the paper they were written on.

"My impression was that Malcolm was lost for thinking that he could bribe John into returning to the Pistols," says Tiberi. "I was happy to go out to Jamaica, but there were things that I didn't know. For instance, I didn't know Don Letts was there. And Don made it his mission—his agenda, if you like—to keep me from getting close to John. There was little love lost between Malcolm and Don Letts. All the talk about Boy, or Acme as it was before that, being competition to SEX is nonsense. Absolute nonsense! It was nothing more than a blatant rip-off!

"Branson was also there, of course.... Branson was all about self-promotion, and feeding into the Pistols' notoriety. Virgin were talking about setting up a reggae subsidiary at the time they signed the Pistols. They had like fifty people sitting around the office all day, so they had to think of something to merit their worth. Virgin wasn't a record label in the true sense, like EMI or CBS. They were just a bunch of hippies. The Pistols' contract was so drawn out. It seemed to go on for ages. Branson had arrived in Jamaica with a suitcase filled with money, which John then handed out to any acts he thought good enough. That's not to say John wasn't a good choice. His interest in reggae wasn't ephemeral of anything, but that whole thing was nothing more than a glorified A&R trip.

"And while it's true that I was thrown into the swimming pool, the tale that I was found hiding in the bushes with a tape recorder was utter fabrication. As was the tale about Malcolm instructing me to get a photo of John lounging by the pool smoking a spliff to ruin his 'punk credibility' in Britain. These were cooked up…. What actually happened was I'd given up on trying getting John on his own. I mean, I was in regular contact with Malcolm by phone, and once I'd explained about the influence Letts and Branson were having on John, Malcolm understood the situation. So I'd given up chasing John and was sitting by the pool reading a book when John and Don ran across and dumped me, the chair, and my book in the pool. They were just larking about."

♪ ♪ ♪

Towards the end of February McLaren was forced to interrupt his filming schedule and return to London in order to deal with the legal proceedings Russ Meyer was seeking his unpaid director's fees on the *Swindle* film. Upon discovering McLaren was back in London, Bob Regehr wasted little time in summoning him and Rotten to LA for a reconciliatory meeting between the protagonists to see if a compromise might at least be reached over the *Swindle* project. With the Sex Pistols existing now only on paper, Regehr knew getting the film completed was the only realistic means to recoup Warners' six-figure investment. Regehr was so keen to get the warring parties around the table that he wired the funds for Lydon to bring his mother to LA with him. (Eileen Lydon had already been diagnosed with the stomach cancer that would claim her life before the year was out. After the meeting Lydon flew on to Toronto to enable his mother to see her sister for the first time in many years.)

Rotten had the greatest respect for Regehr, but reiterated his stance regarding the Pistols, and suggested that Warners' money would be better put to use financing his new musical ventures, whatever they might be. Though happy to listen to Rotten's overtures, Regehr's immediate priority lay in was cajoling the singer to giving his consent towards the *Swindle* project.

Rotten hadn't set eyes on McLaren since their acrimonious tête-à-tête in San Francisco and the latter's sending Tiberi out to Jamaica on a spying mission had merely exacerbated his contempt. When the two came face-to-face the following morning at the Continental Hyatt House Hotel, Rotten took great delight in imposing several non-negotiable content stipulations to which he knew McLaren could never possibly comply. McLaren still had a couple of cards up his sleeve, however, and Rotten was in Toronto with his mother when he discovered McLaren was insisting that the stage name "Johnny Rotten" was the property of Glitterbest. McLaren was also asking for 25 percent of all money Rotten had earned as a Sex Pistol in accordance with the Glitterbest contract.

Rotten wanted nothing more than to put the Pistols behind him and move on with his life and career, but McLaren's pettiness left him seething. He decided to fight fire with fire. On returning to London he hired Brian Carr, a no-nonsense litigation solicitor who specialized in the music business. Carr's first act in the *Lydon v. Glitterbest* court battle that was to endure for the next eight years was to send a letter to McLaren asking him to supply Sex Pistols accounts, as per the band's Glitterbest contract, from the two quarters up to September 30, 1977.

While Lydon, as he'd now reverted to calling himself, was locking horns with McLaren, Jones, Cook, and Vicious shared a stage together one last time performing the title track for the *Swindle* movie. McLaren had hired the pub rock bastion, the Hope & Anchor in Islington, to stage mock auditions for a stand-in singer to replace Rotten. Jones doesn't remember much about the session as by his own admission he was "drunk off my arse…. I suppose that was Malcolm's way of showing Johnny that the band didn't need him, but what it actually showed was the opposite."[4]

Jones and Cook had recorded two songs with Ronnie Biggs (whom the UK press would playfully dub "Ronnie Rotten") while in Rio de Janeiro. The first of these was a reworking of "Belsen Was a Gas" with alternate verses penned by Biggs, while "No One Is Innocent" was a new song featuring a lyric in which the Great Train Robber blithely exonerates the crimes of Moors Murderers Ian Brady and Myra Hindley and Ugandan despot Idi Amin.

During the summer, Jones and Cook worked as hired hands on Johnny Thunders' debut solo album, *So Alone*. The duo would also make several appearances with Thunders' ad hoc outfit Johnny Thunders' Allstars at The Speakeasy, the preferred watering hole of London's music fraternity. Thin Lizzy front man Phil Lynott had also guested on Thunders' album. This in turn led to another collaboration which saw Jones and Cook teaming up with Lynott and his fellow Lizzies Scott Gorham, Brian Downey, and Gary Moore as The Greedy Bastards. A show was booked at the Electric Circus in Camden Town at the end of July, but owing to their respective commitments several months would pass before they performed live again.

(It wasn't until the following year when, finally free of their involvement with the *Swindle* movie, that Jones and Cook were able to channel their energies with The Professionals.)

"No One Is Innocent" (VS 220) was released as a single in the UK at the end of June. As if having a wanted fugitive supplying the vocal wasn't enough to guarantee tabloid outrage, McLaren had wanted to release the track as "Cosh the Driver," in tasteless reference to the train robbers' assault on Jack Mills, the driver of the mail train. Indeed, he and Jamie Reid went as far as preparing the artwork under the alternate title.

Despite a total lack of airplay on daytime radio, "No One Is Innocent" reached # 7 on the UK chart, outselling all four previous Sex Pistols singles into the bargain. However, while the single's performance in the charts appeared to justify McLaren's claim that "anyone could be a Sex Pistol," it was Vicious' rendition of Paul Anka's "My Way" on the flip side that proved of interest to the fans.

♪ ♪ ♪

Vicious had been the first Sex Pistol to arrive back in London (January 21), but unlike Rotten's return several days later, the UK media hadn't deemed the bassist's return of any import. Reunited with his beloved Nancy, Vicious rarely ventured from their Maida Vale drug lair other than to collect his weekly stipend from the Glitterbest offices. As with most bands, the Pistols' sum had proved greater than its respective parts, but whereas Jones and Cook could at least rely on their ability as musicians, Vicious was left to rue his willful refusal to improve on his rudimentary skills.

In late-January, Lech Kowalski and his film crew had arrived at Pindock Mews accompanied by *NME* scribe Chris Salewicz to interview Vicious about the Pistols' break-up for *D.O.A.: A Right of Passage*. Despite Salewicz's valiant efforts, however, Kowalski had to settle for Spungen doing most of the talking as Vicious was so out of it that he kept nodding off mid-sentence. "What was so striking about that visit to Pindock Mews was how tragic it all seemed," says Salewicz today. "Sid was not at all well. He'd collapsed on a plane flight in America, I believe, and been hospitalized with pneumonia. The room that housed the bed on which he and Nancy lay was surrounded by empty prescription cough medicine bottles, including—unsurprisingly—the morphine-based Collis Browne. It seemed pretty clear that Sid had done some of those bad drugs he shouldn't have gone near before we arrived. But he was also pretty ill, in shockingly bad shape."[5]

A lifeline of sorts appeared out of the blue in February when Johnny Thunders invited Vicious to play bass in The Living Dead, another of his impromptu Speakeasy ensembles. Vicious had naively thought of himself and Thunders as kindred spirits, but his return to the spotlight ended in ignominious failure.

One of the songs Vicious was required to learn for the All Stars' set was "Steppin' Stone." The song's simple E/G/A/C riff apparently proved too much for Vicious, however. Only Ones front man Peter Perritt, who had also appeared on *So Alone* and was guesting as an All Star, told Vicious to just play the E and was bemused to find that the ex-Sex Pistol didn't know where to find the note on his bass.

Speaking with Nina Antonia for her 2015 book, *The One & Only: Peter Perritt, Homme Fatale*, Perritt revealed that Thunders had wanted to give Vicious the elbow and that it was only his pleadings for clemency that saw Thunders relent. Thunders had one proviso, however; that Vicious' amp be switched off during the performance. "It was Johnny's pre-condition for allowing Sid to play," Perritt explains. "It became pretty clear at the soundcheck that even learning one song would be difficult for Sid. I persuaded Johnny to let Sid play as he had the enthusiasm of an innocent, and I didn't have the heart to disappoint him. Also, Living Dead gigs had a certain amount of chaos surrounding them anyway, so Sid's silent appearance didn't seem incongruous. After three songs, Sid noticed the absence of bass sound and started haranguing the roadies to fix it. At this point Johnny thanked him for his contribution and he was replaced by Henri-Paul [Tortosa of The Maniacs]."[6]

Thunders had also insisted that Spungen go up on stage topless to introduce the All-stars. Perritt says Thunders hadn't intended to humiliate Nancy and probably didn't notice the hurt in Vicious' eyes. It's since gone down in punk folklore that it was their ejection from Junkie Johnny's court that set Vicious and Spungen on their tragic tailspin, but Perritt offers a different perspective. "Sid worshipped Johnny, and enjoyed himself immensely while he was on stage ... even if Nancy's topless introduction of the band wasn't perhaps to his liking."

Vicious and Jones were reunited again in Paris for the recording of "My Way." McLaren had wanted Vicious to record "Non, je ne regrette rien," the French standard made famous by Edith Piaf, for inclusion on *The Great Rock 'n' Roll Swindle* soundtrack, but that Vicious had insisted on "My Way." An arrangement was worked out which saw Vicious mock-

Ten. Aftermath

crooning the opening verse before speeding things up with Jones' telltale chugging riffs giving the song a Sex Pistols feel. An accompanying promo video was shot at the Paris Olympia music hall on the Boulevard des Capucines.

Aside from "My Way," Vicious would also record souped-up versions of the Eddie Cochrane classics "C'mon Everybody" and "Something Else" for the *Swindle* soundtrack. (Both would be released as singles in the wake of Vicious' death and reach the UK Top 3.)

According to Tiberi, the intention behind the Paris trip had nothing to do with any recording. "Malcolm and I flew to Paris to meet with Eddie Barclay from Barclay Records. [The Pistols had signed a two-year deal with Barclay to cover France, Switzerland, Zanzibar, and Algeria in May 1977.] Warners had stopped the money they had put into the film the moment John walked out of the band, and Malcolm was desperate to get fresh funding. The idea to put Sid in front of a microphone probably came about at the hotel bar. It was Malcolm's way of saying, 'Fuck you!'—at a distance—to John. But there was never any serious intention of establishing Sid as John's replacement in the Pistols. That would never have worked. I mean, 'My Way's great and everything, but Sid and Nancy were beyond redemption by that point, literally beyond redemption."

In late June, Vicious was reunited with Hellin Killer. Killer had been in London several weeks when she inadvertently happened upon Vicious and Spungen on the King's Road. She was unsure as to whether Vicious would remember her, but her fears were instantly allayed when he came bounding towards her and gave her a hug. Spungen surprisingly welcomed her fellow American with open arms and insisted Killer move into Pindock Mews. "Yes, I ran into Sid and Nancy when I got to London. I'd booked a one-way ticket on Laker airlines from New York. I was always going off on my own, but wherever I went I had friends there. It's true Nancy invited me to live with them. She was a real friend to me, and I to her.

"While I was living there they just did ordinary stuff: go out to gigs, or to the local pub, or go out to buy fish and chips. Boogie came round a few times. And Steve English did as well. What a guy! He was a bouncer who looked after Sid. He used to kinda look out for me while I was in London. In fact, he was the one who told me my family was there looking for me!

"Looking back, I feel like I was fated to meet Sid, then Nancy, live with them, and look after them for a while. Sid was a big deal to me."

Vicious was now a free agent as before leaving Paris he'd forced McLaren to relinquish all managerial rights. Seeing Vicious in front of the microphone had convinced Spungen that her beau could be a star in New York. But as Vicious wouldn't be receiving royalties from the sales of "No One Is Innocent"/"My Way" until later in the year, they had no viable means of raising the cash to fund their venture. Help, however, was literally just around the corner.

In a strange quirk of fate, Vicious lived within spitting distance of Glen Matlock, and the two would occasionally meet up for a drink. Matlock, who was in the Rich Kids at the time, remembers it was during one of these get-togethers that the idea to do a show together materialized. Having recruited Matlock's fellow Rich Kid Steve New on guitar and ex-Damned drummer Rat Scabies, the Vicious White Kids, as they would be calling themselves for the one-off show, knuckled down to rehearsals before setting a mid–August date at the Electric Circus in Camden Town. (The repertoire consisted of "My Way," "Something Else,"

"C'mon Everybody," "Belsen Was a Gas," and several other punk rock standards such as The Stooges' "I Wanna Be Your Dog."

In the run-up to the Electric Ballroom show, Vicious and Spungen received a shocking wake up call when their drug buddy—19-year-old studio assistant John Shepcott—overdosed on a "speedball" (street slang for a cocktail of cocaine and heroin). Shepcote's untimely demise not only brought unwarranted attention from the police, but also galvanized Vicious and Spungen to seek help for their crippling addiction by entering a methadone program at a private hospital in Harrow-on-the-Hill, northwest London. Their attempt at rehabilitation would prove short-lived, however, as the week following the Camden show Vicious and Spungen left London bound for New York.

Killer elected to remain in London rather than accompany Vicious and Spungen to New York. Vicious' parting gift to Killer was the tuxedo he'd worn in the "My Way" promo video.

♪ ♪ ♪

Upon their arrival in New York, Vicious and Spungen booked themselves into the notorious Hotel Chelsea on West 23rd Street. The Chelsea had been designated a New York City Landmark in 1966, but by the summer of 1978 the hotel was regarded as the last refuge of wannabe actors and down-at-heel musicians. Spungen was now acting as Vicious' manager, and through her connections managed to secure her lover a string of dates at Max's Kansas City, the legendary restaurant/nightclub on Park Avenue South which had come to prominence in the Sixties thanks to Andy Warhol's patronage.

Prior to embarking for London and snaring herself a Sex Pistol, Spungen had attached herself to Jerry Nolan. Nolan was now drumming with The Idols, the band he'd formed in London with Vicious and Spungen's pal Steve Dior (born Steven Hershcowitz). With Nolan's fellow ex-New York Doll Arthur "Killer" Kane borrowing Vicious' blood-spattered bass for the occasion, The Idols provided the backing when Vicious made his Max's debut on Thursday, September 7.

The upstairs room at Max's held around 600 people, and Vicious' celebrity as an ex-Sex Pistol was enough to ensure a sell-out crowd. There would be two performances each evening, but as Vicious didn't have the wherewithal to keep straight until the end of the night, the second sets were often shambolic affairs. The final Max's date saw Mick Jones co-opted into The Idols' ad hoc line-up. Jones, who was in town with Joe Strummer mixing The Clash's second album, *Give 'Em Enough Rope*, had once shared a squat with Vicious and was shocked to see his friend lumbering about the stage in a somnambulistic state. "We just about managed about five songs. It was a nightmare between shows, it was full on. Sid was sort of semi there. It was a serious drug thing. Me and Joe kept looking at each other 'cos we couldn't believe it. The people there were as far out of it as you can be without actually being dead."[7]

With no other shows until the first of two dates at the Artemis in Spungen's home town of Philadelphia on October 18, she and Vicious withdrew from public view and spent each evening holed up in the Chelsea blotting out their miserable existence with a cornucopia of drugs procured with the money Vicious received for the Max's shows. Heroin remained the couple's drug de jour, and when that wasn't available they could always rely on a daily dose of methadone (a synthetic opioid), which the couple procured from a dispensing clinic in Lower Manhattan. By this time, however, they were both also hopelessly hooked on barbiturates such as Tuinol and Dilaudid—a synthetic morphine normally given to terminal cancer patients.

During the first week of October, Vicious and Spungen's drug fund received a significant boost following a royalty payment of $20,000—$100,000 at today's value—from Virgin Records for "My Way." As neither of them had a U.S. bank account they rather unwisely kept the cash in their hotel room. Needless to say, news of Vicious' windfall soon hit the streets and the Chelsea became a magnet for every drug addict and drug runner in the city.

Late in the evening of Thursday, October 12, Spungen was seen arguing with a third party through a gap in the open door to room 100 by aspiring actor Victor Colicchio (*Summer of Sam*, *Inside Man*, *The Brave One*). Colicchio couldn't see the other party, but assumed whoever it was had arrived unannounced as Spungen appeared ready for bed.[8] At some point during the night, Vicious awoke to find a trail of blood leading through into the room's tiny en-suite bathroom where Spungen—dressed in black knickers and matching bra—lay slumped on the floor between the toilet and washbasin with Vicious' recently purchased Jaguar K-11 knife protruding from her abdomen.

Theories have abounded ever since as to what occurred that fateful night, but as Vicious—either by accident or design—overdosed on heroin in early February 1979 while on bail for Spungen's murder, the truth will probably never be known.

What is certain, however, is that the wound to Spungen's abdomen was far from fatal, and had medical assistance been summoned she would have survived. If Vicious had roused from his Tuinol-induced slumber and stabbed Spungen, why would she crawl into the bathroom instead of out into the hallway to raise the alarm? And what happened to the Virgin royalty cash that the couple kept in a bedside table? The only conclusion that can be drawn is that whoever stabbed Spungen also took the cash and that they remained until she lost consciousness.

New York Police Department officers responding to the 911 call arrived at the Chelsea to find Vicious with his hands and T-shirt (ironically, a Sex Pistols '78 U.S. Tour T-shirt) covered in blood. Vicious was taken to the Third Homicide Division on East 51st Street, where he was processed and charged with second-degree murder under his real name, Simon John Beverly. (Despite Vicious' death certificate—issued by New York Chief Medical Examiner Dr. Michael Baden on March 7, 1979—stating his name as "John Simon Ritchie," his birth certificate states "Simon John Ritchie.")

Having entered a plea of not guilty at a specially convened hearing the following day, Vicious was remanded at Riker's Island, New York's main jail complex, on the East River between Queens and mainland Bronx. Owing to the five-hour time difference between New York and London, it was Friday afternoon in London when the news came through of Spungen's murder and Vicious' arrest. McLaren was at Glitterbest's offices working on the *Swindle* movie when a tabloid journalist called to give him the news.[9]

According to eyewitnesses at the Chelsea, Vicious had told the arresting officers that they couldn't arrest him because he was a "rock 'n' roll star."[10] The sad truth, of course, is that Vicious' star had long been on the wane. Indeed, it was only in death that he would achieve lasting recognition of sorts as punk's doomed poster boy.

♪ ♪ ♪

In another quirk of fate, John Lydon's new band, Public Image Ltd., released their debut single, "Public Image" (VS 228), in the UK the same day that news of Vicious' arrest broke in London. Aside from himself, the line-up consisted of his and Vicious' old college mate Jah Wobble (a.k.a. John Wardle) on bass, ex-Clash guitarist Keith Levene, and Canadian-born drummer Jim Walker. When presenting his new outfit to the UK music media earlier in the year, Lydon revealed that he'd part-lifted the band name from quirky Scottish authoress Muriel Spark's 1968 novel *The Public Image*. (The "Limited" was added as the band was to be run as a company rather than a band, with Lydon, Wobble, Levene, and Walker each serving as directors.)

With Lydon still being contracted to Virgin, there was never any doubt that "PiL," as the band quickly became known, would sign with Branson's label. Although Bob Regehr was as yet undecided whether to pick up the option for Warners to promote the band in the U.S., he nonetheless handed Lydon the cash to enable him to put a deposit down on an end-of-terrace townhouse in Fulham.

Shortly after his moving into his new abode (45 Gunter Grove), Lydon had received a surprise visit from Vicious and Spungen. It seemed Vicious was keen to rekindle their friendship in the hope that they might work together again at some point in the near future. Lydon admits to his having proved amenable to the idea, but Spungen, in her own inimitable way, put a damper on the proposal by brashly declaring that Vicious be the star of any such collaboration. When Lydon had enquired what his role might be, Spungen said he could be the drummer. Lydon was forced to grit his teeth a second time when Spungen dismissed his songwriting as "shit,"[11] but his rapidly fraying temper finally snapped when Vicious asked to borrow some money.

Lydon had sent the pair packing, little caring whether he saw his old friend again. His simmering resentment had dissipated on hearing Vicious had been charged with Spungen's murder. He'd desperately wanted to help—especially upon hearing McLaren would be accompanying Vicious' mother out to New York—but had more pressing matters to attend to as Virgin were keen to get PiL's debut album recorded and pressed in time for the Christmas market.

Chapter Notes

Introduction

1. John Lydon with Andrew Perry, *Anger Is an Energy* (London: Simon & Schuster, 2015).
2. *Daily Mirror*, December 2, 1976.
3. *Never Mind the Sex Pistols: An Alternate History* (Demon DVD, 2007).
4. Steve Jones, *Lonely Boy: Tales From a Sex Pistol* (London: Penguin, 2016).
5. *Ibid.*

Chapter One

1. Interview with author.
2. Legs McNeil and Gillian McCain, *Please Kill Me: The Uncensored Oral History of Punk* (New York: Grove, 1996).
3. Ray Stevenson, *Sex Pistols File* (London: Omnibus, 1978).
4. *The Washington Post*, October 2004.

Chapter Two

1. John Lydon with Keith Zimmerman and Kent Zimmerman, *Rotten: No Irish, No Blacks, No Dogs* (London: Hodder & Stoughton, 1994).
2. Interview with the author.
3. *Daily Mail*, January 4, 1978.
4. www.robertchristgau.com.
5. Interview with the author.
6. Interview with Lauren Griffin (courtesy Lauren Griffin).
7. Interview with the author.
8. Interview with the author.
9. Interview with the author.
10. Interview with the author.
11. Lydon with Zimmerman and Zimmerman, *Rotten*.
12. www.clatl.com.
13. www.robertchristgau.com.
14. Interview with the author.
15. Interview with the author.
16. Interview with the author.
17. Interview with the author.
18. Interview with the author.
19. www.robertchristgau.com.
20. Interview with the author.
21. Interview with the author.
22. www.swimmingpoolqs.com.
23. Interview with the author.
24. *The American Music Press* (March 1994), courtesy Devorah Ostrov.
25. McNeil and McCain, *Please Kill Me*.

Chapter Three

1. *Record Mirror* (January 1978), courtesy Barry Cain.
2. Interview with the author.
3. *Record Mirror* (December 1976), courtesy Barry Cain.
4. Noel E. Monk and Jimmy Guterman, *12 Days on the Road: The Sex Pistols and America* (New York: Quill, 1990).
5. Interview with the author.
6. Monk and Guterman, *12 Days on the Road*.
7. Interview with the author.
8. Interview with the author.
9. Interview with the author.
10. Chris Harrington, *The Memphis Flyer* (January 1978), courtesy Bruce Van Wyngarden.
11. Interview with the author.
12. Jon Savage, *England's Dreaming* (London: Faber and Faber, 1991).
13. Interview with the author.
14. www.lechkowalski.com.
15. Monk and Guterman, *12 Days on the Road*.
16. *The Commercial Appeal* (January 1978).
17. Chris Harrington, *The Memphis Flyer* (January 1978), courtesy Bruce Van Wyngarden.
18. *Ibid.*
19. *Ibid.*
20. *Ibid.*
21. *Ibid.*

Chapter Four

1. *San Antonio Current* (October 2012).
2. Stephen Colgrave and Chris Sullivan, *Punk* (London: Cassell, 2001).
3. www.randysrodeo.com.
4. Interview with the author.
5. Interview with the author.
6. Interview with the author.
7. Monk and Guterman, *12 Days on the Road*.
8. Lydon with Zimmerman and Zimmerman, *Rotten*.
9. *Punk* #14 (May 1978), courtesy John Holmstrom.

10. Interview with the author.
11. Interview with the author.
12. Interview with the author.
13. *San Antonio Current* (January 2013).
14. Interview with the author.
15. Interview with the author.
16. Interview with the author.
17. *The Austin Chronicle* (January 2003), courtesy Margaret Moser.
18. Savage, *England's Dreaming*.
19. *Sounds* (January 1978).
20. www.mysanantonio.com (January 2003).
21. *The Evening News* (January 1978).
22. Jones, *Lonely Boy*.
23. Interview with the author.

Chapter Five

1. McNeil and McCain, *Please Kill Me*.
2. Jones, *Lonely Boy*.
3. Lydon with Zimmerman and Zimmerman, *Rotten*.
4. Robert Day interview with Melissa Eastin in November 2012 (courtesy Melissa Eastin, East Baton Rouge Library).
5. *Ibid.*
6. Interview with the author.
7. Interview with the author.
8. Interview with the author.
9. *Gris Gris* (January 1978), courtesy Melissa Eastin, East Baton Rouge Library).
10. *Ibid.*
11. Interview with the author.
12. Interview with the author.
13. Interview with the author.
14. Interview with the author.
15. Interview with the author.
16. www.rockindopsiejr.com.
17. *Gris Gris* (January 1978).
18. Interview with the author.
19. *Gris Gris* (January 1978).
20. Interview with the author.
21. Interview with the author.
22. Interview with the author.
23. *Baton Rouge State-Times*, January 10, 1978.
24. *Ibid.*
25. Monk and Guterman, *12 Days on the Road*.

Chapter Six

1. www.txmusic.com.
2. www.flashbackdallas.com.
3. Interview with the author.
4. Interview with the author.
5. *The Filth and the Fury: Sex Pistols* (New York: St. Martin's, 2000).
6. Jones, *Lonely Boy*.
7. *Punk* #14.
8. Savage, *England's Dreaming*.
9. Interview with the author.
10. Interview with the author.
11. Interview with the author.
12. Interview with the author.
13. Interview with the author.
14. Interview with the author.
15. Interview with the author.
16. Interview with the author.
17. Interview with the author.
18. Interview with the author.
19. Interview with the author.
20. *Stagelife* (February 1978), courtesy Jim Parrett.
21. *Rolling Stone* (February 1978).
22. *Ibid.*

Chapter Seven

1. Lydon with Zimmerman and Zimmerman, *Rotten*.
2. McNeil and McCain, *Please Kill Me*.
3. "Sex Pistols and America," British Museum, July 2016.
4. www.cainsballroom.com.
5. Interview with the author.
6. Interview with the author.
7. Monk and Guterman, *12 Days on the Road*.
8. www.tulsapeople.com.
9. Interview with the author.
10. Interview with the author.
11. Interview with the author.
12. Interview with the author.
13. Interview with the author.
14. Lydon with Zimmerman and Zimmerman, *Rotten*.
15. Interview with the author.
16. Interview with the author.

Chapter Eight

1. *Stagelife* (February 1978), courtesy Jim Parrett.
2. www.thrasherswheat.org.
3. *The Filth and the Fury: Sex Pistols*.
4. *Ibid.*
5. *Helsingin Sanomat*.
6. *The Sun* (January 1978).
7. Nick Russell-Pavier and Stewart Richards, *The Great Train Robbery: Crime of the Century: The Definitive Account* (London: Phoenix, 2012).
8. Savage, *England's Dreaming*.
9. Interview with the author.
10. www.sylviesimmons.com, courtesy Sylvie Simmons.
11. McNeil and McCain, *Please Kill Me*.
12. God Save the Sex Pistols website's interview with Jim Draper, courtesy Phil Singleton.
13. Interview with the author.
14. Interview with the author.
15. Interview with the author.
16. www.sfgate.com (January 2012).
17. www.laweekly.com (June 2002).
18. Interview with the author.
19. Interview with the author.
20. Jones, *Lonely Boy*.
21. Interview with the author.
22. Interview with the author.

Chapter Nine

1. www.sylviesimmons.com, courtesy Sylvie Simmons.
2. McNeil and McCain, *Please Kill Me.*
3. Craig Bromberg, *The Wicked Ways of Malcolm McLaren* (New York: Harper & Row, 1989).
4. Interview with the author.
5. Interview with the author.
6. Belinda Carlisle, *Lips Unsealed: A Memoir* (New York: Crown, 2010).
7. *Ibid.*
8. Interview with the author
9. Savage, *England's Dreaming.*
10. *Record Mirror* (April 1978).
11. *The Filth and the Fury: Sex Pistols.*
12. *The Filth and the Fury: Sex Pistols.*
13. *Punk #14*
14. *Ibid.*

Chapter Ten

1. Interview with the author.
2. Marc Spitz and Brendan Mullen, *We Got the Neutron Bomb: The Untold Story of LA Punk* (New York: Three Rivers, 2001).
3. *Daily Telegraph* (November 2007).
4. Jones, *Lonely Boy.*
5. Interview with the author.
6. Interview with the author.
7. Pat Gilbert, *Passion Is a Fashion* (London: Aurum, 2004).
8. Interview with Victor Colicchio in *Who Killed Nancy?* (Ipso Facto Films. 2009).
9. Alan G. Parker, *Sid Vicious: No One Is Innocent* (London: Orion, 2007).
10. *Ibid.*
11. Lydon with Zimmerman and Zimmerman, *Rotten.*

Bibliography

Books

Bromberg, Craig. *The Wicked Ways of Malcolm McLaren*. New York: Harper & Row, 1989.

Colgrave, Stephen, and Chris Sullivan. *Punk*. London: Cassell 2001.

The Filth and the Fury: Sex Pistols. New York: St. Martin's, 2000.

Gilbert, Pat. *Passion Is a Fashion*. London: Aurum, 2004.

Jones, Steve. *Lonely Boy: Tales from a Sex Pistol*. London: Penguin, 2016.

Lydon, John, with Andrew Perry. *Anger Is an Energy*. London: Simon & Schuster, 2015.

Lydon, John, with Keith Zimmerman and Kent Zimmerman. *Rotten: No Irish, No Blacks, No Dogs*. London: Hodder & Stoughton, 1994.

Monk, Noel E., and Jimmy Guterman. *12 Days on the Road: The Sex Pistols and America*. New York: Quill, 1990.

McNeil, Legs, and Gillian McCain. *Please Kill Me: The Uncensored Oral History of Punk*. New York: Grove, 1996.

Parker, Alan G. *Sid Vicious: No One Is Innocent*. London: Orion, 2007.

Russell-Pavier, Nick, and Stewart Richards. *The Great Train Robbery: Crime of the Century: The Definitive Account*. London: Phoenix, 2012.

Savage, Jon. *England's Dreaming*. London: Faber & Faber, 1991.

Spitz, Marc, and Brendan Mullen. *We Got the Neutron Bomb: The Untold Story of LA Punk*. New York: Three Rivers, 2001.

Stevenson, Ray. *Sex Pistols File*. London: Omnibus, 1978.

Newspapers

The Austin Chronicle.
Baton Rouge State-Times.
The Commercial Appeal.
Daily Mail.
Daily Mirror.
Daily Telegraph.
The Evening News.
Helsingin Sanomat.
The Memphis Flyer.
San Antonio Current.
The Sun.
Village Voice.
The Washington Post.

Magazines and Periodicals

The American Music Press.
Gris Gris.
Punk.
Record Mirror.
Rolling Stone.
Stagelife.

Interviews

Anders, Smiley. Email, August 3, 2016.
Arguelles, Trudie. Email, March 10, 2017.
Bayley, Roberta. Email, March 6, 2017.
Bentley, Bill. Email, October 4, 2016.
Berlin, Gabi. Email, January 9, 2017.
Blacker, Clarke. Email, March 9, 2017.
Blue, David. Email, March 10, 2017.
Bourgeois, Kevin. Email, March 9, 2017.
Broughton, Don. Telephone, April 3, 2017.
Brown, Hugh. Email, January 15, 2017.
Cain, Barry. Email, September 5, 2016.
Campbell, Susan A. Email, July 26, 2017.
Chapman, E. Winslow "Buddy." Email, November 14, 2016.
Childress, Bob. Email, December 11, 2016.
Cochran, Doreen. Email, August 10, 2016.
Dutton, Tom. Email, September 22, 2016.
Edwards, Thom "Tex." Email, February 16, 2017.
Ellis, Greg. Email, March 19, 2017.
Evans, Donjon. Email, January 31, 2017.
Flowers, Eddie. Email, April 3, 2017.
Flowers, Lannie. Email, September 1, 2016.
Freeman, Carlton. Email, December 7, 2016.
Freeman, Getty. Email, January 10, 2017.
Galbraith, Richard. Email, January 20, 2017.
Gehman, Pleasant. Email, March 26, 2017.
Golightly, Jeff. Email, October 5, 2017.
Gowdy, Vernon L. Email, October 5, 2016.
Graves, Tom. Email, September 10, 2016.
Gray, Nancy. Email, October 2, 2017.

Griffin, Freddi. Email, September 19, 2016.
Griffin, Lauren. Email, September 19, 2016
Groom, Doug. Email, February 5, 2017.
Guarnieri, John. Email, April 10, 2017.
Hall, Stacy. Email, September 30, 2016.
Haslett, Mike. Email, February 11, 2017.
Hibbert, Jonny. Email, October 18, 2016.
Hoffman, Kristian. Email, July 3, 2017.
Hoge, Ken. Email, October 3, 2017.
Holmstrom, John. Email, October 31, 2016.
Houston, Penelope. Telephone, February 2, 2017.
Huebner, Barry "Kooda." Email, February 9, 2017.
Ingraham, Greg. Email, February 5, 2017.
Izbrand, Sig McKenna. Email, October 14, 2016.
Johnston, Rory. Telephone, November 1, 2017.
Keeling, Gaylon. Email, March 12, 2017.
Kereakes, Theresa. Email, January 16, 2017.
Knight, Saran. Email, February 6, 2017.
Lindsay, David T. Email, September 8, 2017.
Living, Jarboe. Email, September 14, 2017.
Martin, Dana. Email, March 11, 2017.
May, Steve. Email, September 25, 2016.
McLaughlin, Sean. Email, October 2016.
Merlis, Bob. Telephone, February, 19, 2017.
Moser, Margaret. Email, October 4, 2017.
Orgeron, Brad. Email, March 5, 2017.
Ostrov, Devorah. Email, April 14, 2017.
Parrett, Jim. Email, February 23, 2017.
Parrish, Tim. Email, March 3, 2017.
Patton, Rex. Email, September 2, 2016.
Perrett, Peter. Email, April 24, 2017.
Powell, Sharon. Email, September 15, 2016.
Pugliese, Joe. Email, October 19, 2016.
Reinhalter, Earl. Email, October 9, 2016.
Rhoades, Darryl. Email, September 7, 2016.
Roessler, Helena "Hellin Killer." Email, January 11, 2017.
Ruth, Cyril A. Email, April 6, 2017.
St. John, Lamar A. Email, January 18, 2017.
Salewicz, Chris. Email, May 10, 2017.
Schaeffer, Larry. Email, March 2, 2017.
Sewell, Greg. Email, February 6, 2017.
Storch, Tony. Email, February 4, 2017.
Stroud, Lynn. Email, September 20, 2016.
Sublett, Jesse. Email, October 8, 2016.
Tiberi, John. Telephone, May 17, 2017.
Valentine, Kathy. Email, October 14, 2017.
Vontillius, Alun. Email, September 24, 2017.
Weatherman, Annette. Email, February 19, 2017.
Weems, Jane. Email, February 27, 2017.
Widner, Ellis. Email, March 16, 2017.
Wiley, John F. Email, October 11, 2016.
Young, Dan. Email, January 21, 2017.

Index

A&M Records 7, 131
Abshire, Nathan 76
Advocate 80
Aerosmith 74, 85
Alfonso, Ralph 96
Allin, GG 38
Allison, Glenn 35, 43, 54, 81, 102
Allison, Mose 72
Allman Brothers 42
American Psycho 43
Amin, Idi 161
Anders, Smiley 80, 81
Anderson, Jennifer "Miro" 135, 136
Anka, Paul 162
Antonia, Nina 162
Archer, Ward
Arguelles, Trudie 90, 101, 102, 130, 145; guest-list at Longhorn Ballroom 93; Vicious infatuated with 92
Arkansas Democrat-Gazette 114
Austin, Mo. 12, 30
Austin Chronicle 52
Austin Sun 52, 53, 62
Autry, Gene 106
Avengers 124, 136, 137, 138, 142, 151
Avengers EP 139

Bacharach, Burt 7
Baden, Michael Dr. 165
Bags 129
Bailey, David 159
Barclay, Eddie 163
Barge, Dave 22
Barrett, Keith 92
Barsalona, Frank 10
Baton Rouge
Baton Rouge State Times 81
Bators, Stiv 149
Bay City Rollers 32, 131
Bayley, Roberta 98, 128, 130, 140, 155, 156; atmosphere inside Longhorn Ballroom 101; atmosphere inside Randy's Rodeo 63–64; invited onto tour by Forçade 55; meeting McLaren and Westwood 56; playfight with Sid on tour bus 82–83; religious protest outside Cain's Ballroom 115; Sex Pistols speaking with fans at Randy's Rodeo 65, 80; Vicious' early death prophesy 89

Beach Boys 69
Beatles 50, 97, 101, 107, 109, 132, 133
Beatty, Warren 149
Bentley, Bill 53, 62, 64, 66
Berlin, Gabi 100, 139–140, 145, 149; dinner with Sex Pistols in Dallas 94; discovered the Sex Pistols 89, 90, 91, 92; "kidnapped" Vicious in Dallas 93; Sex Pistols' arrival at Longhorn Ballroom 92
Bernstein, Sid 11
Berry, Chuck 95
Beverly, Anne 65
Biggs, Ronnie 126, 146, 150, 155, 161; prison break after Great Train Robbery 126–127
Billboard magazine 34, 118
Bingenheimer, Rodney 147
Birdboys 139
Blacker, Clarke 95–96
Blair, Tony 43
Blake, John 89
Blank Generation 156
Bliss 115, 116, 118
Blondie 42, 136, 143
Blue, David 115–117
Blue Öyster Cult 116
Bogart, Neil 12
Bolan, Marc 128
Boomtown Rats 59
Bormann, Martin 155
Boston 116
Bottom, Rock 149
Bourgeois, Kevin 76, 80
Brady, Ian 161
Brady, Tate W. 106
Branson, Richard 7, 159, 166
Broughton, Do: early life 109; filming Sex Pistols in Dallas 109–110
Brown, Hugh 142, 143, 146
Browne, Jackson 134
Burn Something Beautiful 136
Buzzcocks 59, 112, 139

Cain, Barry 69; interviewed Johnny Rotten 34–35; encountering Vicious at airport 36
Cain, Madison W. ("Daddy Cain") 106
Calder, Jeff 31
Cale, JJ 110

Cale, John 11
Campbell, Susan A. 134–135, 146
Capitol Records 30
Carlisle, Belinda 129, 148
Carpenters 7
Carr, Brian 161
Casablanca Records 12
Casale, Bob 159
Cash, Johnny 16
CBS Records 7, 136, 160
Cervenka, Exene 90
Chapman, E. Winslow "Buddy": crowd unrest outside Taliesyn Ballroom 46–47; Sex Pistols in Memphis 40; Sex Pistols' reputation 41; Sex Pistols' worth 49
Cheap Thrills 96
Childers, Leee Black 69
Childress, Bob 97–98, 98
Christgau, Robert 21, 25, 29
Chrome, Cheetah 156
Clarke, Al 157
Clash 11, 18, 22, 32, 50, 80, 101, 109, 147, 164
A Clockwork Orange 48
Cobain, Kurt 156
Cochran, Doreen 24, 29
Cochran, Eddie 60, 163
Cohen, Ted 44, 64, 84, 108, 146, 150
Colicchio, Victor 165
Cooder, Ry 70
Cook, Paul 9, 13, 30, 31, 39, 57, 60, 62, 65; 73, 77, 86, 95, 99, 102, 122, 124, 127, 128, 137, 143, 150, 153, 155, 156, 161; attack on 69; questioned Lydon's claim about rooms at Miyako 125
Cooley, Alex 24, 28
Cooper, Alice 32, 46, 95, 130
Costello, Elvis 16–17
Crash, Darby 148, 149
Crash 'n' Burn 96
Cream 113
Creem 59, 118, 149
Crime 135
Crowe, Sheryl 27
Cruise-O-Matic 24, 26
Crum, Bill 112

Daalder, Rene 155
Daily Express 126
Dallas Morning News 104

Dallas Observer 95
Damned 23, 109, 147
Dangerhouse Records 137
Dawson, Walter 40, 50
Day, Robert 70
Dead Boys 149, 156
Dean, Marilyn 59
Deep Purple 71, 113
Deep Throat 82
Depress, James 62
Detrick, Ritchie 135, 136
Devil in Miss Jones 82
Devo 133, 149, 159
Devoto, Howard 139
Dictators 72
Dior, Steve 164
D.O.A.: A Right of Passage 42, 48, 101, 114, 115, 162
Doe, John 90
Donahue, Rod 149
Doobie Brothers 15
Downey, Brian 161
Draper, Jim 132
Dutton, Tom 111, 114

Eagles 15, 40
Eastin, Melissa
Eddie and the Hot Rods 59
Edwards, Jonathon 22
Edwards, T. Tex 95
Ellis, Greg 71, 73, 74, 79, 81
EMI Records 6, 30, 32, 160
England's Dreaming 126
Epic Records 12
Escovedo, Alejandro 135, 136
Evans, Donjon 59, 60
Evening Standard 89

Faltin, Brian 65
Fields, Danny 131
Filth and the Fury 41, 101, 132
Fisher, Stephen 12, 159
Flamin' Groovies 95
Fleetwood Mac 40
Fleury, Joseph 128
Flowers, Eddie 72, 74, 80
Flowers, Lannie 96–97
Floyd, John 47, 50
Forçade, Thomas King 41, 42, 44, 54, 56, 89, 98, 108, 122, 130, 140, 155
Frampton, Peter 107
Franklin, Jeff 10
Freeman, Carlton 73, 76, 82
Freeman, Getty 73, 74, 79, 80

Galbraith, Richard 107–108
Gehman, Pleasant 147–148, 151
Georgia Satellites 29
Germs 112, 148
Gimme Shelter 121
Ginsberg, Allen 54
Girlschool 58, 59
Give 'Em Enough Rope 164
Go-Go's 58
Goats Head Soup 134
Goldstein, Gerry 56
Goldman, Vivien 159, 160

Golightly, Jeff 45, 50
Gorham, Scott 161
Gowdy, Vernon L. III 111–112, 114, 118
Graham, Bill 87, 124, 125, 134, 135, 136, 143, 145, 146, 153, 155
Graham, Terry 90, 91
Grand, Tommy 70
Grateful Dead 42, 124
Graves, Tom: on Quo Jr. 45; Sex Pistols play Memphis 40; Taliesyn Ballroom 39, 41, 45, 47–48
Gray, Nancy 65–66
Great Rock 'n' Roll Swindle 41, 140, 155, 159, 160, 161, 163, 166
Greedy Bastards 161
Green, Derek 7
Griffin, Freddi 37–39
Groom, Dewey 85
Groom, Doug 85, 93, 98
Gruen, Bob 32, 33, 55, 69, 93, 100, 105, 106, 121, 146
Grundy, Bill 6, 127
Guardian 156
Guarnieri, John 73–74, 75, 79
Gun Club 90

Hahavishnu Orchestra 22, 25
Hall, Stacy 50; discovered Sex Pistols 48; on Quo. Jr. 46; Taliesyn Ballroom 39–40, 49
Harpo, Slim 70
Harron, Mary 43
Harry, Debbie 136
Haskins, Mike 95, 97, 98
Heartbreakers 156
Heaven, Edwin 136
Heaven Can Wait 149
Hefner, Hugh 130
Hell, Richard 13, 55, 89, 128, 156
Helsingin Sanomat 126
Hendrix, Jimi 113, 156
Henley, Don 27
Herman's Hermits 81
Hewlett, John 128
Hibbert, Jonny 25, 26
High Times 41, 42, 54, 55, 98, 130, 156
Hindley, Myra 161
Hit Parader 118
Hoffman, Kristian 128–129
Hoge, Ken 52, 53, 61, 63, 64
Holiday, Chase 128
Holmstrom, John 56, 64, 83, 130–131, 140–141, 145; Cain's Ballroom 114–115, 121; Forçade offers 43, 155–156; launched *Punk* magazine 42; at Longhorn Ballroom 87, 88, 94–95, 100; McLaren's open-mic policy 124; near-mugging in Memphis 55; *Punk* magazine interview with Rotten 43; Taliesyn Ballroom 47; Tom Forçade's background 42, 54; Vicious at Kingfish Club 82; Vicious' death 156; Vicious in Tulsa 121–122; Warners' attitude towards Sex Pistols 45

Houston, Penelope 137, 138, 142
Huebner, Barry (aka Barry Kooda) 95, 97, 100

I Shot Andy Warhol 43
Idol, Billy 32
Idols 164
In the City 111
Ingraham, Greg 136, 137, 138, 142
Izbrand, Sig McKenna 57, 60–61, 66

Jackson, Michael 156
Jaffe, Ted 15, 84
Jagger, Mick 134
Jefferson Airplane 124
Jett, Joan 55, 95
Jeter, Jim 155
Johansen, David 55, 98
John's Children 128
Johnston, Rory: 15, 70, 82, 84, 127, 128, 129, 136, 137, 138, 142, 146; arranged *SNL* appearance, 16; arrival at Lamar St. John's apartment 153; booked Sex Pistols into Miyako 124–125; decision to keep Sex Pistols out of San Antonio 54; and flight to San Francisco 125; and Freddi Griffin claim 38–39; introduction to Sex Pistols 11; Lech Kowalski's film crew 42; at Longhorn Ballroom 108; McLaren's initial visit to A&M's offices 12; mood inside Randy's Rodeo 62–63; press conference in Baton Rouge 75; recruited Dwayne "DW" Warner 16; relocated to US 11–12; Rotten's arrival at Miyako 150; Rotten's reaction to Rio trip 149–150; Rotten's showdown with McLaren in San Francisco 153–154; set up US tour 10–11; Sex Pistols in Atlanta 19–20; ticket-pricing 14; tour logistics 68; Vicious' heroin problem 20, 37
Jones, Alan 11
Jones, Brian 156
Jones, Charlie 69, 105
Jones, Mick 11, 18, 164–165
Jones, Steve 6, 7, 13, 30, 31, 39, 57, 60; desire to fly to shows 86; guitar problems at Randy's Rodeo 62; purchased Gibson Firebird 138, 141, 143, 148, 150, 153, 155, 156, 161; purchased Vicious' bass guitar 65; recorded "My Way" 163; on San Antonio 51–52; tried heroin 69, 73, 77; Vicious' bass-playing 86, 97, 99, 102, 104, 107, 123, 124, 127, 137
Journey 116
Junkin, Todd 135

Kane, Arthur "Killer" 164
Kansas 116
Keeling, Gaylon 77

Index

Keenan, Clyde 40, 41
Kelly, Bob 45
Kennedy, John F. 89
Kereakes, Theresa 129, 146–149
Kertacy, Danny 70, 72, 73
King, BB 85
King, Martin Luther, Jr. 45
Kinks 58, 70, 97
Klein, Howie 127
Knab, Chris 127, 143
Knight, Saran 85, 86
Kowalski, Lech 41, 42, 44, 64, 108, 162
Kral, Ivan 55

Laaksonen, Touko Valio (Tom of Finland) 61
Led Zeppelin 71, 115
Leibowitz, Annie 55, 60, 98, 145, 146
Lennon, John 30
Letts, Don 69, 160
Levene, Keith 166
Lewis, Furry 50
Liebrand, John 112
Lindsay, David T. 27
Lips Unsealed: A Memoir 148
Little Richard 114
Live at Winterland 1978 138
Living, Jarboe 26
Lobotomy magazine 129, 147
Loeb, Henry G. 45
Loud, Lance 128
Lousteau, Jerry 72
Lydon, Eileen 160
Lynott, Phil 161
Lynyrd Skynyrd 74

Maggots 132, 133
Maida, Sal 147
Mallory, Bill 73
Manchester, Melissa 22
Mannheim Steamroller 50
Marley, Bob 42
Martin, Dana 116–117
Matlock, Glen 7, 13, 16, 86, 127, 164
Mau Mau's 149
May, Steve 23, 25
MC5 41, 71
McCaffrey, Richard
McCain, Gillian 13, 33
McLaren, Malcolm 6, 12, 14, 18, 22, 51, 54, 61, 77, 87, 99, 101, 108, 110, 113, 124, 126, 127, 128, 129, 136, 140, 142, 146, 149, 157, 158, 159, 160, 161, 162, 163, 165; arrival at Lamar St. John's apartment 152; distrust of Stiff Records 23; fascination with New Orleans 70; filmmaking interests at Goldsmiths 41; plot to kidnap Nancy 20; press conference in Baton Rouge 75; showdown with Rotten in San Francisco 153; worry about Sex Pistols' becoming "entertainment" 88
McNeil, Legs 13, 33, 130, 145

McQueen, Steve 155
Melnick, Monte 130
Melody Maker 35, 52, 58, 97, 142, 147
Meltzer, Richard 136
Memphis Commercial Appeal 40
Memphis Flyer 47
Mercury, Freddie 80
Merlis, Bob 30, 31, 51, 84, 146
Meyer, Russ 143, 154, 155, 160
Mills, Jack 161
Monk, Noel 15, 19, 20, 36, 39, 43, 44, 53, 61, 68, 81, 94, 102, 105, 106, 108, 110, 115, 120, 122, 128, 132, 135, 140, 150
Monkees 66, 80, 127
Moody Blues 16
Moon, Keith 156
Moore, Gary 161
Morris, Dennis 82, 159
Morrison, Jim 156
Moser, Margaret: Sex Pistols play San Antonio 52–53; Randy's Rodeo audience 60, 62, 66
Mosley, Oswald 17
Mothersbaugh, Mark 149, 151, 159
Mumps 128, 129
My Aim Is True 16

Natividad, Kitten 143
Negative Trend 135
Nelms, O.L. 85, 99
Nervebreakers 95, 96
Never Mind the Bollocks, Here's the Sex Pistols 7, 8, 10, 15, 28, 48, 57, 71, 72, 73, 88, 96, 111, 112, 148
New, Steve 164
New Musical Express 6, 35, 43, 52, 59, 73, 97, 147, 149, 150; see also NME
New York Dolls 13, 32, 56, 75, 87, 95, 97, 113, 128
New York Post 19
Nicks, Stevie 27
Nolan, Jerry 69, 164
Notorious Bettie Page 43
Nunes, Maxine 135
Nuns 124, 135, 136, 137, 138, 142, 149, 151

O'Brien, Danny 137
O'Brien, Glenn 42
Offs 135
Oklahoma University Daily 112
Olener, Jeff 135, 136, 137
Olivarria, Margot 148–149
Olsen, Carla 59
On the Road with the Ramones 130
The One & Only: Peter Perritt, Homme Fatale 162
O'Neil, Mark 76, 81
Only Ones 162
Orbin, Jack 57, 85
Orgeron, Brad 71, 74, 78
Ostrov, Devorah (aka Betty Fremont) 133
Otis, Harold 54
Outcastes 127, 141

Palmer, Robert 72
Parrett, Jim 96, 99, 101, 104, 123
Parrish, Tim: Baton Rouge music scene 72–73; introduction to Sex Pistols 71; Kingfish Club 70–71, 74, 77–78
Patton, Rex 24, 25
Perkins, Jack 30, 31, 127
Perrett, Peter 162–163
Perry, Lee "Scratch" 159
Phillips, Sam 39
Piaf, Edith 163
Pitney, Gene 104
Politics EP 98
Pompili, Jerry 135
Pop, Iggy 26, 89, 113
Powell, Sharon 36; Atlanta punk scene 22; Great SouthEast Music Hall 22, 27, 29, 32
Presley, Elvis 39, 50, 53, 95, 114, 120
Professionals 161
Public Image: First Issue 88
Public Image Limited (PiL) 88, 166
Pugliese, Frank 57, 58
Pugliese, Joe 57, 58, 59, 60
Punk magazine 41, 42, 43, 56, 82, 87, 89, 95, 120, 122, 130

Queen 6, 80
Quo Jr. 45

Rainbow 116
Ramone, Dee Dee 28, 55
Ramone, Joey 37
Ramones 16, 22, 26, 56, 73, 76, 79, 87, 99, 111, 112, 130, 131
Raphael, Jeff 135
Rat, Mary 90
Read, Sir John 7
Record Mirror 34, 150, 152, 157
Regehr, Bob 12, 15, 29, 30, 84, 87, 124, 125, 132, 155, 160, 161, 166
Reid, Jamie 162
Reinhalter, "Electric Earl" 73, 78, 79
REO Speedwagon 116
Restraints 22
Rhoades, Darryl 22, 25–26, 27
Rhodes, Bernard 18
Richards, Keith 134
Richmond, Sophie 86, 125, 153, 155
Ripped and Torn 43
Riviera, Jake 23
Road to Ruin 131
Roadent (Steven Connelly) 23, 126
Roberts, Ebet 33, 39
Roberts, Farrell 27
Robinson, Dave 23
Robinson, Heidi 81
Robinson, Roland 45, 48
Rockin' Dopsie, Jr. 76
Rockin' Dopsie and the Twisters 76, 77; *see also* the Twisters
Roessler, Helena "Hellin Killer" 89–90, 98, 102–103, 145, 149; after-show party at Lamar St. John's apartment 151; Longhorn Ballroom 92–93, 100; Plunger

Pit 90–91; with Vicious at Mabuhay Gardens 129–130; with Vicious at the Miyako 128; with Vicious in Dallas 93–94, 103
Rolling Stone 27, 40, 55, 56, 57, 60, 87, 88, 98, 104, 111, 118, 149, 152–153, 163
Rolling Stones 15, 16, 50, 58, 70, 84, 97, 109
Ronstadt, Linda 112
Rotten, John 6, 7, 8, 9, 15, 20, 24–25, 28, 29, 30, 31, 34, 39, 51, 54, 57, 60, 61, 73, 76, 82, 85, 86, 105, 114, 122, 125, 128, 131, 132, 134, 143, 146, 147, 150, 153, 155, 156, 158, 160–162, 166; A&R visit to Jamaica 159; attack on 69; Cain's Ballroom 118; final visit with Vicious 166; at Longhorn Ballroom 108; penned lyrics to "Sod in Heaven" (aka "Religion") 88–89, 98, 102, 103; possibility of joining Devo 159; reverting back to "Lydon" 161; tried heroin 69; Winterland 132, 141; *see also* Lydon, John
Roxy Music 147
Ruby, Jack 85
Runaways 95, 131
Russell, Rosalind 150
Ruth, Cyril A. 77, 80
Ryan, Pat 135

St. John, A. Lamar 90, 93, 102, 110, 129, 145, 152; after-show party 151; Dallas road trip, 91–92, 94; Longhorn Ballroom 101
Salewicz, Chris 162
San Antonio Current 51
San Francisco Chronicle 143
Sand Pebbles 155
Sanders, Donald B. 113
Saturday Night Live see also SNL 14, 16–17
Savage, Jon 126, 127
Scabies, Rat 164
Schaeffer, Larry 108, 111–112, 115–116; Cain's Ballroom 106–107, 110, 114, 117, 119; speech about getting into music promotion 107
Scott, Carl 12, 125
Screamers 92
Scruggs, Earl 22
Scuffs 45
Search and Destroy 112
Selwin, Joel 143
Sewell, Greg: Cain's Ballroom 118, 120; Sex Pistols in Tulsa, 111
Sex Pistols: Live at the Longhorn 109
Sex Pistols Number 1 124
Sham 69 132
Shelley, Pete 139
Shernoff, Andy 72
Simmons, Bonnie 131
Simmons, Sylvie 130, 145
Simonon, Paul 18
Sinatra, Micol 128
Sioux, Siouxsie 147
Siouxsie and the Banshees 32

Sire Records 12, 36, 136
Skydel, Barbara 10, 14
Smear, Pat 148
Smith, Grady 70
Smith, Patti 11, 55
Sniffin' Glue 43
Snyder, Don 55
So Alone 161
Sounds 25, 43, 130, 147, 159, 160
Spark, Muriel 166
Sparks 147
Spencer, Neil 147
Spungen, Nancy 20, 128, 149, 162, 163, 165, 166; murder of 165
Stagelife 96, 98, 123
Stephens, Scott 58
Steppenwolf 113
Sterne, Cindy 135
Stevens, Joe 54, 55, 106, 121, 127, 150, 153, 156, 158
Stewart, Rod 50, 112, 153
Stiff Records 23
Stooges 56, 71, 72, 95, 97, 98, 101, 111, 136, 164
Storch, Tony 31–32
Strange, Don 52
Strickland, Jimmy 73
Stroud, Lynn 27–29, 36–37
Strummer, Joe 11, 18, 164
Sublett, III Jesse 58, 59, 60, 62, 66–67
Subterranean Records 139
suicide 131
Sun 126, 158, 159
Sylvain, Syl 13, 14, 70

Talking Heads 112
Temple, Julien 41, 109
Thin Lizzy 161
Thomas, Chris 96
Thompson, Sada 75
Thunders, Johnny 69, 79, 106, 156, 161, 162, 163
Tiberi, John "Boogie" 16, 23, 33, 125, 132, 140, 159–161; babysitting Vicious 43–44; D.O.A film crew 108–109; Lamar St. John's apartment 152–153; "My Way" recording sessions 163; and the 101ers 18; Randy's Rodeo 63, 69, 86; Sex Pistols arrived in New York 19; Sex Pistols' break-up 154–155; Sex Pistols departed from Heathrow 19; Sex Pistols performed with Ronnie Biggs in Rio de Janeiro 126; Sex Pistols' songwriting 49; Vicious and Spungen 20–21; Vicious' hospitalization 156; Vicious on probation 21; Winterland 125
Today 6, 86
Tortosa, Henri-Paul 162
Trouser Press 59, 97
Tulsa Tribune 112
Turner, Tina 32, 50

Ubu, Pere 14
Ultra 59

Vaeth Dot 98
Valentine, Kathy 58, 59, 61
Vamps 56, 57, 58
Van Halen 128, 143
Velvet Underground 111
Vicious, Sid 7, 8, 16, 20, 28, 30, 33, 34, 155, 156, 161, 162, 165; arrest for Spungen's murder 165, 166; AWOL in Atlanta 36; decision to quit Sex Pistols 150; with Hellin Killer 151; with Johnny Thunders All Stars 162; Lamar St. John's apartment 151–152; Longhorn Ballroom 100, 102, 103, 104, 105; Max's Kansas City 164; Randy's Rodeo 64; recorded "My Way" 163; Tulsa 106, 122; Winterland 141
Vicious White Kids 164
Village Voice 21, 26, 29, 53
Violators 58, 59
Virgin Records 7, 35, 96, 126, 157, 159, 160, 165; *see also* Front Line (Virgin subsidiary)
Vontillius, Alun 23–24

Waits, Tom 22
Walker, Jim 166
Warhol, Andy 164
Warner, Dwayne 16, 19
Warner Brothers 7, 10, 12, 14, 24, 37, 69, 72, 84, 87, 109, 143, 146, 150, 155, 158, 159, 160, 161
Warwick, Dionne 75
Washington Post 15
Wayne, John 86
We Are the One EP 137
Weatherman, Annette: Cain's Ballroom 114, 118–120; discovered Sex Pistols 112–113
Weems, Jane 132, 133, 134, 141
Wenner, Jann 87
Westwood, Vivienne 11, 41, 61, 87, 126, 128
Who Killed Bambi? 143
Widner, Ellis 112, 114, 118
Wiedlin, Jane 102, 148
Wiley, John F. 29
Williams, Hank 106
Williams, Tex 106
Wills, Bob 85, 106
Wilson, Ed 57, 58
Winehouse, Amy 156
Wobble, Jah 166

X 90

Young, Charles M. 27, 40, 57, 87, 88, 89, 104
Young, Dan 141, 142, 143

Zolar X 90
Zombies 109
ZZ Top 74

www.ingramcontent.com/pod-product-compliance
Ingram Content Group UK Ltd.
Pitfield, Milton Keynes, MK11 3LW, UK
UKHW050526150426
5217IPUK00026B/1813